HOW TO INFLUENCE PEOPLE AND DAILY SELF-ESTEEM AFFIRMATIONS

2-in-1 Book

Learn How to Influence People, Live Your Life to the Fullest, Increase Your Confidence with Positive Daily Affirmations

How To Influence People

How To Influence People And Get What You Want Now

Become The Person Everybody Listens to by Mastering the Art of Influence & Manipulation. Learn How to Persuade Your Partner, Boss or Colleagues

How To Influence People

Table of Contents

Introduction 7

Chapter 1: A Beginner's Guide to Persuasion 12
    Everyday Ways You're Being Manipulated 12
    Manipulation: A Tool for Both Good and Evil 13
    6 Golden Rules of Manipulation 15
    How to Use Persuasive Body Language 21

Chapter 2: Emotional Intelligence 101 25
    What Is Emotional Intelligence? 26
    Why Master Manipulators Need Emotional Intelligence 31
    9 Ways to Develop Powerful Emotional Intelligence 33
    How to Control Your Emotions Like a Boss 38

Chapter Three: Choosing Your Target 43
    What Hooks People In? 46
    7 Qualities That Signify the Perfect Target 58
    The Targets That are Harder to Win Over 60

Chapter Four: Decoding Body Language 63
    Reading the Body's Subtle Signals 63
    The Secret Messages of the Face 66
    Understanding Microexpressions 72
    What Walking Styles Say About Someone 75

Chapter Five: Essential Manipulation Tools 78
    Everyday Manipulation Tricks 78
    11 Persuasion Tricks to Start Getting What You Want in Everyday Life 85
    How to Use the Six Laws of Persuasion 87
    All You Need to Know About Reverse Psychology 90

Chapter Six: A Master in Every Arena 97

How to Secretly Manipulate Your Boss *97*
Killer Negotiation Strategies to Manipulate Your Way to Success *104*
Fractionation: The Seduction Tool of Master Manipulators *108*
11 Less-Known Manipulation Techniques for Seduction *114*

Chapter Seven: Advanced Manipulation Tactics **121**
The Manipulative Power of Reinforcement *121*
Charming Habits to Manipulate Anyone *125*
How to Turn Someone Into their Own Enemy *129*

Chapter Eight: Asserting Dominance **133**
Body Language that Asserts Dominance *133*
How to Talk Like a Top Dog *138*
Dominant Behavior to Show Who's Boss *145*

Conclusion **150**

Introduction

Everyone has a little manipulator living inside of them. If you're feeling insecure about your life, it might be hard to recognize this quality and the power it can have over others. As humans, we have a wide variety of methods we instinctively fall back on when we want to exercise our influence over others. We might make people doubt their own judgment in lieu of our personal advice when we want something; we could make people feel guilty about something we don't like, or we might put on the charm to entice someone to do something they are reluctant to do. It's all part of daily communication and we start relying on it very early in life.

However, somewhere along the line, we become convinced that manipulation has somehow become immoral; that there is something inherently indecent about it and so they change their means of communication. Sadly, this leaves them vulnerable to the devices of those who recognize that the skill is merely a tool that can be used for both good and bad purposes. As a result, they find themselves being manipulated and pushed to do things they don't really want to do. They end up feeling powerless, frustrated, and out of control.

What they are failing to recognize is that manipulation, like any other craft, is a skill that can easily be developed and used in a positive way to help them achieve their goals. Just by making a few tweaks to their body language, speech, and behavior, all of us can position ourselves to become masters of our own lives. It doesn't matter if you're a parent trying to get your child to clean his room or the CEO of a major corporation trying to motivate a massive workforce, getting past your own insecurities and learning how to use this skill can change the whole dynamic of your life.

It has sometimes been referred to as a form of "dark persuasion" as if to imply that there is something mysteriously evil about manipulation. On the surface, it may seem like that is true. After all, when you hear the word 'manipulation' the mind automatically conjures up intriguing ideas. Visions of science fiction movies on mind control play out in your head, hypnotists attempting to get you to do strange or embarrassing things you wouldn't normally do, and unethical people who want to persuade you into some form of questionable acts. But these are all misconceptions of what manipulation is all about.

The most common belief about manipulation is that it involves one person taking control over another as if they were a puppet with them controlling the strings. But what most people are missing is that the true art of manipulation has nothing to do with getting people to do things against their will but is instead a gentle form of persuasion that will convince them to want the same thing that you want. In other words, manipulation is simply deep form of persuasion, something that all of us do in our everyday lives.

Your goal is to get others to believe that whatever action they are taking was actually their idea all along. While there are always going to be people who will use this skill for questionable purposes but doesn't mean that the art of persuasion itself is wrong.

A person can use a knife to prepare a meal for their family or they can use it to cause harm to someone else. The knife itself is not the problem, it is how someone chooses to use it. If you follow the media then you know that historically there have been an endless stream of charismatic people that have put forth a lot of effort to influence and maneuver people to do their bidding. They look to control the behaviors of the masses in subtle ways that may be difficult to notice.

All of us have heard of the horrific stories of the Nazi oppression of the Jews during World War II. How many normally peace loving and kind Germans were duped into believing that the Jews were really a threat to their way of life? Or you may have heard about the record number of suicidal deaths committed at the persuasion of charismatic people like Jim Jones or those that participated in the pact formed in the wake of the Hale-Bopp comet. Our history books are riddled with such horror stories that show just how evil and dangerous psychological manipulation can be. However, those cases are not the norm and do not reflect the reality of what the art of manipulation truly is.

All of us practice manipulation in some form or another. We do it every day and never give it a second thought. In fact, the main definition of the word 'to manipulate' is "to manage or influence with skill," in some process of treatment or performance."

Manipulation is not the evil itself; it is how it is used that can become questionable. Do you have a religion? Do you have a clique that you belong to? Were you ever a part of a fraternity? Or a member of an exclusive club? Did you follow the rules at school? Is there office politics where you work?

All of these things groups were formed and grown by using some level of manipulation. The members were giving you gentle pressure to follow a certain norm, to fit into certain expectations, and to please a certain group of people. You just didn't realize that you were being manipulated because you wanted to be a part of the picture.

But after reading this book, you can be on the other side of that equation. Gently pushing people in one direction or another. The tricks are all there in your mind and how you think. All of that may need to change and our goal is to help you to do that. In this book you will learn:

- What manipulation really is and how to recognize when you're being manipulated
- Non-verbal language you're always sending out to the rest of the world
- How you EQ (Emotional Quotient) plays a part
- How to find out if you're lacking in EQ and how to get it back
- What attracts most people
- How to identify a person vulnerable to manipulation
- How to read body language and micro-expressions
- How the way you walk tells people a lot
- How to stock up your manipulation toolbox
- And how to manipulate others like a real pro
- And so much more

The question you have to ask yourself is why are you here reading this book? What is your goal in learning how to manipulate people. Keep in mind that to effectively manipulate people it will take a serious commitment in time. You will have to be patient and cultivate your art. It may seem easy, but in order for the strategies used here, you must practice them until they feel natural and effortless. This kind of skill takes time to cultivate and involves overcoming your own mental barriers and creating a very specific mindset.

That involves a lot of work and commitment. However, once you have mastered this skill, you will be able to accomplish amazing things. It will be easier for your new business to gain traction and pull ahead of the competition. You will be able to get the kind of support you need to overcome any obstacle. You'll have access to a wide source of resources, and you'll be able to communicate and connect to the rest of the world on your terms.

How To Influence People

If you've ever wondered how someone with just the clothes on his back can seem to take on the rest of the world and win, then you've witnessed first-hand the power of manipulation. You don't need a basket full of tools or a lot of tricks up your sleeve. Whether you're looking to convince your kids to make certain life choices or you're a CEO trying to motivate a team of employees to follow your ideals, the strategies are the same.

What does that mean for you? It means a lot. With the art of manipulation, you'll find it easier to get the job you want, get the types of loans you need, and even negotiate the kind of deals you're seeking. Your goal is not to get people to go against their will and help you, but to convince them that what you have to offer to the world is worth them taking a risk on. That's a powerful tool that anyone can use to get what they need. And it's all about learning how to use your own personal strengths to your advantage. So, if you're ready to take on the world and finally get the things you need and should have, then it's time to turn the page and learn to be a master manipulator in your own right. So, let's get you started so you can take the rest of the world by storm.

Chapter 1: A Beginner's Guide to Persuasion

Most people think of manipulation very negatively. They feel that anyone that is manipulative has a malevolent purpose and can't be trusted. Unfortunately, this is at least partially true. There are definitely those out there who wish to do you harm or take advantage of anyone who gets in their path.

One of the reasons we often associate manipulation with negative intent is because we don't have the ability to look into someone's heart and determine what their true motive is. So, rather than thinking someone is genuinely complimenting you, the mind often becomes suspicious and will adopt the worst case scenario.

Everyday Ways You're Being Manipulated

It would be nice to feel that when we make our own decisions that we are doing it of our own accord, but that is rarely the case. We live very busy lives and as a result, we often defer to the influences of others and use them as a sort of a shortcut or as a guide to drawing our own conclusions about a given situation faster. For the most part, this can work well, but it is rarely the wisest course of action.

For example, you come home and turn on the TV news to hear the latest events going on in the world. You see a media photo of Prince Charles holding up his middle finger to someone in the crowd. People are outraged that someone in the royal family would adopt such an action in public and you agree. Are you being manipulated or is it a real news report. The image in the picture is clear so you join in the crowd and are incensed by the photograph and launch your own protest against an insensitive member of the royal family.

However, while this incident did actually happen, the media did not show the whole story. The same image taken from a different angle, shows that Prince Charles was actually holding up three fingers as if he was counting something while talking calmly with someone in the crowd. It was not the single middle finger and his gesture was completely innocent.

That major example of manipulation had millions of people weighing in on the state of the royal family before the truth was really revealed. However, all manipulation does not come out in such a public way. It can come on a smaller scale as well. Consider those people who act as if they are better than you. Perhaps they have a higher education, or they make more money than you. Some even act that way because of their family line. When they talk to you, they take on a condescending voice as if speaking with a child. Their facial expressions make it clear that they see you as inferior.

Does this strategy work? Only if you accept this behavior and go along with it. If you become nervous and jittery in their presence you are giving them signals that you agree and you do see them as superior to you. How you respond to that type of behavior will let you know if they are manipulating you or not.

Other manipulating strategies may be seen in a person's body language, tone of voice, or even in what they don't say (silent treatment for example). There is a myriad of ways that one can try to manipulate you. If you take the time, I'm sure you'll find countless forms of manipulation being played out with you every day. It's a perfectly normal strategy that we all us throughout our lives.

Manipulation: A Tool for Both Good and Evil

How To Influence People

It is cases like these that make people question whether manipulation is ethically sound or not. The media is notorious for these kinds of tactics. They use photography, carefully worded phrases, and other clever tactics to persuade people to feel a certain way.

However, while the message they deliver has some degree of truth it is not always the whole truth. Because someone uses manipulation for bad doesn't mean it is all bad. A closer look at our communication styles helps us to understand how manipulation has been used far more for good purposes. Once you recognize this, you'll not only be able to recognize it when you see it playing out around you, but you'll want to apply it in your own life as well.

Because our subconscious mind is usually the force that is driving our behavior, we don't often recognize what is really happening during our mental processes. The subconscious mind is always at work, every second of every day, it is collecting information from our senses and putting it through filters, deciding what is important and what is not.

So, as you are scrolling through your computer, checking your social media pages, things are happening in the back of your mind that you're not even aware of. This is a strategy that marketers use to draw you in. A business' marketing team understands that if they put the brand name in front of you often enough, you'll eventually make a connection to it. Have you ever wondered why Coca-Cola has become the number one brand in the world of carbonated beverages? Little things like a catchy phrase, little blurbs in between scenes of your favorite TV show, and their logo plastered at every sports event and entertainment venue.

This crafty art of manipulation isn't something new. It has been around for decades. It is used by businesses, political parties, religions, and even social interest groups. Your employer uses it to get more work out of you, your parents use it to get you to come home by curfew, your teachers use it to get you to want to study, and your spouse may use it to get you to agree with him on any number of things. Simply put, manipulation is the skillful use of persuasion to achieve a desired result. It is the oil on the squeaky wheel that moves our society.

Bottom line, if you're a part of this world, you are in one of only two classes; the manipulator or the one being manipulated. There is no middle ground here. So, in essence, it is one of the most useful skills a survivalist can use to get what he needs.

If you're thinking that you need to have a special amount of charisma or certain talents to employ the strategies we will use in this book, then you'd be wrong. The fact is that everyone has an inborn talent to be a master manipulator. You already have the qualities to get the job done. So, let's start with the basics.

6 Golden Rules of Manipulation

So, how can you tell when you're being manipulated? There are a lot of ways this can happen. Chances are, by now you're starting to get the idea, but let's get a little more specific here. After years of study, researchers have narrowed down exactly how manipulation works.

In the beginning, you probably felt that people made decisions based on the information they have gathered, but that is not always the case. Evidence shows that manipulations has very specific characteristics and the decision-maker uses those characteristics as a kind of ruler to measure the information they collect. This allows them to come to a conclusion by bypassing all the analytical steps involved. There are at least six different rules of manipulation that are commonly used on you every day.

- Reciprocity
- Scarcity
- Authority
- Consistency
- Liking
- Consensus

Once you understand how each of these works and how they can be used you will not only be able to spot when someone is trying to manipulate you but will be able to harness this strategy and use it on others.

Reciprocity: The art of reciprocity allows the manipulator to tap into an inborn characteristic of all of us. If someone does something for you, you automatically feel compelled to do something in return. Even if their gift does not come with an expectation in return, you will still feel as if you have to do something for that person before your mind will rest.

Still, don't expect it to be an equal exchange of gifts or favors. The manipulator may not even ask or expect something from you, but instead will create a situation that will make you feel connected to them in some way. Later, when the circumstances are favorable and they need the service or product you provide, your mind will automatically bring up their name and put it at the top of the list and the odds are good that you're going to throw your business their way.

A perfect example of reciprocity is a practice found in most restaurants today. After you've had your meal, the waiter will usually bring you the check along with a mint for each person in your party – a gift. In most cases, the gift is something small and seemingly insignificant. How do you feel when you receive this gift? What do you do? While the mint costs the restaurant a tiny fraction of the meal you just had, you begin to feel a sense of indebtedness. Your subconscious mind tells you that you have to return the gesture in some one. Evidence of this has been revealed in a number of studies that have shown that diners who receive a mint after their meal often increased the amount of their tip by at least 3%. If they received two mints, they size of the tip actually quadrupled to around 14%.

Another surprising result of reciprocity is if the waiter gives you a mint with the bill and then starts to walk away, pauses and then returns to compliment your party by saying something nice, the tips increase even more up as much as 23%.

This reveals something interesting. That it's not just the gift that makes a difference. Yes, giving a gift will increase your chances of getting what you want, but attention should also be paid to the manner in which the gift is given. This will give you the maximum possible results you receive.

Scarcity: It is a well-known fact that when there is only a limited supply of anything, people will want it more. This natural reaction is built into all of us. We may not even be aware of this inclination, but psychologically when something we desire becomes scarce, we feel compelled to try and get it as soon as possible.

We see how marketers use the art of scarcity in campaigns that have deadlines. You'll receive emails or text messages with phrases like "only 12 hours to go" or "just five seats left." To put it simply, once you realize that you no longer have infinite access to something you want you will be driven to take action and secure it for yourself before supplies are exhausted.

The important thing to remember here is that nothing has changed about the product. It isn't improved nor is it offered at a lower cost.

The only difference is that there is a good chance that the resource would no longer be available. That fact alone made people want it all the more.

So, when you really want to motivate people to action, the Principle of Scarcity is very effective. When people learn about the benefits they would be missing out on, they will be clamoring to get it while supplies last.

Authority: We have been programmed from a very young age to respect and accept the words and advice of people in authority. This is the reason we take the advice of medical professionals without question, we listen to the voice of a teacher, and we comply with the badge of authority whenever it gives us direction.

We do this on a conscious level. It is a decision that we all make at some point in our lives. However, few of us realize that we also do this on a subconscious level. Even a professional who we know nothing about, we give more weight to their opinion and place it higher than any others. It is because it is our way of acknowledging their experience, position, and knowledge.

It is interesting to note that this automatic acceptance can be seen not just in numbers but also in social settings all around the world. Doctors are able to get their patients to follow certain regimens of treatment if their diplomas are openly displayed in their offices when they make recommendations. People are more likely to obey traffic laws if there is a uniformed officer present, and most are inclined to listen to an expert on any subject if there is some indication that he is indeed an expert.

Of course, this strategy can also backfire on you. If you were to go around boasting about your accomplishments or you were to tell everyone that they have to listen to you because you're the expert, it can be off-putting to many people and shut them down. However, if someone else was to point to your level of experience in a particular area and recommend you, people are more inclined to respond favorably.

This is why you see countless testimonials on webpages that want to sell you something. Interestingly enough, you don't need to know the trustworthiness of the person who is making the recommendations. In most cases, just the suggestion from an outside person is enough to convince people of the weight of the authority is all that is needed. Studies that have shown that this type of referral strategy can yield an increase of as much as 20% results in many cases.

Consistency: People generally will always follow the same path they have traveled in the past. They defer to something familiar and comfortable. Therefore, if someone naturally has done something for you in the past, it is quite likely that they will do it again; in most cases, their next action will even be bigger than before.

If you can get someone to make a small and insignificant commitment the first time, then it is likely that they will make an even larger gesture later on. Businesses tap into this natural desire by asking first for small but voluntary commitments like filling out an online form or answering a simple survey question. In one such health center, patients were asked to fill out their own appointment card rather than the staff. As a result, they had an 18% drop in missed appointments. But the act was so miniscule and minor the patient never even realized they were actually making a commitment.

Liking: We all naturally gravitate to the people and things we like. This is because of three essential elements. First, we want to be with those who are similar to us and we can relate to. Second, we are attracted to those who compliment us, and third those people who are willing to work with us and help us to achieve our goals.

Many have become successful by finding ways to point out similarities between their goals and their potential customers. By taking the time to engage in some form of small talk, sharing personal information with each other, you create a bond that will bind the two of you together on some level. The stronger you can make that bond before you begin to make a request, the better chance that the person will be willing to grant your request. Businesses that have used this strategy have seen as much as a 90% positive response as opposed to those who had a 55% response when they just got right down to business.

To use this skill to your advantage, look for common ground that you might share with others and give them genuine compliments rather than canned platitudes, and you should see better results.

Consensus: Consensus is the gentle use of peer pressure. People tend to follow the crowd in their actions and beliefs, especially if they are not sure of themselves. All of us take notice of what other people are doing. We often choose a restaurant because of how busy it is. We assume that if it is always busy it must be good. McDonald's displays the number of customers they've served over the many years they have been in business and you've probably already noticed how Amazon has a list of other products customers are buying when they choose anything you've searched for.

It's all part of our culture of socialization. Applying this to our art of persuasion gives people a sense of camaraderie with us and helps people to connect to not just what we have to offer but also to others who have already become a part of who we are. Whether you're selling a product or you're just trying to get someone to agree with you, one of the simplest ways to get people on board is to let them know that if they join you, they will not be alone. It feels less risky when they know they have someone to join forces with.

Any one of these strategies can help you to achieve better results when you're looking to get certain things. You've probably already begun to realize how many times you've been manipulated in your everyday life. No doubt, you believed you were making your own decision, which is probably true to a certain extent, but there's no question that the idea that germinated in your mind was planted there by someone else.

How to Use Persuasive Body Language

One thing that few people realize is that when you communicate with others, it is not the words that most people connect with. The foundation of your communication style lies not on what comes off your lips but on what your body is doing. Careful attention must be given to how you present your message. A poorly delivered speech can do so much more damage than a poorly developed presentation. To get the most of your message, your aim should be to tap into their subconscious mind on a more physical level. Here are just a few of the most commonly used body language signals. As you read through them visualize them in your head, practice them in a small scale when with others and watch how easily you can bring people into your fold.

Be Superman

The Superman pose works because it makes you stand out from the rest. Practice this in the privacy of your home before going out. Slip into the bathroom and try standing erect, puff out your chest (not too much), and place your hands on your hips with your elbows pointing out to the sides. Your goal is to make yourself look as big as possible. Do this pose before you begin your presentation and notice how your confidence and poise begins to grow.

Stand Up Tall

It can be pretty easy to slip into a slouch but fight the urge. It's important for you to stand tall so you project the best possible image you can. When you speak publicly with your body erect, your shoulders pulled back, and your body straight you'll not only look more confident but you'll feel it too. However, there is another benefit to standing tall that is not so readily seen. When you stand up tall, you align your airway so that your breath flows in and out freely. With all the potential blockages open, you'll naturally speak louder, your voice will be cleaner, and you'll sound as well as appear more professional.

Keep Your Body Open

You do need to be careful with the standing tall pose. You can overdo it and instead of displaying poise and confidence you could come off as being cocky and arrogant. To avoid this, resist any temptation to cross your arms as that will make you appear closed off. Try not to stuff your hands in your pocket, and if you are sitting don't cross your legs. You want to appear confident but also trustworthy so the more open you can keep your limbs the more people will want to respond to your message.

Make Eye Contact

If you want to give your presentation a more personal touch, work hard at making true eye contact. When you look directly into someone's eyes, you are basically inviting them into your inner fold. Direct eye contact creates an unspoken bond that feels more receptive than just talking at a person.

Of course, you don't want to stare into their eyes because that might make them feel a little uncomfortable. So, make eye contact with them, but only hold it for a few seconds. If you're speaking to a group of people, pick out several people in the crowd and make eye contact with each of them. After a few seconds move to the next person and continue this with as many people as is reasonably possible. It makes listeners feel that you're giving them a personal touch and that you are genuinely interested in them.

Move Around

If you're giving a presentation, resist the temptation to stand there like a statue. Whenever possible walkaround and use as much space as you can. It will reflect a more natural movement and give you more confidence. If you are nervous, movement will help you to relax in the environment and get your message across more easily. Movement also makes it possible for you to project your voice into different areas of the room so more people can connect with your message.

Use Your Hands

Remember, let your whole body talk. Communication involves more than words. Keep your hands free so that you can gesture freely. This will draw more people from your audience to you. Let your hands move freely to emphasize the points you want to make. Common gestures you can include could be pointing to your palm to stress a specific point, palms open wide and spread out to the sides to indicate openness or to create a question in the audience's mind and pointing outwards to stress other matters.

It would help a great deal if you were to take some time and observe how you communicate naturally with people you know. Very few people speak comfortably without gestures, you just don't realize you're doing it. However, if you start to take note of how your hands and body move when you speak with friends, you'll know which gestures you can incorporate into any presentation you make to give it the extra push to take your message over the top.

Use Facial Expressions

We say a lot with our face and when people speak to you, they will subconsciously look for those cues to fill in the blanks of what you didn't or can't say verbally. When they ask you a very basic question like, "how are you?" they immediately watch your face when you give the answer. Our faces are like blank canvases and when we speak our message is reflected on it projecting our inner feelings. Without saying a word, a person can tell how we are feeling, what we are thinking, and whether or not they want to trust you.

When you make facial gestures, keep your face relaxed. A calm and relaxed face can give you the appearance of authenticity and make you feel more human.

Keep these facial gestures to a minimum. Too many and people will feel uncomfortable – too little and people will think you are uninterested.

Becoming a master manipulator is just a matter of perfecting an art that we have been learning since childhood. It is not something new, unique, or questionable. It is just refining our way of communicating with the outside world. What we've just discussed in this first chapter are the basics of this skill. Now, let's roll up our sleeves and look a little deeper under the surface to see what really drives people to follow a true master in the art of persuasion.

Chapter 2: Emotional Intelligence 101

For years, the common belief was that the key to success lies in your Intelligence quotient or your IQ. Whether you are book smart or street smart, there is no question that having some level of mental acuity will help you navigate the obstacles that you must overcome to achieve your goals.

But that leads us into a long-standing debate, which one is more important? Those who advocate for IQ as the most important argue that your mental intelligence is what will help you to navigate the system will definitely pave the way for you but evidence is now emerging that shows that emotional intelligence is equally as important in preparing you to deal with people. To clarify this though, we need to fully understand the difference between the two.

Well known psychologist, Howard Gardner points out that one's intelligence is not limited to mastering one single ability. His years of study in how the brain works has identified several different ways one can show intelligence. Read any of his writings and you'll come across his well-known expression:

It's not how smart you are but how you are smart

Where IQ focuses on one or a few abilities, commonly referred to as the "G Factor," he points out that the ability to recognize emotions, understand, and express them clearly is key to how well one may be able to navigate the challenges in life.

If you've ever taken an IQ test then you know that it only focuses on certain skills. Your IQ score was based only on visual, spatial, working memory, short and long-term memory, quantitative and fluid reasoning. In essence, you were tested on the general topics commonly taught in school.

Your EQ, however, is measured on your ability to perceive an emotion, evaluate, manage, and express it. When you have emotional intelligence, you are able to see and identify the emotions in others, reason on your observations to determine how others are feeling and use those emotions as a means of facilitating communication all while keeping your own emotions in check.

For years, we've always placed great store in our IQ and it is still viewed as important even today. However, as our knowledge of how the brain works continues to grow, there is increasing evidence that the IQ alone is not a guarantee of success. It's true, people with a high IQ will usually do better in school, they get the better jobs, and even seem to be more physically healthy. But throughout history, we have repeatedly seen many with high IQs that seem to fail at everything they attempt. It is clear that IQ alone will not get you to where you want to be. Rather it is an entire battery of factors that include your EQ that will give you better assurance at success.

What Is Emotional Intelligence?

We've already determined that at the heart of it, emotional intelligence is the ability to identify and recognize emotions in others and manage your own, but there is more to it than that. In order to have good emotional intelligence, you need to master three skills.

- **Emotional Awareness:** The ability to recognize emotions in others and label them. It's not enough to say that person is upset, you need to know whether they are angry, sad, frightened, grieving, or embarrassed.
- **Redirect:** Once you've identified those emotions, you need to skillfully redirect those emotions by thinking things through,

use them to solve problems, and apply them to the tasks or skills you need to meet.
- **Manage:** The skill in managing your own emotions goes beyond just not throwing a fit when you don't like something. As long as you can manage those feelings and use them to your advantage, you will become a master of emotional intelligence.

When you have a high EQ, you are able to identify a wide range of both negative and positive emotions, even when they are not obviously displayed. You will be in-tune with how other people are feeling, which can give you insight into what they are thinking, and you'll be able to pick up on even the subtlest of cues when you are interacting within a particular social environment. All of these skills can be used to help you become a better spouse, friend, parent, teacher, lover, leader, boss, or anything else you might wish to do.

It would be difficult to get someone to respond to you if you don't know what moves them to take action. There is a delicate art to managing emotions, but it is necessary for anyone who is looking to expand their horizons.

Emotions are extremely powerful and are the force behind all of our behavior and by extension the behavior of all people, triggering both positive and negative reactions. Your EQ will help you to focus on not just your own personal feelings and thoughts, but also on those of others.

If you take the time, you could probably look back and find plenty of examples of how others have used their EQ to manipulate you in the past. The tactic was subtle, you likely had no idea it was happening. For example, how many times have you been watching TV and saw a commercial showing young children from a third world country with distended bellies and flies and mosquitos buzzing around them. It pulls on your heart strings, doesn't it? Or perhaps you met up with a friend who was visibly distressed and after some prodding, told you how he was in a bad financial state and needed some help to pay off some financial obligations.

In each of those cases, the manipulator pulled on your emotional heartstrings because they knew how it would affect you emotionally. They were able to get you in a position to want to help them. In fact, you probably thought that it was your idea all along. Every day, we see these kinds of emotional manipulators all around us, most of them are used in a positive and beneficial way, but there are plenty examples of negatives ones as well.

Consider one example of one manipulation master that caused extreme harm to others. Before Adolf Hitler began his reign of terror as the head of the Nazi regime, he spent years observing human behavior and how his own body language was affecting those around him. He observed the emotional impact of every gesture and position and honed those skills until he turned himself into a mesmerizing speaker.

A leader who wants to take unfair advantage over others will use many things to get them to buy into a specific idea.
They may try to control you by using your own fears against you, even going to the point of exaggerating the truth or telling you outright lies to back you into a corner where you feel they are the only ones you can trust.

They could also resort to outright deception to put you at a disadvantage. They may tell you the truth but only part of the story; the part that shows them in a more positive light. They will say all the things you want to hear. So, they may be the yes person in the office, always agreeing with you on every point, regardless of the logic. They will do you small favors in an attempt to get you to be indebted to them. They will try everything they can to maneuver things to their advantage. This strategy puts you in a setting where they have the power and you are not as at ease as you would be otherwise. Meetings will be at their home, office, club, or any other location of their choosing.

They are not afraid to ask the hard questions. This is an attempt to uncover your weaknesses or to gather information they could one day use to manipulate you further. Often the questions are about personal matters or things you are less likely to discuss openly.

They talk fast to try to throw you off track and may even use uncommon vocabulary in order to undermine your confidence. Think of those fast talking infomercials you see on late-night TV. They usually throw extensive vocabulary at you in the hopes that you won't be able to follow their storyline fully. And the rapid-paced speech doesn't give you enough time to process all the information they are giving you, leaving you unsure of yourself.

They are not afraid of showing their emotions or causing a scene when it will work to their advantage. Negative situations often make people uncomfortable which can give them a huge advantage that they can exploit.

They will pressure you to respond to situations quickly so you don't have time to think about it. They want you to react on impulse even to what may seem like unreasonable demands.

They may even cut off communication altogether in order to unnerve you and give them the upper hand. This gives them a sense of power and forces you to wait until they are ready to continue the relationship.

All of these are tactics that negative manipulators use at will. As you read through them, there is a good chance that you have seen these used on you from time to time. In fact, you may have even used them yourself on other people.

As a master manipulator, it is important that you recognize these tactics. None of these would work if you recognized them firsthand, and if you had a high enough EQ, you would know how to respond in order to avoid being manipulated in ways that you're not comfortable with.

If they try to use fear – take the time to examine the bigger picture, gather more information so you would have all the facts to make a decision.

If they are being deceptive – ask questions to uncover the truth or speak to someone trustworthy to verify the facts of the situation.

If they are being too agreeable – focus on having a more balanced thinking process.

If they are always doing you small favors – don't hesitate to say no and refuse them.

If they always want to control location – insist on a neutral meeting place.

If they ask too many personal questions – avoid saying too much.

If they speak too fast – stop them to ask questions for verification.

If they are prone to emotional outbursts – avoid impulse reactions. Wait for them to calm down and speak to them in a slow and purposeful manner to balance the situation.

If they are pressuring you to make a decision quickly – request more time or refuse.

If they are giving you the silent treatment – be willing to walk away or at least wait until they come to you, giving you the advantage.

Another masterful manipulator of the 20th century was Martin Luther King, Jr. Take some time and read over his *I Have A Dream* speech and ask yourself why it was so powerful. Why decades later, the words continue to resonate with everyone who reads or hears them. It was his choice of words, meant to stir up and touch on the emotions of his listeners. At the same time, as he delivered his message, he was able to keep complete control of his own emotions, letting out only what was needed to stir the audience to align with him.

So, while your IQ may be instrumental in positioning you in the right place to achieve some level of success, it is your EQ that will be most effective in getting others to go along with your grand plan so you can get the results you seek. No doubt, you'll need both, but your EQ will be the bigger indication of success.

Why Master Manipulators Need Emotional Intelligence

Lisa Nowak was a highly intelligent person. By the time she had applied for her job at NASA, she had met all the qualifications. She had completed a Master's program in aeronautical engineering and a postgraduate study in astrophysics at the US Naval Academy. She had spent more than five years accumulating five years of piloting experience. She was physically fit and had all the book knowledge she could have possibly need. She was selected to be in the astronaut program with no problems.

Unfortunately, things didn't work out well for Lisa. In 2007, her inability to control her emotions caused her to make a rash decision that destroyed her chances completely. When she discovered that her then romantic partner was involved with someone else, she took matters into her own hands. She took the 15 hour drive from Houston to Orlando to confront and kidnap the other woman, which lead to her having an emotional breakdown, going to jail ending her career completely.

The evidence is clear, one's EQ dictates how we behave. Our behavior is the end result of a linear process that is played out in our brains.

1. A triggering event occurs
2. Our senses pick up the event and transmits it to our brain
3. We mentally process the event and produce thoughts and opinions about it
4. The thoughts trigger an emotional response
5. The emotion we feel triggers a specific behavior
6. The behavior then triggers another inciting event
7. The cycle starts all over again

The key to becoming a master manipulator is to control behavior and since all behavior is triggered by our emotional state, it is important to manage emotions well. No matter what we do with others, communication, relationships, business, or anything else, the emotions are behind the entire process. If you have a high EQ it will be easier for you to read other people and manipulate situations in order to get them to do what you expect.

Most of us can identify and recognize our own emotions and how they cause us to react to triggering events in our lives. However, where we often find ourselves lacking is in the ability to see those same reactions in others. One of the most important factors in mastering a high EQ is to identify emotional reactions in others.

According to one study conducted by Johnson & Johnson, higher performers in the workplace were those who showed a higher emotional intelligence. The numbers were quite impressive showing 90% of the best workers were those with a high EQ and 80% of the lowest showed a low EQ.

No matter what your goals are or how you plan to use your manipulation skills, a high EQ can be one of the most significant factors in getting you to where you want to be.

9 Ways to Develop Powerful Emotional Intelligence

Because emotions are so powerful, they have a direct effect on how well you interact in social situations. They can also dictate your coping strategies, the amount of money you spend, and what you do with your time. As you can see controlling your emotions could be one of the most important factors in determining your success no matter what you do.

Keep in mind that there is a big difference between developing emotional intelligence and suppressing your emotions. If you feel sad or you try to hide your feelings, it could cause you more harm than good. Suppressing emotions are generally what leads to damaging coping skills like over-eating, gambling, and drinking.

Managing your emotions and developing a high EQ is not hiding or suppressing your feelings but is recognizing those feelings and not allowing them to have the power to control you. In other words, you control your emotions not the other way around. So, if you find yourself in a bad mood, you need to take the helm and change it by choosing to display another emotion. But learning how to manage them will take an investment in time and practice. Here are a few skills that will help you get started on the right path.

1. **Identify Negative Emotions First**

Generally, the emotions that are most likely to get us into trouble are the negative ones. When our negative emotions take control, we often make impulse reactions. We need to take the time to analyze what is going on inside our heads. By taking the time to stop and think about what's happening internally before you become overly emotional, you are less likely to have a knee-jerk reaction to a triggering event. Learn to breathe a little and try to look at things more objectively. Practicing the art of mindfulness can help you to slow down and analyze a situation objectively from different perspectives. Once you have identified your emotion and labeled it, you cross a mental threshold that makes it easier to move forward.

2. **Change Your Vocabulary**

Your choice of words you use to communicate says a lot about who you are inside. Analyze your language to see which words you're using to relay what you want. Those with a higher level of emotional intelligence are very specific when they speak while those with a low EQ tend to be very vague, sounding like they are skirting issues rather than addressing them. The next time you're in a conversation with someone else that didn't go well, take the time to analyze the words you used. How could you have been clearer in your communication. Chances are you will start to see your own communication deficiencies, but also recognize emotional triggers in others. This will give you a better chance of addressing the problem rather than allowing your emotions to catapult you into a cycle of negative behavior.

3. Learn to be More Empathetic

Start watching other people more closely. People subconsciously give you both verbal and non-verbal cues letting you know what emotions they are feeling. This can give you invaluable insight into what actions you need to take or words you need to say to change the dynamic. Before you react though, take the time to put yourself in their place and ask yourself how you would want someone to react. This can be a key communication tool that can lead to better connections with others and remind yourself that every situation is not always about you.

4. Learn Your Stressors

All of us have our own triggers, events that cause us stress and anxiety. These stressors are what can take you out of the game so, if you know what they are, you can develop strategies that can address them before you react negatively. So, if you know that looking at the bills gets your blood boiling, put it off to a time when you are less likely to have to interact with other people. If you know that the phone ringing during dinner time causes you to get angry, unplug the phone until dinner is over. By being proactive in these situations, you can avoid negative altercations with others.

5. Don't Allow Challenges to Bring You Down

No matter who you are, we all are faced with challenges. That in itself is not an indicator of the kind of person you are. It's the behavior that those challenges trigger that can tell the world who you are. How you address uncomfortable issues can either put you on the path to success or bring you down. So, when faced with unpleasant situations, learn how to take a more optimistic view rather than a critical one. For example, if you find you are having difficulties with your employer, you can either leave the office constantly complaining about what he or she said, or you can ask yourself constructive questions and try to come up with proactive strategies to diffuse the situation. Learn how to address the conflict before it arises and take on a more optimistic approach. This will gradually start to change your personal behavior and will start to draw more people to you.

6. Strive to Understand the Reason Behind Your Emotions

Once you have been able to identify which emotions you are experiencing, you need to try to understand why. Your goal is to discover the triggering event that caused these emotions to form. It may take a little time, but rarely is the triggering event the true cause of the feelings. You may find that you have to look further back in your life to find out why certain events cause you to react the way you do. Quite often it is not the event that causes your distress but the fact that the situation does not honor your personal values in some way. This will require you to develop some cold hard honesty to help you uncover your own hidden truths.

7. Resolve the Issue

Sometimes all that is needed to diffuse a difficult situation is to learn how to look at it from a different perspective. Remember the cycle – thoughts lead to emotions which lead to behavior. If you are feeling bad about something, go back to your thoughts to change the dialogue. After you've identified the triggering thought, try to think of different possible thoughts that can change the outcome. Focus on the positive and the negative feelings usually will go away. Other times, you might find that much of the negativity you've built up can be alleviated simply by understanding what's happening. This redirect process is key to gaining command over your emotions and usually leads to a much calmer personality.

8. Make a Different Choice

After you've resolved the issue in your mind, you need to make the decision to react a different way in the future. This can be quite difficult, because we know that in the heat of the moment, rational thinking is never truly the case. But a lot of our behavior is actually the result of habits; we have automatically behaviors with certain situations and we have done so for so long that we don't even stop to consider if our response is working or not. No one wants to be the guy that flies off the handle at the slightest provocation; it's stressful on everyone including him. Make a choice today, to not allow your emotions to hijack you and lead you down the path towards destruction. Learning to master this skill is not something you can just read about and the next day you know exactly what to do. You will fail many times, you will struggle with restraining yourself, but you will gradually make a change.

9. Minimize Negative Moods

When you do find yourself in a bad mood, readjust as soon as possible, otherwise you could find yourself engaging in behavior that will isolate you. Avoid being evasive, this can actually work against your attempts to become a master manipulator. You might find yourself complaining about the people around you or slip into a scenario of not talking or lashing out at others.

So, it is smart to plan ahead. Think of the things that generally put you in a better mood so you can start doing those things when negative feelings start to rise up. For example, you might want to talk about pleasant things with a friend, listen to your favorite music, take a walk, or meditate. It will keep your mind focused on what's important so that you can get away from the negative feelings before they become a problem.

It is one thing to identify emotions and understand them but managing them can be very difficult. Our emotions are not constant and can rise and fall like the waves of the sea so it can be hard to keep them under control. No one is pleasant all the time and no one is always a hot head. We all have certain triggers that bring out the ugly in us, but if you practice these steps often enough, eventually you will begin to see the tide changing and you'll get the mastery over them. As you do, your EQ will become stronger and you'll be more in-tuned with your own inner demons. This will give you the needed confidence to handle uncomfortable situations by shifting your mood and give you more control over any situation you find yourself in.

How to Control Your Emotions Like a Boss

When you feel like the world is closing in on you, there is a powerful but overwhelming sense that you are losing control, which can be a very frightening thing. It doesn't matter if it deals with something at home or in the boardroom with a team of professionals. The pressure from a constant stream of things piling up can make you feel claustrophobic causing you to do something quickly to change it. It can be these times that cause us to make our biggest impulse reactions, which are usually the ones to get us into trouble.

At times, taking a few deep breaths or a walk around the block just doesn't cut it. As the cortisone in your body starts to increase, you feel your chest tighten or the knot in your stomach starts to grow. You start to yell and scream at anyone within your vicinity, whether they are responsible or not. You may threaten, or you could storm out of the room, slamming the door behind you in a child-like tantrum. That is the moment when you are on the verge of exploding. How can you reclaim your life and make sure that your emotions stay in check even when everything seems out of your hands.

We've all had that scenario or something similar happen to us. Later we are riddled with guilt and shame for our behavior. But what we may not realize is that your emotions have triggered a chemical reaction in your body, which started a snowball effect that once started was almost impossible to control.

On the other hand, we have all seen that one boss, parent, teacher, or other authority figure that seems to maintain their composure no matter how desperate the situation may seem. What's the difference? It comes down to one simple factor. They were able to control their emotions so that the negative behavior never starts in the first place. The truth is that managing your emotions can literally transform your life and personality, enabling you to bring out the best qualities within you rather than the worst.

If you can relate to either of these situations, it should become clear to you that emotions are not inherently bad. We all have them for a reason; they are there to warn us of situations that are uncomfortable, dangerous, or unpleasant. But, since schools are primarily focused on teaching us book knowledge, most of us have to learn to manage our emotions on our own and we never outgrow those temper tantrum habits we displayed as a child.

It doesn't have to be this way though. By making a concerted effort to take charge of your emotions, you can literally begin to take charge of the situation. Rather than allowing your own emotions to direct your behavior, you direct your emotions. How can you do this?

By developing something called emotion regulation skills. In essence, these are unique skills designed to manage those impulse urges and emotions that rise up in all of us. The more you master these skills the more confidence you'll have in managing your emotions and controlling them. This will be a major step in your training to become a master manipulator. It's a X step process:

1. Identify your feelings and accept them for what they are

You can't manage what you can't understand. But it is not enough to say, "I'm angry" or "I'm frustrated." This is a starting point but aim to be more specific in your identifying process. Are you angry because you're afraid? Are you frustrated because of the workload or because you feel unqualified to manage it? By identifying the root cause of the negative emotion, you begin to understand what your true emotions are. Rarely, are the ones we reveal to the public a true image of who we are.

It is important that you get rid of the need to judge yourself. Your goal here is to merely identify the situation, not justify, explain, or judge. Acknowledge it for what it is, don't resist them, just accept them for what they are and move on. You'll address the correction of these habits later on.

It is important to do this as soon as you notice an emotional surge begin to rise. Work at expanding your vocabulary and go beyond just stating the obvious. As you work on developing these skills, you will soon be able to discern even the slightest changes in your mood swings.

a. Identify that you are having an emotion
b. Pause and analyze
c. What thoughts are running through your mind
d. What sensations are you feeling in your body
e. Identify the emotion
f. Try to discern the nuances and what changed
g. What is the reaction you are trying to suppress
h. Observe

Here, you are working as an outside observer. Rather than allowing the emotion to unfold within you, use your imagination and allow it to play out in front of you as if it was an actor on a stage. Let happen, watch it intensify and then dissipate without making yourself a part of it.

2. Take Positive Action

Once you are familiar with the emotion, you will find it much easier to manage it. As you observe the emotion playing out in front of you, pull back the curtain to see the bigger picture. In most cases, you will be able to bring your mind to a calmer state. Often just taking the time to identify and look at the bigger scope is enough to bring you into a more stable frame of mind.

If that doesn't work, you can take the next step and find something that can distract you from your negative feelings at the time. Try to have a calming task you can do on hand to bring your mind back into balance. Many people turn to something they instinctively enjoy like walking, journaling, deep breathing, crafting, or coloring. The key here is to have something that will naturally relax you. All of us are different so your calming activity may be something unique to everyone around you.

By mastering your emotion regulation, you will naturally become more confident and empowered. Once your emotions are no longer controlling you, it will be easier for you to see how you can master manipulation. The bottom line is that you can never hope to manipulate others until you are able to manipulate yourself. Once you have developed your EQ well, you will not only see how it changes you internally, but by extension have a positive effect on everyone around you. It will take dedication and hard work. You won't be able to accomplish it right away and it will take a lot of practice, but the results will pay off for you many times over and you will be able to see the advantages in the changes as you progress.

Chapter Three: Choosing Your Target

After going through the process outlined in the last chapter, chances are you've come to learn something new about yourself. Most people are surprised to learn what really makes them tick, and it's even more surprising to discover what their triggers actually are. Now that you understand yourself better, it is easier to determine exactly what you need to change your circumstances and move towards your goal. You can't manipulate or influence other people, if you can't manipulate yourself.

Another advantage of mastering the skills in the last chapter is that you become more aware of others around you. By paying more attention to both verbal and non-verbal cues they give, you will almost feel like you're a mind reader. You will be able to discern their moods, wants, fears, desires, etc. This knowledge can be used to find your first target for manipulation.

When choosing a target, look for certain traits that the individual demonstrates to show they are open to receiving and responding to your powers of influence. So, as you scope out potential prospects, look for these characteristics. Don't assume that if someone is displaying these qualities that they are in some way inferior to you or others. To the contrary, many of the following qualities are quite admirable. As we've already stated, any facet of a person's character can be used in both a positive and a negative way. We are only looking for a doorway to enter and implement a possible means of exercising your powers of persuasion.

They are Conscientious

People who are conscientious are not likely to be focusing entirely on themselves. Conscientious people are concerned about the quality of their work, the welfare of others, and their commitment to any task that has been assigned to them. While they may be concerned about how events will affect them, their primary concern will be determined by their moral compass. In order to exercise some level of influence over them, you need to tap into their powerful sense of morality. Once you can show them how they can achieve their goals in relation to that, you will have a powerful means in which to persuade them to do what you want them to do.

They Have Empathy

A good target will have strong empathetic tendencies. Empathy can be viewed as the emotional fuel that you can use to propel you towards your goals. People with empathy often are given praise, attention and valuable resources freely, putting you in a state of comfort as you make your requests or needs know.

Empathetic people are excellent at putting themselves in your shoes. They can feel your pain in their heart and because of this, they will do everything within their power to relieve you of it. You can use that empathy to your advantage by telling a store, apologizing, or carefully framing a scenario to gain their sympathy.

They Have Integrity

A person with integrity is true to their word and can be of immense value to you. They are not inclined to cheat or steal, nor are they likely to break off a relationship until it is absolutely necessary. Even if they realize later that you have taken unfair advantage of them, their sense of integrity is usually what keeps them from retaliation. The relationship you build with them will be strong and their entire sense of being will keep them from betraying it no matter what.

They are Resilient

A good target will be resilient enough to bounce back from any incidents that may cause them harm. This resiliency makes them strong enough to stand up against of the pressures you can put on them. Even if they are faced with difficult challenges these are the people who are less likely to give up. While all their instincts may be telling them to run the other way, they are more likely to stay the course in spite of it all.

Establishing a relationship with them is the same as obligating them to you. They are unlikely to turn on you even if they discover that they are being manipulated.

They are Sentimental

A person who is very sentimental leads with his heart in everything he does. A manipulator can use flattery and praise to position the target and set them up for persuasion. The words used need to address their unique needs and desires. By idolizing them from the very start of the relationship, you can garner their trust and appeal to their most basic need for love. Creating pleasant memories together pulls at their heartstrings and bonds them into a relationship you can use later to get what you want.

They best way to influence a sentimentalist is to carefully study them, determine their individual qualities and the things that they value the most. By establishing a relationship with them and picking up on their verbal-and non-verbal cues, you can uncover their insecurities and weaknesses.

These are the basic characteristics you will find in those who are easy targets for manipulation. It doesn't mean that they are the only one you will be able to work your magic with, but these are the ones you will most likely find success with as you start to apply the manipulation strategies will we be discussing throughout this book.

What Hooks People In?

Anything that draws our attention can be used as a key tool of manipulation. So, when choosing a target to persuade in one way or another, it is important that you use those things that will naturally hook people and draw them into you. Your hook, however, needs to be something that your target won't have to think too much about. In fact, you don't even want them to get even the slightest inkling that you're pulling them in. With the right skill, you will be able to subtly draw them into your circle without ever making them consciously aware that they are caught in your web.

Whether you're trying to entice a love interest or you're trying to get your foot in the door of your next job, your first task is to draw the person in. This can be tricky and the answers can vary depending on your target. However, there are common threads you can find in all sorts of people. Since most people are more inclined to listen to you when they feel respected it's a given that if you can tap into their personal sense of self, you'll be halfway there. Consider these very basic qualities and test them out to see if they will work with your intended target.

Become a Good Listener: People will naturally be drawn to you if they feel that you are listening to what they have to say. But this involves more than just giving the appearance that you are interested in what they have to say. When you are a dedicated listener, you are fully engaged in their message.

This does several things that can work in your favor. First, you'll become a better communicator but you will also be building up a level of trust between you and the other person. That rapport will work on a subconscious level slowly building up a deeper and more meaningful connection between the two of you.

An active listener requires commitment and focus. It may not be easy at first, but to show keen interest in what the other person is saying. That means not responding to distractions or interruptions but being completely present in the moment. You may have to ask questions for clarification, regularly insert words in the conversation so they know you're still with them, turning off or not answering your phone when calls come in, and giving your whole attention to them.

Being Observant

Active listening also means watching the other person's non-verbal cues as well. You will be paying close attention to their body language and verbal intonation. In other words, you want to not only hear what they are saying to you but how they are saying it. This will give you valuable information about their emotional state of mind.

For example, if they are whimpering or speaking in a low tone of voice it may be a sign that they are worried or fearful. However, if they are shouting it could be an indication that they are angry or frustrated.

But in order for these observations to draw them in, you need to find ways to show them that you are committed to them. By mirroring back some of their expressions, and clarifying your understanding of those points, you are demonstrating to them that you are kindling a new relationship with them. It will endear them to you on a subconscious level. The more they are able to believe that you value their input and their message, the more attractive you will be to them and they will respond to you accordingly.

Kindness

We live in a world where true and genuine kindness is hard to find. If you want to really hook people in, just a simple act of kindness may be all that is needed. Kindness does not necessarily mean the giving of gifts. While that may be a part of it, sometimes just the habit of saying kind words, smiling, or showing a genuine active of consideration may be all that is needed to show people that you care.

This should not come as a surprise to you. You've probably already experienced how you respond to people who are kind to you. You should think no less of those who you are trying to lure into your circle. In fact, it has been scientifically proven that both men and women are more drawn to people who are compassionate and selfless. It is actually quite a powerful means of attracting others and can literally influence a person even if the kindness is not shown to them. In other words, it can also work if they are just mere observers of your acts of kindness even if they are not the recipient.

The concept of kindness can be extended beyond the obvious. A 2013 study showed that both men and women were drawn to people who had a more helping spirit, actually finding them to be more attractive on all levels. Demonstrating a preference for others in a helpful manner can appeal to people on the most basic of levels as this is an indication that a helpful person will fill need for protection in a dangerous world.

Smiling

Hooking people can be as easy as smiling. It is the one act that will cost you nothing but can yield you lots of results. Smiling not only makes you stand out as kind and helpful, but it also releases your own endorphins and serotonin in your body. Both of these naturally produced chemicals will not only improve your own mood but is infectious enough to improve the mood of those around you, including your target.

Studies have shown that just seeing a smiling face can activate the pleasure center of the brain giving your target a sense of satisfaction and reward. According to the School of Psychology conducted at the University of Aberdeen in Scotland, those who received smiles from others (even if indirectly) were naturally drawn to the smiler.

Consistency

People crave stability in their lives. If you're serious about drawing other people to you then consistency is the key. Instability in jobs, home life, even our diets cause people distress. Life becomes unpredictable and confusing. A person who has an inconsistent person in their lives never gain the ability to feel secure.

Your target will naturally be drawn to you on a subconscious level if your behavior is consistent and reliable. To reinforce this gravitational pull, if your consistency is in line with their personal attitudes, beliefs, and core values it will be that much easier to draw them in.

Obligation

People can also be hooked and drawn over to you by obligating them to you. This is interesting in that quite often the obligation starts even before you do anything directly. Think of the company that offers a free gift of very little value. Sometimes referred to as the theory of reciprocity, it is a concept that is deeply ingrained in us from a very early age. When someone does something for us, we feel indebted to reciprocate in some way. They may not expect anything in return, but the power is so strong that it compels us anyway.

This power is so strong that there is only one way to rid ourselves of this need to return like for like is to do something for the other person. Even if you don't want or even like the gift or favor, you feel compelled to follow through quite often with a sense of urgency. It is a kind of psychological debt that can sometimes be so strong that it drives a person to sometimes exceed the original gift many times over.

Connection

It's a natural inclination in all of us. The more connected we are to others the more influence they have over our decisions. By creating a bond, you create comfort in others. Even if you've known them only a short time that bond can make it seem like a lifelong relationship.

There are four main elements to a strong connection:

- Attraction: By choosing a single positive quality and using it to influence the general perception, people will naturally feel connected to you. By displaying qualities like kindness, intelligence, and loyalty, people will find you more attractive.

- Rapport: Rapport is a little bit more difficult to define. It is a hidden quality that puts you on the same mental wavelength as the other person. It's that feeling you get when you meet someone and instantly hit it off. That secret something that automatically bonds you to another person. Sometimes rapport is readily recognizable as in a physical attraction or a common understanding. Other times it is a little harder to identify. You've probably seen cases where two people have no obvious common ground but they develop a rapport just the same.

- People skills (EQ): Your ability to work well with people can forge a strong bond with them. According to some research, at least 85% of your success will depend on how you interact with others; the other 15% can be related to your intelligence and specific training. As we discussed in the last chapter, your EQ is crucial to your ability to take that knowledge and skill base and connect it to other people.

- Similarity: People are naturally drawn to things they are familiar with. So, by utilizing those characteristics that people feel comfortable with, you can connect to more people. Studies have revealed that people are naturally attracted to things they can relate to and understand. By matching your personality traits with their lifestyles, they will be impelled to connect to you.

When all four of these elements are in play you can build a strong bond that long-standing relationships can be founded upon.

Social Pressure

Because we are social creatures by nature, all of us, no matter how shy, have an inborn desire to belong to something. A good manipulator will definitely look for someone who is searching for some form of inclusion to his advantage. For all of us, if the desire to become a group is strong enough, it can easily cause us to change our viewpoint and perceptions just so we can fit in.

We all care to some extent, about what others think of us and we all seek validation, even if we don't want to admit it. It is this inborn desire to fit in with the main crowd that determines our view of what is considered "correct" behavior. If our actions go against the mainstream of the masses, our behavior is frowned upon, but the more we fit in, the "correct" others will perceive us and the more likely they will be willing to conform to what you want. It is a natural part of human nature, and the more you can create an approved form of social pressure, the more your targets will feel validated and bond with you.

Scarcity

People have an inner drive to not miss out on things. This is why limited time offers usually work very well when it comes to sales. The natural tendency is to put things off until a later time when there is no real immediate need, but by creating sense of urgency, you can trigger an impulse reaction that will compel people to move even if their own minds tell them it's not necessary.

Scarcity triggers that inborn fear of missing out or FOMO. Think of how things work in an auction. Usually at an auction, there is a limited supply of a specific item (often only one). When another person outbids you, a sort of panic starts to set in. What if you can't find this item again, what if someone considers the item more valuable than you? Perhaps you missed something? All sorts of thoughts start to running through your head and suddenly, the drive to obtain that item becomes more powerful than your own common sense. No matter what you planned before the event, it can quickly go right out the window when this factor starts to put pressure on you.

This factor can be extremely powerful when played the right way. The more scarcity you can create, the more valuable it will be in the eyes of others.

Language

Your choice of words also has a great deal of influence on other people. Because we are social creatures, at least 60% of our daily lives is spent on oral communication. By choosing words that appeal to the ears of your target, you can capture their attention and bring your story to life. Words can generate a powerful source of energy and convince people to respond to your message. By the same token, the wrong words can crush all of your hard work in mere seconds.

The more adept you are at using the spoken word, the more persuasive you will be. While body language makes up the lion's share of our communication skills, do not underestimate the power of your words. They have a direct impact on the beliefs, attitudes, and perceptions of those around us. Used in the wrong way, you could lose a lot more than you bargained for. Even newscasters are specifically trained to use certain inflections in their voices to project a sense of authority and knowledge.

Elements of voice control also influence people. Consider how you emphasize words, your pitch, pace, fillers, volume, articulation and even where you pause when you speak. Even your lack of words has power. Knowing when to speak and when to let the silence have power says a lot about your own level of confidence.

Creating Contrast

Contrast is usually something that is better understood in art, but when applied in persuasion can literally bond someone to you with little effort. When you present someone with two scenarios that seem like they are worlds apart you are creating a contrast. Imagine realizing that you need thousands of dollars to redecorate your home, and then later learning that most of the cost can be eliminated by using a different designer. This is creating contrast. Chances are you will feel indebted to the new designer or contractor that saved you all the money, even if you later learn that none of the other expenses you thought you needed were even necessary.

They key to the success of using contrast is to use the two scenarios close together. If too much time is allowed to pass before the favorable option is presented, contrast loses much of its power. Because people will naturally be drawn to positive news, when they hear negative reports they are usually emotionally thrown. Here, timing is key. If you submit your concept in quick succession with another great idea, your message will have little impact. There is not enough contrast between the two ideas. However, if you submit your idea immediately after someone else presents a bad idea, the power of your message will cut right to the heart of the listeners and you will see an immediate reaction.

Creating Expectations

Many people make decisions based on what they know others will expect them to do. We see this often in children. If the parents expect them to behave poorly in a given situation, they will usually oblige them. The same is true of all of us. If your target is aware of your expectations, they will usually act accordingly.

People have all sorts of ways to show what they expect of you. Some will tell you directly what they want and others will use more subtle means. For example, if you are meeting someone for the first time, how you introduce yourself lets them know exactly how you want to be addressed. If you use your title and surname, then they know you want to be addressed that way. However, if you tell them a nickname or just a first name, they are more likely to feel more at ease and comfortable around you. The casualness of your words can put them at ease.

Whenever you communicate with others, you're letting them know what your expectations are.

Involvement

You have much more influence over another person when they are involved in what you are doing or saying. Efforts to engage the other person requires you to tap into their sensory perceptions. We all have five senses that is continually feeding the brain. The more of these senses we are able to engage in, the more involved and committed to you the other person will be. By creating a very specific atmosphere you can yield a powerful influence over them.

Just talking to the other person is not sufficient enough to influence people because listening is merely a passive exercise. It doesn't evoke any emotions or connection. However, if the other person is listening, smelling, tasting, and feeling all at the same time, it would be nearly impossible for their mind to drift off and focus on something else.

There are several ways you can create a sense of involvement in the other person. If you're in a discussion with them, make sure the conversation is not one-sided. Ask information questions that will naturally compel them to contribute to the discussion. You can engage their creative mind by telling stories designed to touch them emotionally. By creating an atmosphere of suspense, you can keep them hanging on to your every word until you achieve your set goal. The more involved a person is in your goal the more likely they will do whatever is necessary to give you what you want.

Build Self-Esteem

One might think that a person with a weak self-esteem is easy to manipulate but that would not be entirely correct. The general belief is that anyone that is lacking in self-esteem craves acceptance. The reality though is that acceptance, praise, and recognition is a common need shared by all of us. It speaks to the core of what it means to be human.

Watch what happens when you praise anyone, even with the smallest and most insignificant expressions. You can literally see their spirits lift and their mood change. All humans need praise and recognition. In fact, it is the only way a person gets built up psychologically over time. Praise from others satisfies our need to be a part of something bigger than ourselves.

When persuading others, presenting your message in a way that edifies your listeners will take you much farther than you might imagine. The more you build them up, the more they will be inclined to follow you through to your goal. This rule is true for everyone regardless of their level of self-esteem. But the mere fact that self-esteem is key to their connection with you, your goal should be making your listener feel needed and respected.

You will have to walk a fine line here though. There is a big difference in helping to build someone's self-esteem and boosting someone's ego. So, don't go overboard when it comes to this practice. Make sure you understand the difference because this quality could easily backfire on you.

Association

As social beings, our brains subconsciously look for connections in everything we do. We do this so quickly we rarely recognize that we have automatically categorized people as soon as we make a connection. These categories instantly put some people closer to us and others far away. We categorize based on a myriad of options. We might decide where they fit in our lives based on the colors they wear, the people they are with, the jobs they have, the music they listen to, or even emotions they express. We use these associations to make judgments about them and how deep our relationship with them will be.

When you are trying to apply your powers of persuasion you utilize this internal and instinctive need to create the type of relationship you need. You can tap into it to bring out certain emotions you need them to employ to bond them to you. Obviously, everyone's idea of association will be different so before you can use the art of association, you need to learn enough about that person to figure out what kind of associations you need.

Balance

When you are manipulating your target, your focus needs to be on their emotions but that does not mean that you can neglect their ability to reason on things. There has to be some level of balance in order to get your desired results. You may be able to evoke a powerful emotional response that may last for a while but no one can maintain intense emotions all the time. By the same token, you may be able to use careful reasoning and logic analyzing a certain situation but that will eventually become boring and they may lose interest.

Emotions can stimulate a person to action, generating the necessary energy to move them in the direction you want them to go. Logic works by laying a foundation they can rely on to make their decisions. By creating a careful balance between the two, you can create the perfect environment for evoking the right response.

To become a master manipulator, you will need all of these qualities, but you will use them each to different degrees depending on your target. Everyone needs them in order to tailor their message for the best results.

7 Qualities That Signify the Perfect Target

With the above qualities, just about anyone can be manipulated. However, there are some people that will stand out as the perfect target for persuasion. These people will show some express vulnerabilities that will be easy to identify.

The need to please: Some people crave attention so much that they will be more than eager to please others. This may stem from a need to be accepted or a low self-esteem, but these people are pretty easy to pick out from a crowd. Push just a few of their buttons and they will usually fall in line pretty quickly.

Fishers of compliments: Along with that need to please, many will also be constantly fishing for compliments. In other words, they will constantly be creating scenarios where they will earn praise and approval from those around them.

Fear of their own negative emotions: They will fight very hard not to display any sign of negativity in their lives. They may resist the tendency to express disapproval of something they seek, their disappointment, frustration or anger. They will apply avoidance techniques in order to not show that they feel uncomfortable about a given situation. They may work hard to find the right words to say what you want to hear in order to not lose their connection with you.

Lack of assertiveness: Assertiveness is one's ability to feel self-assured and confident about themselves and to have the kind of control that keeps them from being aggressive and overpowering others. People who are assertive do not need to demand or force others to do things. They have a quiet and controlled demeanor that naturally draws people on. However, those who lack assertiveness are very unsure of themselves, struggle with saying no to anyone even when they are uncomfortable about the situation making them the ideal target for manipulation.

No clear personal boundaries: Those who are willing to compromise on their personal boundaries can make easy targets for manipulation. They lack an established sense of identity and therefore are inclined to bend to the whims of others. When anyone is not clear on who they are or what they should stand for, they tend to stand for everything. They have no firm grounding to base their decisions on and therefore are easily swayed.

Low self-reliance: They lack independence and therefore are always in need of help from others. In essence, they are always in need of other people to help them get through even the most basic things in life. They struggle to survive if someone is not there to provide the basic necessities for them.

Belief in their own self-control: Sometimes referred to as locus of control, it does not reference one's level of control over certain events but rather to one's belief that they have control. This is a very big difference. When one believes that outside factors have more control over a situation than they do it leaves them open to all sorts of persuasions.

A person that believes he has control will more likely believe that anything he does has in some way been caused by him. When something goes wrong, he'll accept the blame rather than shifting it to someone else. However, if he believes that the fault lies in external factors, he will likely not want to take responsibility even if it is pointed out that he is responsible.

Any one of these qualities will make a person a pretty easy target for manipulation. In most cases, they won't be hard to find, they may even have a form of nervous behavior that will put their low self-esteem on display. An effective manipulator should first take the time to observe potential targets and look for these specific characteristics to identify them.

The Targets That are Harder to Win Over

No matter how careful you are in choosing your targets, there will inevitably come a time when you're going to find someone who resists your attempts to manipulate them. It's true, everyone will fall for the strategies of manipulation at one time or another, even those who you might feel are relatively wise. However, there are those few that will not succumb to your attempts no matter what you do. Trying to influence these targets can literally leave you with a headache as you struggle to overcome their resistance.

However, there are those who have been "burned" before by past manipulators. So, while you may be able to overcome their objections, their defenses will be up and they will be on guard for any other possible forms of influence.

Think about it. A common manipulation strategy is to promise them relief from whatever stresses or worries they are trying to overcome. However, those who have been burned have a highly suspicious nature and will question everything, even seeing ulterior motives in your efforts. You will have to work pretty hard to overcome those objections.

Their past baggage will cause them to approach every new relationship with an anticipation that something is wrong. It will take a lot of work to get them to believe in any promises you make, no matter how reasonable you sound. They may even insist on solid evidence, physical proof, or even more time for you to show that you are worth the trust you are asking for.

Another person you may have trouble reaching are those who are "loners." It is human nature to find a place within a social network. The common and often unspoken belief that there is safety in numbers is what makes a person an easy target. People who are loners, content with their own company have somehow overcome that need and are less likely to succumb to the same tactics that others may follow.

A person who is not part of a family, team, religion, or tied to any other group does not feel the need or is resistant to inclusion. While this is a natural inclination that we are all born with, they have learned to survive without it. In order to reach those people, you will have to rekindle that need in them in order to get them on your side.

A good manipulator seeks out weaknesses and works at them until they can trigger an emotional reaction. Your main goal is to get them so emotionally involved that they develop a sort of tunnel vision that gets them to push their own logical reasoning ability aside and respond emotionally to your needs. In essence, you are creating a narrow-minded focus in them, so they only see what you want them to see.

Those people who are resistant are strong willed enough to carefully think through every scenario will be your most difficult targets. They may actually be manipulators themselves and will therefore recognize your tactics as soon as you apply them. It doesn't mean that they can't be overcome with these strategies, but you will likely have to work longer and harder to get them to where you want them to be.

It's true, there are some targets that will seem impervious to your efforts, but don't let that discourage you. Where you can't find success with one person there are plenty others that you will be able to influence.

Chapter Four: Decoding Body Language

Communication is much more than just words. Inside of all of us there is a hidden code that we inherited at birth that allows us to communicate even when words are not available. In fact, this hidden form of language is far more reliable than the words we choose to speak. Through it, we let others know how we are feeling, what we are thinking, and our innermost desires.

Body language is more than just gesturing because its roots are embedded deep in our subconscious. One movement can relay more meaning than a thousand words strung together, no matter how poignant. Still, few of us have learned how to read this language and use it to our advantage. We are often so focused on the verbal message people are delivering that we fail to notice what is right in front of our eyes.

This form of non-verbal communication is done on a subconscious level and the messages others are sending to you can be very valuable to a manipulator. Not only can you read and interpret what others are saying, you can learn from your own actions what kind of messages you are sending out. Either way, understanding the underlying mean of these body signals can give you a wealth of information that will make it easier to create a persuasive strategy you can rely on.

Reading the Body's Subtle Signals

There are two kinds of body language cues you can look for: positive and negative. Positive body cues tell you if the person is feeling confident about what he is saying or comfortable in his surroundings. You will see them in all sorts of settings so whether you're talking one to one or you're in a group, these will easily be observed.

- Standing erect with head high and shoulders back
- Making good eye contact and smiling eyes
- Comfortably gesturing with hands and arms while engaged in conversation
- Speaks clearly with a moderate tone of voice
- Nodding his head to indicate is listening and interested in the conversation

Negative body cues are an indication that there is some level of discomfort either with you or with the setting. Look out for these signs:

- Avoiding eye contact
- Minimal hand or arm gestures. They keep their arms close to the body as if in a defensive mode.
- No nodding or smiling while listening or when speaking
- Arms folded across the body – this tells you they are closed off or are unwilling to accept what is happening.
- Nervous tapping of hands or feet
- Clenched fists
- Speaks quickly or at a high pitch

There are signs that may not relay comfort or confidence, but rather how interested a person may be in your message. Recognizing these can help to determine if you are really reaching a person or if your words are falling on deaf ears.

- If they're head is down and there is no eye contact it usually indicates a lack of interest
- Signs of active listening or concentrating on what is being said involves getting the whole body involved in the conversation. Signs of active listening:
  - Repeating or paraphrasing your words

- Leaning forward or to the side while listening
- Slight tilt of the head or if sitting, resting the head on one hand
- Mirroring your facial expressions
- Steepling the fingers – sign of authority and control

When there is a lack of interest, you will see other signs.

- They may be easily distracted
- Constantly checking the time
- Doodling
- Playing with their hair
- Picking at their fingernails
- Not asking questions
- Staring at something else
- Fiddling with small objects

Before you can become a master manipulator you have to become a master at body language. Skillful use of it can help you to decide on the spot whether you need to change tactics or not. It doesn't matter what your goal may be, knowing the message can tell help you to land that perfect job, negotiate the best price, win an argument, or whether you should proceed with a relationship.

It is important to note here that these are the subtle cues founded in modern western culture. Body language signs are not universal and therefore can vary from one culture to the next. If you are not living in the modern western culture like in America, the UK, or Canada, it would be smart to take the time to learn these cues before you attempt regular communication. One gesture in one area could mean something entirely different where you are.

The Secret Messages of the Face

Our faces are also very expressive sending out messages that words can never convey clearly. We all know about smiles and their meanings, but did you know that there were different types of smiles, each one with its own unique message? A smile can show you're happy, shy, warm, or fake. There is one smile called the "Duchenne" smile that is considered the most genuine of all. It is the one that the corners of your mouth pull upward while you squeeze your eye muscles making crow's feet in the corners. Fake smiles do not have the crow's feet in the corner of the eyes – when you see that, you know that the person is not sincere in his expressions. Fake smiles tend to show more teeth than genuine smiles.

Frowns on the other hand, show disapproval, unhappiness, or doubt. A person may tell you he's feeling good about something but the look on his face could be sending you an entirely different message. Body language can tell you a lot about what someone is feeling but facial expressions tell you clearly how a person is feeling.

Unlike gestures and movements in body language that do not cross cultural boundaries, facial expressions are universal. No matter what background or history a person has these expressions can clearly be seen in every part of the world. Research has even indicated that most of us, without realizing it, make judgments based almost entirely on a person's facial expressions. We conclude that if someone's face reflects joy and happiness, they are more intelligent than someone who is constantly showing anger. This helps us to understand how valuable it can be to learn and understand true facial expressions. It speaks to the core feelings of your target so that know exactly what you are dealing with.

Eyes: There is a reason why people have described the eyes as the window to the soul. There is so much expression in them that sometimes people do not have to say a word but their thoughts and feelings come across very clearly. When you are involved in a conversation take the time to observe their eyes. The way they move will give you a glimpse into what's going on in their brain.

- Gazing: When they are making direct eye contact with you, they are showing interest to what you are saying. However, the length of time they gaze can also reflect meaning. Have you noticed how uncomfortable you become if someone gives you prolonged eye contact? That's because we naturally perceive this type of gazing as a threat, much like a predator would feel uncomfortable if a dog was watching you intently.

  Breaking eye contact also shows you that your listener is bored, distracted, or is trying to hide his true feelings about the discussion.

- Blinking: We all blink frequently throughout our waking hours, but when you notice someone blinking too much or not enough, they are sending you an unconscious message. Too few blinks means that they are deliberately controlling their eye movements. Gamblers often do this to resist the temptation to appear too excited about a potential outcome. If you notice rapid blinking it is usually an indication that they are feeling nervous or uncomfortable.

- Pupil size is an amazing sign that most people have no idea they are using. Pupils react to environmental lighting but beyond that, they also reflect emotions in their small changes in size. If they are highly dilated, it could be a sign that they are keenly interested or aroused.

- If they are moving up and to the right when answering a question, it could mean they are lying. Up and to the left usually means they are being honest with you.

- Disgust can be seen when the eyes narrow. It is a negative response and when it is accompanied by tight lips it can mean anger or hostility. Usually the narrower the eyes become the more intense the negative emotion.

- Eye blocking or the covering his eyes after you've made a request usually indicates that they are uncomfortable with something you've just said or that they disagree with your viewpoint.

- Arched eyebrows often show happiness, especially if it is accompanied by a smile or by the pupils getting larger. You will notice mothers do this often when they see their children.

- Fear is also showed with arched eyebrows but is accompanied with wide open eyes and the absence of a smile. There is also a quick and fleeting look and the pupils will dilate as a result of a quick burst of adrenaline flooding the system.

- Probably the most important thing you want to see in the eyes is their focus. When they are keenly interested in your message, their pupils will start to constrict. The opposite is also true, if they are not interested you can expect to see the pupils dilate.

These non-verbal cues can be awesome tools when it comes to reading people's emotions. The next time you are engaged in conversation, start to take notice of these subtle little glimpses into their soul. You will begin to see a whole new world unfold right before you and what you learn can help you to understand exactly what you need to do in order to achieve your goals.

The Mouth: The mouth also says a lot even when the person is not speaking. Every expression has a meaning and learning how to read them is essential for anyone who is looking to persuade someone.

- Covering the mouth: This is usually an attempt to be polite. People do this when they are coughing or sneezing, but they also do it when they are bored or yawning, which could be a warning sign that you need to change tactics. One thing you want to watch out for is covering the mouth as a sign of disapproval.

- Pursed lips: When they tighten the lips, it is a sign of distrust or disapproval of some kind.

- Biting lips: This is a cue that they are worried or stressed about something.

- Turned up at the corners: Indicates that they are happy or optimistic.

- Turned down at the corners means sadness or disapproval. If the gesture is prominent it could mean extreme distaste.

Gestures: Gestures, like the eyes, are usually some of the most obvious signs that reflect a person's inner feelings. We automatically read gestures without giving them a second thought. No one would question the meaning of a wave or pointing or even counting on the figures. Those are quite easy to understand, but there are also cultural gestures that you might encounter. If you've traveled a lot, you'll notice that a gesture in one country does not always translate to gestures in another country. These are common gestures found in the United States.

- *Clenched fists:* in some instances, it could be a reflection of anger. However, if it is made with the arm upraised it usually means solidarity or unity.
- *Thumbs up:* approval
- *Thumbs down:* disapproval
- *Pinching thumb and forefinger together:* This is a sign of approval or saying everything is okay.
- *The V sign:* This sign, made by holding up the index and middle finger in the shape of a V means victory. It some areas it can also mean peace.

The Extremities: Arms and legs are excellent communicators. For example, Crossing your legs and turning them away from the other person lets you know that the other person is taking a defensive position and is wary of you. By paying attention to what the extremities are telling you it will be easy to determine if what they are saying is matching their feelings.

- *Crossing the arms:* the person is feeling defensive or is closed off, not willing to open up to you.
- *Hands on hips:* a sign that they are in control. If the posture looks more defiant it could also be a sign of aggression.
- *Hands clasped behind the back:* this gesture could be a sign that they are bored or anxious. Sometimes could be a sign of anger and frustration.
- *Fidgeting or tapping fingers:* When done rapidly, it is a clear sign that they are impatient or frustrated.
- *Crossing legs:* indication that they are closed off or that they need some separateness or privacy.

Posture: Our posture is another way we unconsciously communicate to others, How we hold our bodies can reflect many things from the state of our health to our sense of confidence. There are two types of posture to watch for.

- *Open:* when the trunk of the body is exposed it tells others that they are open and friendly. An open posture usually means that they are willing and ready to comply.
- *Closed:* When the trunk of the body is closed off by stances like hunching forward or crossing the arms the legs, it can be a show of hostility or anxiety. Usually not a friendly gesture.

Personal Space: In America, people take their personal space very seriously. If you stand too close, they are likely to feel very uncomfortable. It is best to maintain a respectable distance between you and the person you're interacting with. A little too close and they will become defensive and wary, a little too far and they are likely to get the sense that you are being closed off and uninterested.

- *Intimate conversations usually require a distance between 6 to 18 inches.* This distance is acceptable for those in a close relationship and allows for more intimacy and private discussion. The close proximity allows for intimate touching, hugging, and whispering.
- *When it is not an intimate discussion but can still be considered a personal relationship such as with family and friends a distance of 1.5 to 4 feet is considered acceptable.* The amount of distance you maintain between the other person reflects on how close the relationship is. The closer you are the more intimate the bond.
- *In social or group settings, maintaining a physical distance of 4 to 12 feet is acceptable.* This is the acceptable distance for personal acquaintances like co-workers and business

associates. When dealing with people who you are unfamiliar with or those you interact with infrequently, it might be best to stay on the further end of the range.

- *Public distance of up to 15 feet is maintained when you don't need to have direct personal contact. For example, when you are giving a presentation or speaking to an audience you wouldn't want to be too close to your listeners. The distance allows you to make brief eye contact with different people in the audience without making them feel like they have been singled out.*

While you won't need to go out with a measuring tape to determine the proper distance to allow for personal space, you can take your cues from those around you. This is especially important when you are dealing with cultures from other countries. For example, personal space in most Asian cultures is not as important as it is in North America. The same is true with those from Latin America. The more you observe this distance the more effective you will be at reaching your target audience.

Understanding body language will naturally make you a better communicator but it will also help you to understand the signals you're sending out into the universe. This is by no means a full selection of possible gestures so it would be a good idea to do additional research on the topic. That said, just by applying these listed here you will be well on your way to understanding what needs to be done to persuade others.

Understanding Microexpressions

Before, we discussed the importance of facial gestures in understanding communication. However, one area of facial expressions that we are now beginning to get a better grasp on is that of microexpressions. These are involuntary gestures that happen very quickly when a feeling or emotion is first felt. These generally are more reliable than any other facial gesture as they are impulse reactions that the person has no time to think about. They happen quickly and usually occur within the first fractions of a second after the emotion arises generally starting at ½ of a the first second and lasting 1/15th and 1/25th of a second before fading. Because they appear and disappear so quickly, they are good indicators of any emotion that a person is trying to hide or suppress.

Learning how to detect these microexpressions is key to becoming persuasive but before you can master this skill, you have to understand the dynamics of the human face and what you should be looking for. According to Dr. Paul Ekman, these expressions are pretty universal. Everyone, no matter where they are from, shares at least seven common expressions that have exactly the same meaning. While there are plenty more microexpressions to learn, knowing at least these seven will give you a pretty good picture of the person you are dealing with and what to expect.

Surprise: This common expression is seen by the raising of the upper eyelids, the eyebrows raised and curved. You should also see the mouth partially open when the jaw drops but the lips and mouth muscles will remain relaxed. The length of this expression tells you if the person is surprised or fearful. If it lasts longer than a second it is more likely a sign of fear.

Fear: Similar to surprise, fear can be seen when the upper eyelids are raised up. The eyebrows are lifted and pulled together making a flat line. The mouth opens slightly and the lip muscles are tensed and pulled back tightly.

Disgust: This classic look is easy to recognize by the wrinkles that form around the nose. The eyebrows are drawn down and the eyes narrow. The upper lid, cheek muscles, and the lower lip are tensed into a sneer making the teeth visible.

Anger: When a person is angry both the upper and lower eyelids are drawn tightly together. The eyebrows are pulled down in the center and drawn together tightly. You'll see vertical lines appear between the eyebrows and the eyes themselves take on a strong stare or start to bulge out. Some people have a habit of thrusting the jaw forward when they are extremely angry.

Happiness: This emotion is seen when both sides of the mouth pull up in the corners making a symmetrical smile. Many people try to pretend to be happy by forcing a smile but you should be able to tell the difference by looking at the corners of the eye. Genuine happiness also shows in the eyes as well as the mouth. Look for the corner eye muscles to engage showing the tell-tale signs of crow's feet. Expect to see more engagement of the face muscles when happiness is genuine than you will with a forced display of emotion.

Sadness: This feeling can be seen when the corner muscles of the lips pull down at the sides and the lower lip juts out in a pout. You may also see the inside corner of the eyebrows lift slightly.

Contempt: This emotion can be clearly identified by the classic raising of one side of the mouth making a sneer or a smirk.

Microexpressions are universal and common. They differ from regular expressions in that they are very difficult to intentionally create. People can readily hide their innermost feelings with regular facial gestures but microexpressions are formed in a different part of the brain and are impulse reactions. They are fleeting at best and disappear as quickly as they come so to notice them and identify them will require you to pay very close attention to your target so you can catch that one instant that will reveal everything you need to know.

What Walking Styles Say About Someone

Most of us do not spend a lot of time worrying about how a person walks but a recent study published in *Social Psychological and Personality Science,* gives us good reason to consider it. The study conducted in 2017 by a health and wellness expert at Maple Holistics reveal that one's walking speed could tell us at least five different personality traits. These traits: agreeableness, openness, extraversion, conscientiousness, and neuroticism can tell us a lot about the kind of people we are dealing with.

There is a great deal to be learned when you analyze their speed, stride, and how they hold their arms when they are walking. By analyzing these characteristics, you can reveal something about them that you may not otherwise be able to pick up.

Fast Walkers: People who walk fast tend to be more outgoing and maybe even more conscientious. In fact, the faster they walk the more outgoing they tend to be.

Slow Walkers: Those who move at a slower pace reflect a more cautious personality. When they take shorter strides at a more leisurely pace it could reflect a little bit of me-ism as they are classic signs of a self-centered personality. However, this does not necessarily mean that it is a bad thing. It simply reflects a person who is looking out for his own best interests. Those who are more introverted may also walk slow but their body language reveals a lack of confidence. They keep their head down and pull into themselves. A cautious person is not an introvert but rather more careful about his decisions. He walks with his head held high so he can see and analyze everything in his environment.

Veering to the Left: People who gradually veer to the left as they walk tend to be showing signs of anxiety and stress. The further they veer off the straight path the more anxiety they are feeling. No one fully understands this phenomenon but it is believed that the right side of the brain is more fully engaged in solving problems or dealing with their worries or fears than the left side.

The Saunter: When someone takes a more leisurely stroll, literally sauntering down their path with their head held high but no clear destination in sight it is a powerful sign of confidence. These people fall into a slow and easy stride reflecting the calm state of mind.

Energetic Walker: Those who move with a high energy in their step are super conscientious and are more detail oriented. They walk quickly even when covering short distances. For instance, they may move just a few steps to a chair or across the room. Their gait is quick but it is not smooth. Their movements will be jerking as they switch their attention from one thought to the next.

Graceful Walkers: Graceful walkers reflect a quiet and inner sense of confidence, but how you read them will depend on the direction their feet are pointed. When their feet are pointing outwards as they walk it is a sign of high self-esteem. This position is not a natural gait but is one that is taught. Toes pointing inward is a sign of insecurity.

Slumped Shoulders: If their posture has them in a slightly bent forward position with their shoulders hunched over it is a classic sign of discomfort. It is a position that is designed to protect the vital organs of the body. They may have suffered some sort of trauma in their past either physically or psychologically but have not yet recovered.

When it comes to body language, the more you learn the more you realize that every movement, every nuance, and every slight little twitch or gesture is working like a mirror to the reflecting what is going on in the mind and the hearts of the people you are interacting with. While learning these things won't make you a mind reader, you can get pretty close to it when you apply them to your art of persuasion.

Chapter Five: Essential Manipulation Tools

The art of manipulation has a very specific goal. You want to change the mind of your target so that you can affect the kind of behavior you want to see. Learning how to read other people and detect their emotional state of mind is only half the battle. Once you understand your target it's time to select the proper manipulation tools to use to your advantage.

There are several different approaches that are very effective in persuading people. The ones included in this chapter work subtly on the subconscious mind so the target never fully realizes what's happening, but they yield the best results.

Everyday Manipulation Tricks

Foot in the Door: The main principle behind this concept is to get someone to do what you want them to do. In essence you are laying the groundwork to ask for a favor. It starts small by asking for a smaller and less important favor first. By doing this, you're building a small but simple connection between the two of you based on an unwritten rule of commitment that you can fall back on later.

The Chinese have been practicing this strategy for centuries. It follows that by doing small but insignificant favors for someone over time causes them to be indebted to you. It's like putting money in the bank so you can make a bigger request later on. While in China, this tool runs much deeper than in western society, it is a powerful weapon in indebting someone to you.

A good example of how this can be used can be seen can be seen in all walks of life. For example, you might find yourself in unfamiliar territory and ask someone for directions. This simple request creates a connection with you. After a simple and brief conversation, you might make your second request by explaining that you're not very good with directions so would rather they showed you instead of telling you. The person may decide to draw you a map or even personally walk you to your destination. There is a good chance of this working if you asked for the smaller favor first. However, if you had just approached a stranger and asked them to walk you to your destination, you almost certainly would have been unsuccessful.

This theory was tested by researchers back in 1966. A group of 156 women were divided into four groups. They started by asking the first three groups to answer a few basic questions about the kitchen products they used. After several days, they asked permission to go through their kitchen so they could catalogue the products they used. The fourth group was only asked the second question. The results showed the effectiveness of this approach with a 52.8% success rate for the first three groups and only a 22.2% success rate for the fourth one.

You can see this applied everywhere you look in marketing. Most online websites start by asking something that doesn't seem to cost you anything. They may ask you for your email address and then later ask for something bigger. Someone may ask you to "like" a page and then later ask you for a comment, which could later lead to a sale.

Door in the Face: The main principle behind this technique is to ask for something extremely big and unreasonable and then when declined, ask for something smaller. It works on the opposite scale of the Foot in the Door technique. In this case, you are requesting something so large that you know you're going to be refused and then you make a request for something that is much easier for them to comply with.

A case in point would be if you asked a friend for a large loan and then when refused, ask for a significantly smaller one. This works primarily because just by making the initial request, you have moved your relationship up to another level causing them to feel some sort of obligation to you. Then it becomes much easier for them to comply with your second request without hesitation.

This fact was verified in a case study performed in the retail market. Researchers used one saleswoman who was selling cheese to people in the Austrian Alps. She first offered hikers passing by two pounds of cheese for eight euros, and when they rejected the sale, she then downgraded her request by offering one pound for four euros. The results were impressive with only a 9% success rate with the first request and a 24% success rate after the second.

Anchoring: The main thought behind anchoring is to create a cognitive bias by creating familiarity with the same or a similar product so your target can make a decision based on this knowledge. There are several ways you can apply this technique from marketing to landing that dream job you want.

It works similar to the Foot in the Door technique. Stores often raise the price of certain products by 15% prior to a 10% sale. People see the price at a discount from the actual posted price not realizing that they are paying even more for the product than they would have before the sale.

Evidence that this works was seen in a study where 100 subjects were given three different options for subscriptions. The first option was an online cost of $59, the second option was for a printed subscription for $125, and a third option was for print and web combination for $125. The results showed that out of the 100 subjects only 16 chose the first option and 84 chose the third option. Then the second option was removed and the same exercise was given to another 100 subjects where only 32 chose the third option with the remaining 68 choosing the first.

The results showed that when option B was a factor it was merely used as an anchor. No one would seriously consider it, but it clearly showed the value of the other two options. This process is an effective means of transferring learning experiences. It its core, it gives people a stimulus or a personal experience from which to base their decisions on.

Commitment & Consistency: The basic principle here is to tap into your target's internal sense of consistency. As creatures of habit, if you are able to get them to commit to something small and insignificant, then you can use that to motivate them to do something more in the future.

All of us do this to some degree in real life. When we go shopping, we buy the same products we are familiar with, we take the same route to work every day, and we usually eat the same things with few variations in every meal. Because of this internal need for consistency, we rarely try things new. By getting someone to do something for you once you start a precedent that they will follow to maintain consistency.

Many online websites use this principle in their marketing efforts. They start by asking potential customers to sign up for regular emails from their company. You've seen them on the screen when you visit their sites with words like "Yes, I like free money," or "Yes, I want to know more." Sometimes they will even give you options that make you feel like you have to choose one over the other. For example, you may be given two options, "Yes, I want to know more about how to make option," and "No, I don't want to be successful." The second option is so far from the truth that you feel compelled to choose the first one. But once you've made the decision, no matter how insignificant, you will feel obligated to stick to it.

To get the best results, the first commitment should be easy to make. It won't cost them much or anything at all. A charity may send out a petition to get people to increase their commitment to their efforts. The initial cost is minimal at best. Later, they can ask for larger donations and most will comply just to keep their level of commitment involved.

Social Proof: We've all heard of peer pressure, right? Social proof is a perfect example of peer pressure at work. The prevailing principle here is that you don't want to be the odd man out. This concept is based on the thought that before anyone makes a decision, they will stop and think about what decision their peers will make and will usually act accordingly.

If you are working in a restaurant and there is an empty tip jar present, you could start the tips coming in by adding the first coins of your own. Customers are much more likely to add to a jar that already has money in it than to be the first to get the ball rolling. You are more likely to leave a comment on an article or video if you see others are doing it as well.

A 1935 case study bears this out. Researchers took several subjects and placed them in a dark room with the only source of light a pinpoint 15 feet away. They were asked to watch the light and give an estimate to how much that light moved. Each participant gave different answers about the movement.

The second day of the study, they were put into groups and asked the same question. This time they all came to a singular agreement that was far removed from the estimates they gave just the day before.

Authority: We learn from an early age to listen to those who have authority. Regardless of the area of expertise, establishing yourself as an authority on a subject will have a powerful influence on others.

Marketing experts use this very effectively with phrases like "9 out of 10" doctors approve this medication. Or they may say something like "our product won 8 out of 10 awards for being the best." Websites and blogs often enlist the endorsement of recognized authorities in their area of expertise, or they post testimonials from past customers to give evidence that they are the professionals they claim to be.

One Yale University psychologist proved this very effectively in a series of studies called the Milgram Experiment. The studies consisted of three different people, the experimenter, the teacher, and the learner.

The teacher's role was to ask the learner questions. If the learner gave a wrong answer, the teacher would give them an electric shock. The experimenter then would press the teacher to continue to use the electric shock even if there was evidence that the learner was in pain.

In the majority of the cases, the teacher would continue to administer pain even they it went against their conscience. In fact, 8 out of 10 teachers would continue to give the electric shocks regardless of the circumstances. This gives evidence that most people are willing to cross even a moral boundary if their instructions are given by someone in authority.

Scarcity: The fear of missing out is a powerful one and it is the principle that scarcity is built on. People use it to create a sense of urgency and compel their targets to make a decision sooner rather than later. In reality, the tendency to want something when it is in short supply is very strong so by convincing someone that soon something is going to run out within a certain amount of time is more likely to drive them to buy it.

Scarcity is probably one of the most often used persuasion techniques in the world today. We see it used in marketing, in relationships, and in the social world. If you've ever tried to book a vacation online, you'll probably be greeted with there are only a few seats left on this flight, or this offer expires at midnight, or you can only buy these at this time a year. The whole premise is what America's Black Friday is based on.

In one study, 180 student subjects were separated into two groups. The first group was given a product and told of its scarcity while the second group was told that there was an abundant supply. The result showed that most subjects were eager to buy simply because they were afraid that it would no longer be available.

A classic example of this is a case discussed by psychiatrist of a car salesman who made it a point to have several people show up for a car at the same time. This created an aire of competition and anxiety between them making the actual car seem more valuable than it really was.

When used successfully, there is unique sense of power for the victor. The theory is that this principle protects one sense of freedom to choose. Whenever freedom of choice is limited, we have an inborn desire to protect it. By increasing scarcity, we instinctively recognize that our access to that item is restricted unless we do something quickly.

Reciprocation: Reciprocation is the act of obligating one to you because of something you've done for them. Regardless of what the gift is, just the act of giving it generates a powerful need to return the favor. We automatically feel indebted to the giver and the manipulator can definitely use it to their advantage.

This can be used in a wide variety of ways. For example, you might offer a free gift for the first contributors to your cause or you could be given a free download of a book before being asked to make a larger purchase.

Evidence bears this out in a study conducted at a New York city restaurant where the waiter would give a small gift before providing the bill. In most cases, this saw an 18% increase in tips. In a similar setting, when the waiter would leave a mint and then walk away, turn around, and give them an additional piece the increase in tips went up to 21%.

These are not the only persuasion techniques there are but they are the most commonly used. Use these to lay the groundwork for your next persuasion strategy and see how much your power of influence will increase.

11 Persuasion Tricks to Start Getting What You Want in Everyday Life

We live in a dog eat dog world. It doesn't matter who or where you are, you will fall into one of two classes: the manipulator or the one being manipulated. We call them mind games and they are being played out all around us. You need to know them just to make sure that you're not caught in the latter group. Not that being manipulated is always a bad thing, but at least if you are being manipulated you know and recognize the signs and you can then use them to your advantage.

How To Influence People

Once you learn these persuasion tricks, you'll be able to use them to get everything you want out of life.

1. **Hardly Evil:** By helping someone else to achieve their own goals you make them indebted to you. The general concept that we all believe in is that you can get what you want from life as long as you help other to achieve their own goals.
2. **A Little Manipulative:** Asking for favors in a more public setting can make people feel more inclined to do things for you. Rather than asking in a more private setting, making a public request is less likely to be turned down.
3. **Bait and Switch:** Using a decoy offer to hook people then offering them something of higher value, and then making a final offer that seems to be of the same value but less effective in order to get them to purchase what you want.
4. **Focus on the Win:** Get your target to realize what he is gaining in the deal rather than what he is losing.
5. **Mirroring:** Mirror the other person's body language to get them to be comfortable with you. They are more likely to connect with you and do what you want.
6. **Watching:** Make them feel as if they are watched. This can be done by showing them an image of eyes. Subconsciously, when we see eyes as in an image or in a video, they will feel as if they are being judged, which will make them alter their behavior to something they feel will be more accepted.
7. **Tap Into Insecurities:** Your choice of words can tap into how they feel about themselves. People tend to think more of their personal identifies when they hear nouns but they think more of their behavior when they hear verbs. If you want to tap into their insecurities, choose more nouns in your conversations than verbs and you'll weaken their defenses.
8. **Deception:** Speak rapidly if you want them to agree with you. Use lots of words to overwhelm them so they will lower their

guard. Many times, they will agree with you because they just can't keep up.
9. **Scheming:** Approach them at the end of the day when they are tired and ready to quit. When people are exhausted, they're more likely to comply with your request because their energy to resist is pretty much spent.
10. **Fear:** Tapping into their fears is an effective way to get people to comply with your request. Expose their fears and then immediately offer a solution.
11. **Confusion:** Deliberately confuse them. Most people's pride won't allow them to admit that they don't fully understand. The easiest response for them is to agree. Offering prices in unfamiliar terms will make them give up because they struggle to mentally process it.

How to Use the Six Laws of Persuasion

The laws of persuasion are constantly in use all around us. It is at the core of every business negotiation, every relationship discussion, every parent-teacher or parent-child debate, and the center of every social media interaction. It is a fact of life that is essential for every one of us whether we're in business or not. Every one of these aspects employs skill negotiations on some level.

To be successful at using these laws, you need to first understand yourself (your EQ) and the goals you want to achieve, but you also need to understand what's in the heart of your target. This will create a platform from which you can launch your influence over others and affect the kind of change you want to see in your world.

But successful manipulation should not be just about what you want. While you will be able to gain a modicum of success thinking only of yourself, your best results will come when you create a situation that will be mutually beneficial for both you and your target. How well you do this will determine the extent of your success and how efficiently you can ensure that all parties are winners in your negotiations. To do this, you need to develop your expertise in employing the six main laws of persuasion.

We don't realize it, but the average person makes around 35,000 decisions every day. Of course, the majority of these choices are made on the subconscious level and therefore do not require any conscious thought. They provide us with ways to simplify our lives, gives us shortcuts, and are designed to save us either time and/or money. However, it is those conscious decisions we all must make that will allow us to have influence over others and give us what we want. Here is where the six laws of persuasion can hold sway. We talked briefly about them in the last section, but we're going to examine them a little more closely here.

Law of Reciprocity: The law of reciprocity compels others to return favor for favor. By giving someone something they will feel obligated to repay you. To increase this sense of gratification, if you make sure you give them something, they want their connection to you will be even stronger.

Applying this in your life could be pretty simple. Keep in mind though that getting someone to agree to something without asking for something in return sets a pretty bad precedent that will cause the other person feel entitled and you feeling at a loss. By giving them something it gives them a sense of having some bargaining power. So, using a quid-pro-quo works best and can help to establish a longer standing relationship. The sooner you create this understanding, the easier it will be to persuade that person again and again. It is an extremely effective way of bringing your target into your fold and closing the deal whatever it is.

Law of Commitment and Consistency: Using consistency as a means of easing your targets discomfort is important. Once you've established a relationship with that person, it's important that you stick to it and not deviate. Showing the other person that you are committed to a decision (no matter how significant) gives them the assurance that you are not going to abandon them at the first sign of change. Salespeople are very good at this. By getting their customers to agree on several smaller things one right after another they set a precedent of commitment. So, when they do ask for the big sale, it is almost impossible for them to say no.

Law of Liking: Whether you want to attract another person and kindle a new relationship or you're looking to land that dream job of yours, you will probably use the Law of Liking. This basic law of human nature dictates that we are drawn to those people who are more like ourselves. The more similarities you find with someone else the deeper your desire to want to please them. When applying the Law of Liking work to establish a good rapport and make it clear that you are like two peas in a pod. The more similarities you can show them the deeper the bond will be. This works well with home-based sales parties, religious groups, and social groups. Remember the old saying, 'birds of a feather flock together.' Once you've made this type of connection with them, the less likely they will want to disappoint you by saying no.

Law of Scarcity: You don't necessarily have to have a limited supply of something to make the fundamental law of scarcity work for you. You can apply the same pressure without it. You could let the other party know that you will be available to answer questions for a limited time only. This works well for seasonal offerings or things only available during a certain time of the year. You just have to create the idea that something is scarce to get the result so they believe that if they hesitate, they may miss out on the privilege entirely.

Law of Authority: When applying this law, it is important that the other person knows that you are the "expert" in this field or you are acknowledged and recommended by recognized experts. This can be done in several different ways. Marketers often use the "testimonials" of past customers, bloggers use the credibility of other more well-known bloggers, and there is certainly nothing wrong with advertising or posting your own credential that establish you as a knowledgeable person in your area of interest.

Law of Social Proof: The dynamics is any social group is quite powerful. It can be quite unnerving to go against the crowd so people are more inclined to conform when necessary. Once people understand what is the accepted behavior in any social group, they are rarely inclined to go against it. Think about how you feel when you are in an unfamiliar social setting. Your first instinct is to look around you to see what other people are doing and then you copy them. Establishing a set of guidelines for your social group will almost always end in conformity that will be difficult for anyone to break.

All You Need to Know About Reverse Psychology

You've probably heard about using reverse psychology to get people to do things. The principle is very simple. You tell them something opposite of what you want and if they are resistant to your efforts, they will usually do what you desire. The tactic can be quite successful in many different forms of persuasion. However, while simple, it can backfire on you in a pretty big way.

Part of the reason for this is its simplicity. In fact, it is so simple that many will begin to rely on this strategy far too much. Once people begin to understand what you're doing, it can leave a pretty sad taste in their mouth. As a result, you may find that rather than connecting more people to you, it could end up pushing them away leaving a string of broken relationships in its wake. If you do decide to use reverse psychology, make sure that you use it only on rare occasions and not as a regular habit and even then, only in the most serious of situations.

That said, here are some simple ways to use this strategy to get what you want.

To Change Someone's Mind: To do this you have to think beyond the idea of changing the person's mind. Before you can begin, you have to implant your ideas into their head. Even if it is something you know they are resistant to they need to at least recognize the idea as an option.

- **The set-up:** start by presenting the two options they must choose from. For example, we have two options for dinner on Saturday night. If you know that your target has an affinity for Japanese food but you're more interested in Italian you already know what their preference will be.

    Casually present your idea in a matter-of-fact sort of way. You might say something like, "Did you know that there is a new Italian restaurant opening up on Fifth Street this week?"

    When you present your option downplay it to create a negative effect. "I've heard it's pretty good but it'll probably be packed by the time we get there. We might have to wait an hour or more to get a table."

- **Subtle Enticement:** Find subtle ways to build a desire in them. You could happen to have a menu from the new restaurant to look over. Point out some pictures and dishes that you would like to try. You could even start with an Italian night to see if you can imitate true Italian food. This will help them to see just how flavorful Italian food could actually be.

You could also make everything else sound more appealing. Talk about past experiences in Italian restaurants, pleasant memories about the Italian culture, and how "real" Italian food should taste.

- **Add Non-Verbal Cues:** A few days before, start by adding in a few visual images about Italian culture. You could drive by the restaurant on the way home to plant the idea of going there. "It doesn't look as crowded as I thought it would be." Take them for a walk in the area where they can get a whiff of the aromas as they are wafting through the air.

- **Take the Opposing Viewpoint for the Choice You Want:** Once you realize that you have caught their interest, don't give up too quickly but be slightly argumentative. This will compel them to push harder for what they want. This works much better than immediate capitulation. When a person has the natural tendency to resist it gives them a sense of fighting for the choices, they make creating a win for them.

When the event arrives, chances are they will already have made their decision. Introduce the subject again by saying something like "What do you want to do? We can go to the Italian restaurant or we can go to the Japanese." If they are still resistant to Italian you can add something like, "We get to eat Japanese all the time so it won't be anything different, but how often do we really eat Italian?"

Finish with "what do you think?" "I can't decide so it's up to you."

- **Closing:** Finally, you want to resist long enough that the other person is forced to decide. While your goal is to get what you want, the other person must think that it's their decision. After you ask your last questions, wait for them to answer. It may create a bit of discomfort but resist the urge to fill in the silence. Your target is also feeling the pressure too so wait it out until they make the choice. If they are a naturally difficult person then in most cases, they will make the decision you want to do.

When to Use Reverse Psychology: Reverse psychology doesn't work on everyone. Some people are more likely to respond to a direct request while others will be more contrary. This is why it is so important that you understand the personality of the people you are targeting. They behavior will dictate which persuasive strategy you should use. This strategy works best with people who have a naturally obstinate and stubborn nature. Here are some questions you might want to ask before you decide.

- Do they usually go with the flow?
- Are they independent thinkers?

If they are naturally fluid and agreeable, using reverse psychology will likely backfire on you. But if they are more independent thinkers and are not usually comfortable with the status quo, they are more likely to be the best subjects for reverse psychology.

Make it Light: This works well when you're using reverse psychology on children. Keep the topic lighthearted and fun so that they will believe that they're actually smarter than you. Children love that.

For example, you're trying to get your child to clean his room without having to ask him to do it. Start by setting some rules. "Don't start cleaning your room until I've finished cleaning mine." This sentence might start off sounding like that's all he needs for an excuse to "not" clean his room. He'll be happy. But then you will add something like, "I know you're too young to do it right so I'll come in and help you."

Then leave the room and go about your business. In about an hour, you can return to the room "to help" him and you'll most likely find that he has already finished or is well on his way to proving that he's not too young and he can do it on his own.

Using this same tactic with an adult can be similar. Your goal is to allow them to feel as though they are asserting their own independence in the situation. You might be trying to choose between two different TV shows; one may be serious dramatic film and the other could be a light comedy. Your preference is for the drama so you could say something like "I'm not sure I have the emotional stamina for a really serious drama tonight. If your partner is a naturally resistant person, he may want to convince you that you do have the emotional fortitude for it. He may even go as far as he could to prove it. By allowing him to apply a little resistance for a while then you'll most like end up getting exactly what you want.

Think About What the Other Person Needs: Whenever you choose to use reverse psychology, you need to consider what the other person needs or wants in the situation. In some cases, you may have to do a little bobbing and weaving before you get him to give up on his goals. Your strategy is not just to apply the opposing viewpoint but to assess of your desire for what you want is strong enough to overpower their need to resist. If you haven't thought this process through your efforts could easily backfire on you.

Your friend may be interested in visiting or driving through a rather seedy part of town that you know is dangerous. If his desire is extremely strong your efforts at reverse psychology may not work.

However, by analyzing the situation first, you could probably find other ways around the challenge.

As you consider the possibilities start by thinking about all the possible arguments you might come up against in the situation. Then think about the end result you want to achieve. Your goal is to help him to see the risks involved in his decision, not necessarily to prove that you are right or smarter. Sometimes reverse psychology will work and sometimes it won't. Possible things you could say.

"I can't tell you what to do and I can't make you do anything that you don't want to do. I pretty sure that the area is dangerous but only you can decide how much risk you're willing to take to get to where you want to go."

Your goal is achieved. Leave the decision in their hands. If you've applied the right amount of pressure, then there is a good chance that he will decide not to go.

Keep in mind that you won't win every argument this way. Reverse psychology works well only on those personalities that are naturally resistant to going with the flow. Strategies do not always turn out the way you expect them too. Occasionally the situation may escalate into an argument and in the heat of the moment you could lose sight of your goals. Try to avoid this and keep reminding yourself of what you're trying to accomplish and you'll find yourself having more successes in this strategy than not.

Remember, this strategy only works in certain situations and should be used subtly and rarely. It is easy, after achieving a few successes, to want to use it as a fall back but that could get you into trouble and could start to create negative inroads in your relationships. Once others realize this is your fallback position it could cause resentment. You have to learn to let the other person have their way sometimes or they may tire of you always having the power of them.

Try to use this type of tactic in situations where there is not much to lose. Don't use it on something that will dampen your relationship over time. For example, use it when deciding on what to eat or what to do for an afternoon at home. Don't use it when deciding on what car or house to buy.

Never Lose Your Temper: It is important to stay calm when using reverse psychology. It could easily escalate into arguments where you can become frustrated or feelings can get hurt. This is especially true when dealing with young people. Be patient, it may take a while before they come start to see things from your point of view.

Emotional outbursts are natural so make sure you can handle them yourself before you begin. If the other person loses it, you need to remain calm. All them to finish their outburst before you continue your discussion.

Most important of all, make sure this is not done in extremely serious situations. It could not only backfire but could cause irreparable damage as a result. A good example of this is someone with a serious medical condition who is resistant to going to the doctor. Your partner's resistance could be stronger than his desire to get help and you might find yourself supporting his fears rather than getting him to do what he seriously needs to do.

Chapter Six: A Master in Every Arena

Manipulation can be a pretty touchy subject these days. Never before in history have, we seen so many people trying to manipulate others to their advantage. People are constantly on guard against salespeople, bloggers, social media gurus, marketing experts and others. Everywhere you look there just seems to be someone who is trying to hold sway against others for their own advantage.

However, to become a master manipulator, you need to cut through all of that chaff and still find ways to get people on your side. It can be quite unsettling when you end up as a victim of some type of dirty negotiation tactics, especially when it's going to cause you to lose months or even years of your hard earned time and money.

Rest assured, if you're not manipulating there's a good chance that you are being manipulated. It's at the heart of every negotiation whether it is getting your two-year old to use the potty or getting your boss to give you a raise. In this chapter, we're going to teach you how to use manipulation strategies in any type of negotiation situation. That way, you can recognize manipulators when they're trying to sway you and you can hone your skills in a way that will turn the table to your advantage.

How to Secretly Manipulate Your Boss

If you're dealing with a rather difficult boss it can cause a great deal of stress. Difficult bosses are notorious for being die-hard narcissists, playing favorites, and at times even throwing a temper-tantrum or two. These kinds of people leave you feeling insecure and anxious and you end up spending much of your valuable time complaining rather than working towards achieving your own goals.

It's time to change all that. First, you must accept the obvious. Your boss is not going to change no matter how much you yell back or how hard you work to please him. It's because he doesn't want to change. His child-like antics have worked for him so far, so rather than wasting your energy working to get him into a new frame of mind, you need to change your own tactics.

No matter who you want to manipulate, it is important that you understand where they are coming from. You need to find out what is fueling his difficult and challenging behavior. What is he afraid of and what does he want? This goes back to building up your own EQ. You might have to spend some time observing him in his natural habitat in order to fully understand what he secretly wants.

What are his secret fears and/or desires: In nearly every case where a boss is a tyrant, those negative emotions spring from an underlying fear. In fact, desires and fears are the two strongest emotions to deal with. When you look very closely, everyone is either running or hiding from some secret fear that is buried deep in his psyche or they are running to something they secretly want. This is what drives our behavior. Once you understand what these two elements are in your bosses life you place yourself in a position of power. You need what he wants to avoid and you know what he wants to achieve. You can now predict his reaction to any number of situations so you can develop a strategy that will turn the tables in your favor.

Let's take a brief look at some different types of bosses to see how this works:

- The Finger-Pointer: This boss spends his time blaming those who work under him because he is afraid, he doesn't have enough of his own skills to be a success.
- The Egomaniac: usually believes he is perfect in every way. However, a closer look at his work will usually reveal someone who leaves behind a lot of projects that were started but never finished. This person has a strong desire to be loved and admired but secretly feels he is not deserving of any of it. He feels if he loses his control everything will fall apart. He

believes he is just merely an average person trying to pass himself off as being special.

Become his ally: Once you know your boss' fears and desires you need to use it to become his ally. You can do this by feeding his desire or shielding him from his fears. By becoming an ally, you are actually taking back the power he is trying to steal from you. It will give you leverage and put you in a position to demand more and likely get what you want and need.

For the boss that spends his time blaming his underlings, you need to learn to control your own emotions and not fight back when his ire is up. People who blame and shout are trying to instill fear in others, when you don't react in fear, he begins to realize that he cannot overpower you in that way. He will calm down.

Once he is calm you can present yourself as his personal problem-solver. Take the initiative and offer to "fix" the problem. When the problem is solved, he will feel like a success and you will gain his trust in the process. After several of these attempts, you will have become one of his most important assets and a tool he will need to achieve his own level of success.

For the egomaniac you will need a lot more strength and intestinal fortitude to withstand the pressure. Try going with the flow so you can fuel his need for employees that are loyal to him. This type of boss needs to feel like he is in control 100% of the time, by following his cues you can smoothly turn a world of chaos into peace and order. If you are good enough at it, you can position yourself as the trusted wingman that he won't want to do without. In time, when he moves up there's a good chance that you will move up at the same time.

Keep in mind that your goal is not to destroy your boss and let him know that he's not manipulating you. That would be counterproductive to your goals. You're trying to use his fears and desires in a way that will support your goals. As a result, you create a win-win situation that you both can gain from. It will relieve much of the stress from work and give you a higher level of job satisfaction.

The Meeting Hack: Sometimes your boss is intent on causing you embarrassment in a meeting or he is just set on refusing to hear your viewpoint. In that case, you'll have to prepare a strategy before the next meeting so you can get your point across.

Start by making sure that you have a consensus group before the meeting begins. In other words, find your friends and allies among those who will be attending. If you don't feel you have enough of those on your side, convince your boss to widen the scope and invite more people, make sure your supporters are on that list.

Prep your people and encourage them to support your ideas. When the meeting begins volunteer to be the one to take minutes. That way, you can frame the follow-up to support your ideas. After the meeting, send an email detailing the events of the meeting and make sure it is written to show that a consensus was reached in your favor.

It doesn't really matter what actually happened in the meeting. Based on the principle that most people will follow the flow; people will usually reframe their memory to match what is written in your minutes. However, it is important to make sure that when you submit your minutes, you have at least given some recognition to the points of view of the others in the meeting.

Be prepared if someone does accuse you of changing the flow of the meeting. In your minutes, cover you bases by using phrases like "the general sense of the meeting was...." Or "several alternative suggestions were put forth including...", "there was a difference of opinion on..." "However, there were no major objections to the concept that...." This will show that other ideas and suggestions were considered.

If you think this is an unscrupulous strategy then think again. Go back through your mind to consider how many meetings have already been planned to discuss one issue and in the end, the main topic of discussion was one thing but, in the end, the majority of people ended up discussing something entirely different. It is a common practice in business meetings and you probably thought it was just an accident that it happened. The only difference is now, you know that it was a planned strategy.

Bury Information: Another classic strategy for manipulation is to find ways to hide crucial information in order to create a basis for "plausible deniability." Information that may appear detrimental to you or to a case you're working on is, in most cases, essential that you inform your boss. However, there are ways you can do it without getting your or your boss into trouble.

If your boss is like most people, he is constantly on the run. If you give him a stack of papers, he will not likely have the time or the desire to read through them all before giving his signature. By adding the information you are required to report hidden a few pages before the end of the document you're pretty safe that he won't see it. In addition, if you add the document to another report as an attachment.

If your boss does take the time to read it, he's likely just going to give it a cursory glance and then move on to something else. Once he's made his decision, based on the information you made obvious for him to see or he learns of the negative information later, you can honestly inform him that you provided the data in said report and assumed that he had already read it and had no questions about it.

This form of manipulation may also seem a little dishonest but it is a common practice in corporate offices. How do you think that many of these corporations are getting away with millions if not billions of dollars from legal contracts that keep the average customer from figuring out. One telecommunications company has a contract they give to their customers for a simple monthly phone service that is sixty pages long. Don't think you're the first one to try this and don't expect that others are going to let opportunities slip through their fingers by not doing the same.

Create an Illusion of Choice: When you want to be sure that your boss will make a decision in your favor, you can create an illusion that makes him think he has a choice.

Start by preparing three possible methods for dealing with a specific situation. However, you want to be sure that at two of the options you give him only seem like possibilities but if actually put into force would prove to be non-starters. You might offer an option that puts his bonus in jeopardy, or you might present an option that everyone on the team would object to. The third option would be the one you actually want him to make. Your boss will usually consider all three options and then make his choice.

While this is a very effective approach, your boss will likely appreciate your hard work in doing such thorough research in helping him, you need to exercise this strategy with caution. You can't make what you're doing too obvious. If your two additional options are not believable or within the realm of possibilities, your boss will figure out what you're doing and it could end up causing you more harm than good.

Wording is key in this arena. By phrasing the two options that are not viable with words like "courageous" or "bold" it will give him the idea that you think he's strong enough to handle such a bold decision but will cause him to feel more cautious in his approach. The trick to success is in carefully creating seemingly viable bad choices that seem equal in nature to the one you want him to make.

Overworked: This one works well when you want to get out of doing assignments you don't really like. Start by adjusting your appearance. When you're in the office, make it a point to walk around with a large stack of papers in your arms. As a habit, walk fast and give the appearance that you're always on your way to do something, even if it's just a trip to the bathroom.

If he asks you how you're doing, answer with a roll of the eyes and a quick answer. "I'm frazzled," "I don't know how I manage to muster up enough energy to do this or that." "I'm muddling my way through it." If your office has additional meetings to sign up for, try to get in as many as you can so that you can honestly say you're too busy. Your goal is to give the appearance that you're just too busy to take on any additional work.

What usually happens is that you'll develop a reputation for always working hard and you'll gain the sympathy vote. Your boss will see this and as he hears comments from others about your diligence at your job, he'll be reluctant to add any more to your workload and give additional work to someone else in the office.

This is a very effective strategy but it will only work with the kind of boss who values hard work over measurable results. If you have the kind of boss that wants actual reports and solid proof of what you're doing, this is not going to be the best approach.

Wrong place at the wrong time: This is a deliberate strategy that puts you in the wrong place at the wrong time. Your goal is to make it inconvenient for your boss to respond as he usually would to your suggestions. You might pitch an idea at a time when he's in a meeting with a client or on the phone under the guise of being helpful.

Just before the meeting begins give him a large stack of information to throw him off balance. You could also make an expression just before he's ready to launch into his spiel. As you hand him the information add a phrase like, "I just heard that he didn't like the last presentation someone gave him, so it's up to you to kill it in there. Here, I thought this information would help."

The message will be so unnerving to him that he will lose his focus. He will go in the meeting but his inability to concentrate will cause him to fumble or make a major mistake as a result.

Here there are two things that are important to happen at the right time. First, your timing has to be exactly right. Too soon and you give him a chance to recover, too late and you miss your window. Second, your message has to be vague enough that he won't have any way to verify it.

Other than that, you need to make sure that he understands you're not trying to undermine his work, but that you only want to be helpful.

Killer Negotiation Strategies to Manipulate Your Way to Success

The art of negotiation is one area of business where manipulation can prove to be very powerful. If fact, it is the one place where manipulation is not only effective but also necessary. Whether you're buying a new car or you're closing a major multi-million dollar deal on a prime piece of real estate, learning the psychology behind manipulation and negotiation practices can save you a massive amount of money, time, and energy.

Disappointment: Letting the other person see disappointment in you can be very effective. Studies have shown that just the appearance of disappointment is all that is needed to boost the size of your concessions made in your favor. If you're considering a new car for example, you might notice the salesman appear like he isn't pleased with your offer. There is a method to his madness. He may be very happy with your offer but acting disappointed makes you feel guilty and compels you to offer more or opens the door for him to ask for more. It also lowers the chance of you changing your mind and having second thoughts about lowering your offer.

When this is done on the first offer, it puts you in the power position in the negotiation process. Since power people rarely accept the first offer given, the direction the offers move will be based on how you respond. Fake disappointment lets you decide which way the next offer will go.

The Anti-Negotiation Buster: When the other party plays the disappointment card on you, how you respond could put the ball back in your court. By responding with a statement like, "I'm sorry, I don't have the authority to respond to such a good offer, I'll have to defer to my superiors." They will usually respond with a number they want, and the ball is back in your court again.

"You can do better than that": Silence is a great tool for any negotiator. We are psychologically hard-wired to fill in the blanks when there is too much lag time between conversations. That's why when bill collectors call, they usually will say something like we haven't received your bill for this month," and then they will remain quiet.

The don't push or ask what happened, and almost always you will feel the pressure of the silence to say something. That's when you start to make excuses or explain why you haven't paid your bill.

This same tactic works well in negotiations. When you tell them that they have to do better and then wait, more often than not, they will make the concession. Silence makes you the master of the negotiation.

The Defensive Strategy: This strategy uses reverse psychology as its foundation. Manipulators use this when they are dealing with a person, they haven't been able to gain their trust or when other forms of manipulation haven't worked yet.

By telling them that they are "being defensive" and then follow it immediately with a joke at their expense, it takes much of the stress out of the situation. Think how you would react to a statement like this in the middle of a negotiation.

"My goodness don't be so defensive. Just relax a little, we're just discussing a great deal for you. If you accept it, you'll bankrupt us unless we can get you to put down your defensive walls se we can get something out of it too."

The statement is designed to get the other person to lower his guard and maybe even laugh a little. It also gets him to think that the negotiations are already going in his favor and he may lose the deal if he doesn't start making even more concessions.

If someone uses this tactic on you, how would you respond? In most cases, one might find himself compelled to let down his guard in an effort to prove him wrong. Don't fall for this trick. The best response would be to say something like, "The way you are pushing this deal is what is making me defensive. If you want me to take this a little further, this is why...."

This kind of defense puts you back in the driver's seat and you have control once again of the negotiations. You could also make a joke. "Don't take it so seriously. We're all friends here, if things don't go your way, you could always come over to my place. You do cook, don't you?"

Getting to the higher authority: In most cases, when a person says they have some freedom in deciding a price, you can pretty much bet that they won't have the final say on anything. In fact, it means that they don't have much power at all. You need to find the person who is really in charge of what happens in the negotiations. This is usually someone who is just pretending to be a small fry.

They may be the silent one at the table who is pretending like he has no control at all over the situation. They do this so they can use the "fly on the wall" strategy to find out information and play all sorts of games with you.

By presenting yourself as a fake higher authority, you can successfully:

- Delay the negotiations until a time when you're better prepared.

- Take a stronger stance without looking like the bad guy.
- Offer a last minute concession if necessary.

There are several ways to respond when someone uses this negotiation strategy on you:

- Go along with it but make a mental note of the game he's playing. You could respond by saying, "You're not going to play the good cop/bad cop game on me, are you?"
- You could agree and then tell them, "when you do meet with your boss let him know I'd like to meet him."
- Or you could call him on it and tell him you now he's the boss.

Last Minute Approval: On nearly every occasion if someone is pushing for a last-minute concession, you know you're dealing with a master manipulator. There are many ways, they can show their hand. They may agree to the transaction and then inform you that they need an additional approval from someone else. They will give the appearance that the agreement is done but then hold back on finalizing everything. Later, they will come back and tell you that their boss is being very difficult.

If this happens to you, when they return, tell them that you also have a higher authority and you need to defer to them for a final decision. When you return, ask for your own concession. If they need the deal more than you do, this could turn into a final showdown. You could put yourself into a position where you could easily blindside them with a little pressure.

For example, "Listen, I gave this some serious consideration and I really want to hold my position here. I don't like going against my word, but I think I need to ask for 10% more." Then later, you could feel guilty about it and then make a small concession. "Because I quoted you a different price before, I can give you a 5% break, but I need an answer soon. Can you get back to me by the end of the week?"

Good Cop/Bad Cop: This is an expression that all of us know and we usually associate it with legal authorities, but it works well if you have a partner at the negotiation table too. In each case, the bad cop is the one who is firm in his position and doesn't want to budge. When too much demand is on the table the bad cop feigns anger and storms out of the room leaving the good cop to play the nice guy. The good cop then plays the higher authority card and defers to the bad cop for the final decision.

If someone plays this game on you, don't be afraid to present your own bad cop. If that doesn't work, pretend like you're giving in and use what they do next to your advantage. For example, if the good cop presents an offer you then know what they consider a good deal and what they want, but you also know what you won't accept.

Fractionation: The Seduction Tool of Master Manipulators

Have you ever wondered why "that guy" was the one to always get the girl? Why he or she seemed to always have someone hanging off of their arm, but you never seemed to be able to get past first base with anyone? No matter who you are or where you're from, there always seems to be someone who is able to do what you felt was close to be the impossible when it comes to relationships.

In order to have a close relationship with anyone, you need to be able to draw people to you. The common belief was that attracting people was a matter of looks, mannerisms, and sex appeal. However, now according to studies in modern psychology, attraction appears to be well within the reach of anyone and everyone through developing the manipulative skill of fractionation.

The name is derived from its basic scientific definition: *a separation process in which one mixture is divided into a number of smaller parts.* This seems an unusual term to use when trying to attract the opposite sex, which most of us would agree needs some level of skill in the art of seduction, but if you stick with me here, you will see how it fits.

When it comes to relationships, fractionation combines several theories all into one. With the careful use of psychology, persuasion, and the mysterious art of hypnosis, you can attract almost anyone to you. Basically, when you boil it down to the basics, it is simply the manipulative side of seduction. Because of its power to attract, many will question whether it is right or wrong to use it. However, the decision of if or how you use it is entirely up to you. Many claim that you can attract another person in as little as 15 minutes.

With all the hype surrounding fractionation, it almost sounds scary and mystical as if it were a part of the dark arts. In reality though, it could just as easily be described as a conversation technique designed with the sole purpose of bringing out strong emotions in the other person. Emotions so strong that will automatically connect them to you.

The Preparation: If attracting someone of the opposite sex were as easy as just walking up and talking to them then everyone would have someone by their side. In order to effectively use this strategy, you need to dedicate some time to preparation. Before you begin, there are certain skills you should work on developing:

- Leadership skills: Especially if you are a man, most women are not interested in a follower. If you are a woman, most men are interested in an independent woman but not an overbearing one. Learn to be more balanced and flexible.
- Your uniqueness: You don't want to appear as someone that just fell out of a mold. You need an interest that will ensure that you stand out from the crowd.
- Social skills: Build up your confidence in speaking with the opposite sex while in a crowd. Practice talking to both men and women in different settings until you are able to

comfortably develop a casual conversation no matter where you are.
- Know the playing field: Learn about all the hot spots where people you're interested in like to gather. Be familiar with various options so when these places come up in discussion, you can easily participate. It also gives you a few great places to recommend if you want to invite someone out.

All of these qualities can only be done if you approach every encounter with confidence. Note, the word used is confidence, not arrogance. Statistics show that confidence is the most attractive quality to people. If you seriously want to attract someone into your life, get rid of your awkward shyness and let to present yourself in a more positive light.

Your goal with this type of preparation is to position yourself so that you will look desirable in the other person's eyes. Note, all of these things should be done before you open your mouth and say your very first word.

Make it a habit to always look your best every time you walk out your door. Spruce up your wardrobe so you have something trendy and appealing. While looks don't account for everything when it comes to attracting the opposite sex, it does matter. No one wants someone unkempt and slovenly on their arm. This doesn't mean you have to wear the most expensive clothes or the latest styles, but at the very least, make sure the clothes you wear are or were stylish within the last decade and are net and clean.

Your Emotions: The art of fractionation is very similar to the style of writing used in those addictive soap operas watched every day. Ask yourself, why are people glued to the TV set to watch a fictitious story come to life. It's because it is easy, the characters are those they can relate to and the story line taps into their **emotions.** This works because at the core of seduction is always emotion. There can be no seduction if emotions are not involved. This means more than saying pretty words, you're evoking a form of mind control so you'll need to pull out all the weapons in your arsenal including using your body language, controlling your tone of voice, and even some subtle forms of hypnosis.

As you choose your target, don't let your own insecurities get in the way. Never downplay the value of what you have to offer to a relationship. That means, the general idea that "she's out of my league," should not be part of the thought process. Instead, you want them to think they are not in your field, but you want them to feel confident enough that they can reach for it. This creates an area of challenge that will have them believing that you are worthy of the chase.

When you have carefully chosen your target, you are ready to employ your skills in fractionation. Begin with your conversational style. This is where you will apply your excellent conversational skills. Remember, conversation is more than just spewing out the right words but you need to learn to speak with your body as well. Your aim is to not to create a physical attraction but to establish a relationship. Your new relationship should be built on trust, which will be vital if you ever hope the relationship to last more than just a few days. This will require having to ask a lot of questions in order to get her involved in the conversation but be careful. It is not a job interview, just enough questions to show that you are interested, but not enough to make them feel like you're prying, nosey, or a busybody.

Conversation should be compelling and emotionally diverse. What I mean by that is that it should never display one emotion, you want to stir up a range of feelings. Your goal is to build up the kind of conversation they would want to be a part of. Choose topics that will have the emotional ups and downs and use them as an anchor to hold them in. From there you can pivot in any direction you want and they will follow.

Getting started is the tricky part. Start by asking probing but non-invasive questions to get the conversation started. You could ask them to tell you about something that makes them happy. Or you could ask her about something relating to another powerful emotion. After skillfully doing that they will happily follow you through a whole barrage of conversational topics. By tapping into both positive and negative emotions one right after the other and employing your other conversational skills like voice inflections, tone, and body language, you've hooked them in.

So, how do you choose a topic that is going to be the initial draw and then keep it moving forward. Think polarity or focus on alternating with a sequence of opposite emotions. Pleasure/pain/pleasure/pain and so on. The longer you can keep this string going the stronger the bond you will build.

For example, "Have you ever been very close to someone. So close that you felt like you were two sides of the same person and then suddenly they were gone? They just died?" This sentence starts off with something full of joy and happiness and then ends with an emotional downturn of loss and sadness.

Another example: "Have you ever met someone and was sure that they were the one for you? That the two of you were destined to stay together? And then suddenly they left? Something happened to break you apart?"

As you can see from the above examples, your questions have to have some level of depth to them. Don't settle for the superficial expressions commonly heard. Look for ways to introduce topics that will be intriguing and get them to express their innermost feelings.

It's not always easy to find ways to weave these types of questions into a regular conversation and it will take practice. However, once you do, you have started a new relationship with someone that you can now start to build on over time. Fractionation can be a challenge but eventually you will be able to master it and as a result, make yourself more attractive and interesting to others.

The whole idea behind fractionation is to create an aura of suspense. Think soap operas. Don't charge in right away with statements like you're really into them. These rarely work because you can't be interested in someone you know nothing about. It only tells them that you want to get them into bed. People want a challenge they can work for so make don't make it too easy to gain your interest. If they feel too comfortable, they will quickly lose interest and move on to someone else.

Confusion can also be very effective in attracting others. If you're very interested one minute and nonchalant the next it creates a question in their mind. They'll want to get to know you better to find out what's really under the surface.

What to avoid: This is only the beginning of a relationship. As time passes, you will have to continue to find new ways to keep interest. As you build on the foundation you've laid, try to avoid the following:

- Using bad manners: we live in a world where manners have been thrown out the window but that should not be your excuse. Always fall back on courtesy and respect.
- Talking about your exes: no matter how much you've been hurt or disappointed in the past, it should never be part of a conversation with a new relationship.
- Downplaying their emotions: An angry person never likes being told to calm down. While you may not agree with how they feel, their emotions are real and valid to them.
- Posting pictures with other women or men

You get the picture. Remember, you are trying to draw them to you. Men complaining about women's monthly period or her mood swings is just going to put a damper on all your hard work. By the same token, women who challenge his masculinity will rarely be a basis for a long-standing relationship.

There is no question that starting a new relationship is difficult. The combination of nerves and emotions can be hard to cope with. However, if you feel you're ready to embark on this adventure, it is not impossible. Build up your confidence and give it your best shot. If once you've started, you don't feel comfortable in the new relationship, don't be afraid to walk away. It is much better than dragging out a bad match to spare their feelings. It will only hurt more later on.

11 Less-Known Manipulation Techniques for Seduction

Going just a step further, after you've drawn the person in, your next goal is to keep them there until they are just as committed to you as you are to them. This is not always easy, but if you've kept your EQ high, it can be easier than you think.

There are a lot of ways to keep someone by your side but if you want to employ tools that will make the **want** to be by your side, then you should pay close attention to the patterns of their behavior. Observe what they do when they are just being themselves and use these as cues as to what you can do to keep them interested. Depending on your observations you can use any one or a combination of the following manipulation techniques to advance your relationship to the next level.

Flattery: Flattery is different from giving a regular or a genuine compliment to someone. It is actually giving compliments that are not necessary. Be careful when you flatter someone; it can have dangerous repercussions. By flattering someone so as to fuel their own insecurities, they may be drawn to you or they may start to view you suspiciously. A good example of this is if you flatter a man who is not very confident in his own sense of masculinity, he may enjoy hearing your words of praise but he may be equally suspicious about the sincerity of your words. Ideally, you want to find out what makes them insecure and give them just enough support to bolster their confidence but not go overboard.

Ex: "You're such a tough guy, you intimidate everyone around you." This will flatter a man with who is insecure about his masculinity.

Ex: "You're my little baby doll." This will flatter a woman who may be insecure about her weight.

The Trojan Horse: Some might describe this tactic as a bribe. If you keep showering them with gifts, no matter how small, they will feel obligated to stay with you. This can be done very subtly as in the case of buying a meal. This will make them feel obligated to have regular conversation with you but some have actually gone to extremes. For example, some have paid to support the other's entire lifestyle, putting them in homes, giving them cars, etc. In such cases, the extent of indebtedness grows. In those instances, they may feel as if they own the other person, which carries with it its own set of risks.

The Silent Treatment: The absence of communication can have earth shattering effects when they have become accustomed to regular conversation. This type of manipulation can easily unnerve a person and make them feel they have done something wrong and they will go out of their way to fix it for you.

The Mirror: People have also put on pretenses in order to keep someone with them. They may pretend to share the same values or demonstrate that they like the same things. Manipulators have even been known to fabricate a completely new story line in order to attract others. The sole purpose of the mirror is to give the other person exactly what they need to hear to boost their emotional stability.

Make the Decision for Them: Man are usually the ones to take this tactic. In an effort to assert their masculinity, they may make decisions for the other person. By deciding what they will eat, where they will go, or what they will do, the other person over time will become dependent on them and they won't want to leave.

The Big Question: This involves asking them for something that is far more than you know they can afford to give. You know they will be forced to refuse but, in an attempt, to compromise, they will settle for the very thing you want from them in the first place. For example, you can ask them to move in with you, which you know it is too early in the relationship for that. Then you can ask for something that is less risky, like going away for a weekend together.

The Logical Fallacy: Planting the idea in their mind that if they don't do what you want then they don't have feelings for you or they don't love you. Teenagers often use this manipulation tactic quite effectively. "If you loved me you would do this or do that."

The Expected: You might attempt to keep them by telling them it is only normal that you do this or that. "We've been together for six months now. It's only logical that we start living together."

The Guilt Trip: There are often attempts to make the other person feel ashamed for not continuing with the relationship. By making them feel like they have taken advantage of you, they will feel guilty for their own behavior and will stick with you. This tactic only works when you know the other person well and you know exactly which buttons to push, but when used properly, it can be very effective.

The Remote Control: Every time the other person starts to talk about leaving change the subject to something you know they are keenly interested in. They won't be able to resist switching with you and the fated conversation will be put off to another day.

The Board Game: When they ask to do something you don't want to do, you can also shame them by questioning their motives. "Is that what you really want?" Done the right way, it can make the other person feel like they were being unreasonable for even bringing the subject up.

Keep in mind that these tactics will only work for you temporarily. There are few manipulation strategies that will keep the other person connected to do indefinitely if there is not a genuine and compatible match. So, while manipulation may have its place in a new relationship, in time, you will eventually have to work on building that relationship on honest conversation and a real emotional connection between the two of you.

Love Bombing: The art of "love bombing" does not necessarily apply exclusively to romantic relationships. In fact, it's origin started in a church setting where religious leaders developed it to attract new parishioners to their pews. They literally "bombed" them with lots of attention and affection. Over time, parents started using it as an innovative way to education their children through kindness and care. Over time, others grew to see that it could be a powerful tool that can be used to control people in all sorts of settings. Whether it's through the use of kind words, the warmth of a tender embrace, or through the corny actions the success was impressive as more and more people started being drawn into people they would never have given a second look at before.

The basis of love bombing is to display your target with lots of affection and attention in an effort to show that you are the partner of their dreams. Once they are convinced that you are a hopeless romantic and your target is convinced that you are the ideal partner for them they are ready to enter into what they expect to be an ideal relationship.

For this strategy to work, it must be done in several stages. In the initial stage, everything must be flawless in every way. This would involve performing acts specifically designed to gain their trust, giving them encouraging words to build them up emotionally, and giving them the needed support and patience when needed.

Over time, these acts can pull a person closer to you until the point when you are able to emotionally dominate them. Evil manipulators will slowly begin to extend that control and keep them tied to them through a barrage of text messages and phone calls when they're not together. By the time this begins to happen, the other person is so hopelessly dedicated that even if they do detect something is not right, their own insecurities will be so powerful that they will find it hard to break it off. They have become addicted to those large doses of praise and kindness. That's the point when a manipulator can start to take advantage of the situation.

This is an extreme form of manipulation and those who usually practice it are generally those who have a very low self-esteem to begin with. They only use love bombing because they don't believe that they can seduce a person all on their own. They feel the only way they can have a relationship is by trickery, lies, and mind control. They recognize if they have complete dominance over the other person there is no way they will ever be abandoned.

The cycle of love bombing is difficult to miss. It can be easily identified if you know what you're looking for. The resulting relationship is not based on any form of true connection but is mostly founded on the idea of a romantic relationship. The concept of "soulmates" is at the heart and the person begins to believe that everything is so perfect that it must've been fate that brought you together. Once the target accepts this belief, the relationship can quickly turn toxic.

In the beginning, everything seems like a dream come true to the victim as the manipulator dazzles them with a chaotic array of attention and affection. The onslaught of romantic words and phrases are so frequent and steady that the victim may come to believe it so strongly that they are blinded to many of the faults even when they are played out right in front of their eyes. Once it reaches this point, it is nearly impossible for the victim to break free from the hold they manipulator has on them.

There are several phases of love bombing:

Devaluation: This stage happens after the initial phase of compliments, affection, and lots of attention. In the devaluation phase, the manipulator turns that attention to disapproval and anger. This easily can escalate into threats, which is a huge part of the psychological conditional that allows them to become a dictator of the other person's behavior.

These first two cycles could repeat themselves over and over again until it reaches a major climax.

Letting go: After the relationship has escalated into abuse, victims begin to ignore their own needs just so they can stay attached to the manipulator. Given enough time, they will break away from family and friends, and give up all the things they once loved just in an effort to avoid or break away from the conflicts that may arise.

Sometimes it can take an intervention to help the victim separate themselves from the relationship. If the person has some level of emotional strength, they may find a way to break it off on their own. They may grow tired of being controlled or they may just be feeling the pressure from others to help them to break free.

If you're truly looking for a lasting relationship, you want to avoid trying the love bomb strategy. While it may draw a person to you, it won't ever be for the reasons you want. If you suspect someone is love bombing you, use your senses. They may shower you with compliments and gifts, even if you don't know them very well. They may give you a classic line like "I know we're just made for each other."

They also know how to identify someone who would be susceptible to their witty charms. They may openly talk about a past relationship on the first date. They may lament about how the other person didn't appreciate them or how they felt misunderstood, detailing all the elements of their breakup. When that happens, beware. They are trying to pull you in and play the sympathy card. Their words are carefully chosen so that you will listen to them and feel their pain.

Once they can convince you of their "feelings" it is just a matter of time before they start to control you.

Breaking up from a love bomber is difficult but it can be done. However, they will continue to ply you with affections in an effort to win you back. If you want to keep separate from them there is only one way to do this. You must break all ties with them and avoid any contact whatsoever. You also need to get support so pool together those who you trust to help you resist the temptation to go back. And no matter what you do, don't blame yourself for falling for this highly effective trick. Just be happy you were able to break free and move on from there.

Chapter Seven: Advanced Manipulation Tactics

Psychological manipulation can be very subtle and it can be quite obtuse. Depending on your aim, you will decide which tactics will work best to get you what you need. Up until this point, the manipulation strategies we have discussed have been pretty simple and basic. A lot of these things can easily be picked up on your own simply by observing the interactions of the world around you. However, when these other more basic methods fail to work, there are several advanced methods you can try.

The Manipulative Power of Reinforcement

One key element of manipulation is the art of reinforcement. It's a form of behavioral psychology that allows the user to help mold his target's future behavior by giving them some form of reinforcement. By applying this strategy, you can gain a measure of control over your subject and by extension mold his conduct himself in ways that you want to see.

There are two types of reinforcement that can be applied. Positive reinforcement is the kind of stimulus that will encourage them to continue conducting themselves in a way that you approve of. Negative reinforcement would give stimulus that has been chosen to change their behavior to something else.

Of course, there are many different degrees to the type of stimulus you can provide depending on the type of results you seek. If you want them to perform the behavior more frequently or to continue the behavior for a longer period of time then you would use positive reinforcement. If you're looking for them to change their behavior or to lessen the frequency of the behavior you would use negative reinforcement. Depending on the type of reinforcement you use, you can get a wide range of results.

Rewarding Stimuli: The stimuli you use as a reinforcement must be chosen very carefully. If you hope it can be at all effective, you need to understand what your subject wants and likes. The reward has to tap into their basic needs for desire and pleasure or their use will be ineffective. We all have basic needs that drive us to do the things we do so when your reward taps into that inner need, it is more likely to encourage more of the behavior you want. In essence, reinforcement happens only if the subject sees the stimuli as a reward or in the case of negative reinforcement, as a loss.

Parents are very effective at using reinforcement to get their children to do their chores. They may offer an allowance for doing work around the house or they may offer a weekend at an amusement park for exceptionally good behavior. But when you look around you, we see the art of reinforcement playing out in every field. Few of us go to work just because we enjoy the work and it makes us feel good. We go for the paycheck/reward. Few of us are in relationships where we're not getting some form of satisfaction out of it. And we rarely spend our free time doing things we hate. When we get a moment free to ourselves, we naturally go for the things that we feel are most rewarding to us. Getting a raise or a promotion at work is a powerful incentive for getting you to work harder on your job. By the same token, losing your job for undesirable behavior can be a strong negative reinforcement as well.

In most situations, the use of reinforcement is relating to behavior but it can also relate to memory as well. A good example of this is something called "post-training reinforcement" where the reward is given after the subject has learned something new. A manipulator can use reinforcement to help improve their memory of the breadth, duration, and specific details of the lesson until it is firmly planted in their mind. In such cases, the reward needs to be something that touches the subject emotionally. That way, they connect the lesson with their personal feelings.

We've all experienced this type of reward before. If you are of the older generation, you can recall without much hesitation where you were when the Challenger exploded or the 9/11 tragedy occurred. These have been described as "flashbulb memories" because they were both events that give us intense emotions. If you look back through your own personal life, those memories that are the embedded the deepest in your mind are the very ones that have touched you emotionally. This can be an extremely powerful emotional tool when used in the right way.

In order to use reinforcement successfully, you will need to fully understand where your target is vulnerable. This information will help you to decide which type of reward you will give them in order to mold their behavior. Once decided, you must be careful not to be too over when giving the reward. When it is too obvious, the subject is very likely to understand what's going on and squash your efforts almost immediately. However, by playing a subtle and more passive role, you can gently nudge them in the direction you want them to go.

Applying Positive Reinforcement: One of the easiest forms of reinforcement is when you encourage continued practice of a desirable behavior. Your reward will be given as a means of encouraging the subject to continue or to escalate a certain act. Some examples of positive reinforcement:
- You can give words of praise encouraging them to continue.
- Money
- Approval
- Gifts
- Personal attention

- Public recognition

Positive reinforcement does not have to cost you anything. Small children for example are happy with just an approving smile from their parents. Don't get into the habit of thinking that positive reinforcement has to have a monetary value. Look for what that person needs and use that to encourage them. Even adults are not always content with monetary value. People see value in all sorts of things.

Applying Negative Reinforcement: When you want your subject to cut back or cease a certain behavior then you would apply negative reinforcement. In such a case, you would remove a reward or you would prevent them from achieving the reward they seek. Negative reinforcement could also include giving them something they don't find desirable; something that will either make them uncomfortable or find to be unpleasant. Such reinforcement is less likely to keep them continuing with the same behavior for any extended period of time.

- Nagging
- Intimidation
- Yelling
- Swearing
- Guilt trip
- Silent treatment
- Sulking

You will notice that all of the behaviors listed above can make your subject extremely uncomfortable. They play on his emotions and erode their personal self-esteem causing them to cease their behavior. Consider what happens when a parent nags their child about doing house chores. If every time the child enters the room, the parent nags, yells, screams, embarrasses, or threatens the child will eventually start doing his chores. The reward happens when the chores are done and the parent stops berating them.

Another example, an employer has a policy that all work must be completed by the end of the week or they can't have the weekend off. This is a powerful negative reinforcer and gives many workers incentive to increase their productivity during the week so that everything will be done on time.

Extinction: Reinforcement can also take a neutral position too. Positive reinforcers are used to encourage the behavior you want, negative reinforcers are designed to discourage certain behaviors. Extinction reinforcers, however, happens when you don't acknowledge the behavior at all.

For example, a child refusing to acknowledge a bully at school. With neither a positive or a negative reaction, there is no fuel for the bully to work with and he will quickly lose interest in his target. It can also be seen when employers do not recognize the work that an employee is doing. In time, the employee will lose interest in his work and will give up trying.

Keep in mind that reinforcement is not the same as punishment. Punishment is designed to correct certain behaviors and reinforcement is designed to encourage behaviors. You could think of them as the opposites of the same coin.

Charming Habits to Manipulate Anyone

Charisma can be an excellent tool for manipulating anyone. When you can be charming you are also endearing to others and they will be drawn to you. However, there is a big difference between being charming and acting charming. Some people just have a natural way of pulling people in while others may have to work at it. It's not as easy as they make it appear to be.

When you can put on the charm, it is easy to blind someone to your true intentions. By nature, people tend to listen to only those things they want to hear. They often make decisions that they know are against their best interest yet they do it anyway without giving it a second thought.

There are those who already know how to use their charm to draw us in, giving us a strong sense of confidence. Others use their charm to get you to let your guard down so you will believe everything they say. And others will use their charm to make you feel like you've been friends for years even when you've only just met. All of these people are highly skilled at turning it on and off at will making it very difficult to recognize it when it's being put to use. If you're not one of these people you will have to develop these skills that are classics for master manipulators.

Mirroring: Mirroring or matching the other person's body language sends them a signal letting them know that you are very interested in them. It builds a bond of trust that you can use later on when you want to get something from them or get them to do something for you.

In a normal setting, people will automatically do this without even realizing it. However, it can be one of the most effective ways to win someone over when you are using it to connect with the other person. Think of how many times you've smiled when you caught someone mirroring you. Perhaps you both reached for the same book at the same time. Your hands touch and you can't help but smile when you realize what happens. On a subconscious level, you are letting the person know that you have more in common than they may have realized.

Gazing Into Their Eyes: We all know how important making eye contact is when trying to communicate. It is one of the best ways to get people feel like they matter to you. When using this technique when you are trying to persuade someone you can lock your eyes with theirs with an intense gaze that can seem almost hypnotic. For the best effect, timing is important.

For example, locking eyes with them immediately after saying something that might may them feel uneasy can temper the kind of response they give you. It throws them off their game and disorients them for a minute. That will give your initial thought time to sink in.

Breaking the Rules: There is a reason why the bad guy always seems to get the girl. There is a certain charm quality they all seem to have. They may be breaking the rules but they are doing it in a playful way. They are not breaking the rules just to break them though; there is a method to their madness. They may try some intimate moves with you on the first date. Touching you in a way you would not normally permit.

This kind of behavior is really a fishing expedition. They are pushing the boundaries so they can see where you stand. How committed are you to your decisions. How you respond to these tests will determine the method of manipulation to use in the future. If you permit intimate touching on the first date, you can fully expect the intimacy to escalate in the future.

As a general rule, manipulators will use these charming qualities to invade your space, draw your attention, and to show their power over their target. Think of it as playing a game of chess where they are making a play for control over the subject's mind and heart.

Confessions: One thing charming people know how to do is talk. They are very eloquent speakers and know how to pull you into a conversation and hold your attention until they have made their point. They are avid attention seekers and to do this they need to know how to tell a story that will keep you hanging on every word.

Manipulators will do the same thing on a more personal level. Rather than telling a good story they will tell you about confidential matters to keep you coming back. They make you feel as if they trust you so much, they will share their innermost secrets with you. This is usually the first part of a manipulation strategy. They start by getting you to connect with them by confessing all their past deeds. They will continue until you are so involved you look for them to tell you more. Then they stop, literally pulling the rug right from under your feet, refusing to even discuss such things anymore. This leaves you feeling like you've done something wrong and you will do just about anything to get back to that same level of communication you had before.

Using Pet Names: On the surface, calling your significant other by pet names seems endearing and affectionate, but in reality, it is devaluing your role in the relationship. Calling someone baby, or sweetie, or darling shows that they are not seeing you as an equal in the relationship. It makes you feel lesser than you really are.

If they continue this habit for a long time and then stop, you begin to feel as if you're in the wrong and wondering what to do about it. At that point, they have maneuvered you into a position where they now have control over you and you will become their puppet and do exactly what they want just to hear those endearing words again.

Excessive Complimenting: Sometimes excessive complimenting is truly sincere but this tool in the hands of a master manipulator can be covering over questionable motives. This form of manipulation is usually done by those who are lower on the totem pole than others within the infrastructure. Children will do this to their parents, employees to their bosses, and students to teachers.

Be cautious when using this technique, most people in positions of power will be on guard so you will have to exercise a little self-control and use it gradually over a longer period of time. If you can effectively do this subtly then your chances of getting a harder more difficult person to soften up will be a lot easier than if you go in guns a blazing and gushing all over them.

Validating Negative Emotions: Helping people justify negative emotions is a powerful weapon in the hands of a manipulator. If they are feeling depressed about a mistake or something they feel they did wrong, rather than encourage you to change, a manipulator will validate those feelings so that you will stay in a negative frame of mind. Then when they have you fully committed to them, they will be your redeemer and rescue you.

This type of manipulator is not interested in making you feel better but wants you to believe that they are the solution to all your problems. They want you to believe that you cannot resolve the issue on your own so they will try to keep you trapped in that negative emotional state so they can rescue you.

It may take some time to develop these skills to a degree where you can turn them on and off without much though however, once you do, you will have all the charm and grace that you see so many others engaged in.

How to Turn Someone Into their Own Enemy

Our memories are a tricky thing. We often question whether we remember events accurately anyway, so it can be relatively easy for a manipulator to play on that natural tendency to turn someone's own recollections against them. This method of persuasion is called "gaslighting" and it is used to get someone to trust you more than they do themselves.

You can see gaslighting going on all around you. It is used by lawyers, relationship partners, religious leaders, and other with the sole purpose of making the other person believe that their memories or recollection of events is fallible. When you can convince someone that there is something wrong with how the recall events it erodes their confidence in themselves so you can then implant in them your own script for them to play out.

Addiction: It is one thing to call a person crazy and it is another thing entirely to convince them of it. They are not likely to believe you just because you said it so, you will need to start doing things to convince them of your truth. Before you can do that, you have to get them to trust you.

This starts with triggering the brain to release endorphins and dopamine. When a person gets excited a chemical reaction starts in the brain and it releases those hormones. These are the same hormones that are released when people take drugs. By doing things to trigger the same chemical release, you can cause a person to become addicted to you. Your first step in gaslighting is to create an addict by providing them with enough excitement that they will attach themselves to you just so they can continue to get that high from the chemical release in their brains.

Work on Your Own Memory: Now you have to work on yourself. It is a given that we all make mistakes but that doesn't mean that we remember them all. An effective manipulator is very meticulous and will remember every time a mistake is made by their subject and any misinterpretations or misunderstandings they may have developed.

You need this so that you can use this as evidence that their memories are not legitimate and not to be relied upon.

By frequently pointing these normal flaws out, your subject will eventually begin to see how frequently they are in the wrong and will start to rely on your memory and solutions when problems come up.

Act Confused: When your subject raises an objection to your representation of the facts, you can act confused and feign a lack of understanding. Or you can dismiss his recounting as exaggerated, illogical, or completely false. Then you can present your own answer as a simple but logical account of the events. After doing this several times, the subject will start to turn to you for help more and more as they lose their own confidence in their abilities.

Forget: When they tell you they did this or that, simply tell them you don't recall it. Use phrases like, "I don't remember that," or "I didn't see you there." Be persistent even when it comes to the smallest detail. The more insistent you are the less likely they are going to resist your influence.

You could also do the opposite and convince someone that they really did do something you know they didn't do. This will confuse them even more because they will struggle to recall events that never happened. Again, if you project confidence and persistence in your belief they will begin to doubt their own memory and eventually fall in line with your thinking.

Minimize Their Concerns: Over time, gaslighting will drain your subjects to the point of frustration and depression. It will bring out a lot of negative emotions, which can be thoroughly exhausting. Once that happens, they will begin to talk about their concerns and they will turn to you because 1) they're now addicted to you. 2) they lack confidence in their own memory, and 3) you have positioned yourself to be a trustworthy ally. When they come to you with their concerns, dismiss them by telling them that they are "taking things too seriously," "overreacting, or getting too emotional.

This can turn out to be one of the most effective manipulation tools you can have in your arsenal. The best and most efficient way to use it is slowly over an extended period of time. You may not be able to master it correctly the first time, but after several tries, you will be able to turn someone's mind into his own enemy. Then you have them in a position to do whatever you want from them.

Chapter Eight: Asserting Dominance

It is relatively easy to see the kind of people that are drawn to us. We tend to gravitate towards those who are similar to us in behavior and thought. There is a lot of truth in the old saying "birds of a feather flock together." We surround ourselves with people who are going to relate to us, understand us, and support us. It saves us from constantly having to live with a defensive stance over all of our decisions.

However, as a manipulator, you will want someone around you that will behave in a certain way so you will need to exercise some level of control. You will have to assert your dominance from the very beginning so that they will follow your every instruction without question. You not only want to be able to direct their behavior but you want them to accept it too. For this you need to develop some very strong skills.

Body Language that Asserts Dominance

Your body is your largest form of communication. How you move or position it will cause others to react without question. One of the reasons to exercise dominance with your body is because it is subtle, almost invisible, so it is unlikely the other person will even realize what you're doing. We react to body language instinctively, without thought, so once they respond to you, their thoughts will naturally fall in line.

Use of Space: When people are being described as being "larger than life" it's not referring to their physical size, but the amount of space they are using. If you want to exercise dominance make sure that you are using as much space as possible. When you are standing, place your hands on your hips with the elbows pointing out so you occupy more space. When you sit, stretch your legs out as far as possible. When you lean, walk, or find yourself in any other position, make sure that your body is occupying as much space as possible.

Women however, should exercise caution with body posing. More often than not, they will be labeled as taking on a less feminine role and/or of a less reputable position with open body language. She then would want to take a more closed pose but still exercise her dominance by using her body in other ways.

It also depends on the goal of the manipulator. If it is in a business environment, she would need to consider her audience. If she is in a group with many men and few women, a closed stance can be read as being defensive and she would want to avoid that at all costs. On the other hand, if she's in a more social setting with a balanced group around her, her closed body language could make her appear to be more open to a new relationship.

Touching: There have been a number of studies that have shown how touching others while in conversation shows as more dominant. The act itself indicates that you are comfortable around them and are not intimidated or worried about invading another person's space. Of course, all of this is cultural and each environment needs to be taken into consideration. So, make sure that you understand the cultural dynamic of the people you're interacting with before you just decide to reach out a touch someone.

For women, touching men in any way could be perceived in the wrong way. If you're in a business setting avoiding even the slightest touch below the waistline. It is a powerful way to stimulate arousal. Again, women cannot use the power of touch as much as men without sending out the wrong vibes. And she should avoid touching strangers at all unless touching is viewed as acceptable in their culture.

Holding Your Ground: When you're in a small or crowded space, it is normal to give a little to allow others to navigate. To assert your dominance, try to move a little as possible. In social settings, who moves for whom lets you know exactly who is the alpha.

- If you meet an old friend and they approach you, you are on the power side: try not to move.
- If you're in a group that needs something and others retrieve it, they are on the power side: move to accommodate them.
- If you're in a meeting in your office, you are the alpha: don't move.

This same rule can be applied in all types of settings. Whether in business or social settings these guidelines are based on how people naturally move when interacting with each other. We all instinctively know that we must move for the boss but be observant when you're in groups where there is no assigned rank to each person. This is where you can assert your dominance. People will automatically move for the person who acts more dominant or for the larger person.

Eye Contact: Your eyes can also let people know that you're the top dog in the room. The longer you are able to hold eye-contact is usually an indication of your position in the setting. This is because the higher authority figures are quite comfortable maintaining eye contact with those under them. If you want to assert your dominance in a particular setting or group, don't look down.

If you do feel the need to break eye contact, make sure that you break it in the right way. If your eyes move up, it is read as a sign of dismissal. If they move to the side it is considered neutral and the two of you are on equal footing. However, if you break downwards it is always viewed as submissive, so never look down.

However, if you're a woman and looking to seduce, then looking down and then back up again is a clear signal that you want him. So, if that's your aim, then by all means, go for it.

Comfort: The more comfortable you appear the more confidence you project. Nervousness sends a message of fear and anxiety. Try taking on a calmer and slower style to exude more confidence.

It is true that people who move fast and seem to exude energy can send out a message of fear, the person who moves slowly does not reflect any type of anxiety and appears to be much more grounded and in control. The message they send is that others can feel safe and relaxed around them.

There is also the concept of "locking in" where you use the most comfortable position you can in the setting. That could mean leaning against a bar or a railing, sitting on a stool, or leaning against a desk or a wall.

Open Body Language: Asserting your dominance through open body language tells others that you are powerful. When your body is closed (hunched shoulders, crossed arms, and legs close together) it reflects an image of fear, anxiety, or unapproachable. However, when you display a more open body (arms out, legs apart, shoulders back) we appear dominant yet approachable. We let people know that we are confident and are in control.

Relaxed Body Language: Also, a body that is relaxed sends a message of authority. When you show signs of comfort you appear more relaxed. Avoid sending displacement signals like scratching, touching your face or the back of your neck, wringing your hands, or unbuttoning the collar of your shirt. All of these signals show signs of nervousness and anxiety.

Maintain Good Posture: Not only is good posture good for your health but it is also good for your image too. Your level of confidence is easily reflected in how you hold your body. When you stand erect and tall you exert a dominant and confident position but if you stand with your shoulders rounded, your head leaning forward (almost as in a permanent bow) you are taking a submissive position.

If you have been in this habit in the past, you need to start adjusting this stance as soon as possible. However, you need to be cautious and avoid over correcting. Extending your spine too far back can give you a swayback posture. Sticking your chest out too far will make you look cartoonish. Try making the adjustment in the mirror until you find the right balance.

Do the Power Walk: There is some disagreement as to whether a power walk is fast or slow. A slow walk exudes more confidence as long as it represents your natural walking style. However, if you are moving slowly in a busy work environment it may send the message that you're lazy or unmotivated. By the same token, a fast walk can also exude confidence if done correctly. Still, it can be misconstrued as nervous or anxious depending on your environment.

So, while the speed of your walk can send a strong message, it is best to focus on how you walk. Make sure that as you move your shoulders move with you. A sway of the shoulders makes them look broader taking up more space. Use your arms with a smooth back and forth movement keeping them just slightly away from your body. When your arms are too close it is a sign of fear.

Keep the legs slightly apart allowing enough room for air to circulate and keeping the thighs from rubbing together.

Always stand up erect with your feet pointing slightly outward. You don't want to do it too much because it will give off an aire of disdain for those around you.

Keep you gaze staring straight ahead and focused to give you the appearance that your walk has a purpose.

The Upward Nod: Make a habit of nodding with the chin thrusting upward rather than down. It gives you more of a rough appearance but only use it when necessary because in some crowds it can appear confrontational, which could cause more problems.

How to Talk Like a Top Dog

Your physical positioning tells others you are confident and ready to tackle anything that comes your way. People will often defer to you when you display these physical body languages even if they don't understand why. But once they do come to you, it is important for your conversation to match the message that your body is sending out. How you express yourself will further solidify your dominance in any social dynamic.

Lead the Conversation: When you speak, you must think about more than the words you choose to express your point of view. There are several variables that are important to regulating your conversation. As you assert your dominance, you need to be careful of your tone, tempo, subject matter, and who speaks the longest.

This is even more important when you are talking one on one with someone. In a group dynamic, there will always be a variety of characters to interact with however, when in a more private conversation where there are only two players, how you respond to questions and what you do will weigh heavily on who will have more dominance.

- **Tempo:** To exert dominance you need to control the speed of the conversation. You want to speak fast enough that you don't waste time but slow enough that you message is clearly understood. This means not only managing and regulating what you say, but your voice will set the tempo for the other person as well. In a group setting, it is your responsibility to make sure everyone is engaged in the same topic and on the same page. You also want to make sure to include everyone in the group. If you notice someone taking over the conversation, step in and cut them off with confidence.

In other words, you appoint yourself as the director of the conversation. Take control and gracefully interrupt when things start to go the wrong way. You could intervene in several ways.

When one person is cut off by another: "Wait a second." Then address the person who was cut off, "please, go ahead and finish your thought." Or "Let's hear what Janet has to say."

When a person is talking too fast: "Slow down, you're speaking to fast."

By taking the initiate to direct the conversation, you place yourself in a powerful dominant position and soon everyone in the group will be looking to you for direction even after the conversation has concluded and you've gone your separate ways.

- **Setting the Frame:** By the same token, directing the conversation also means deciding what's right to discuss. You decide what's fair, what's acceptable, and what's considered to be normal and appropriate conversation. The more power you exude at this stage the more people will respect and want to follow you.

- **Asking the Right Questions:** How you ask questions also plays a major role in asserting dominance. When engaging in conversation, always ask plenty of questions. In any conversational dynamic, the person who asks usually dominates the conversation and they person who answers is the subordinate.

- **Don't be Afraid to Offer Correction:** When you correct someone, you're making your power move. In essence, you are asserting your right to dictate the rules of the game. The more corrections you offer the higher your position of authority will be in their eyes. Only subordinates avoid correcting others or afraid of being viewed as taking a stand against authority.

It is also a demonstration of your higher intellect, which is key in any dating dynamic. How you offer correction can make a difference too. For example, if you offer it in a way that shames the other person, they may see you as an authority but will lose respect for you. On the other hand, if you offer it with sincerity and with a feeling that you genuinely want to help, you will gain the respect you want.

- **Contradictions:** The same rules apply when you are contradicting another person. Whenever you are going to say something that is the exact opposite of what the other person believes, you are throwing down your dominance gauntlet. It is an extremely powerful move that if not done correctly could sever the entire relationship.

While this may be acceptable in some settings, those who have a higher social EQ understand just how risky this move is. Instead, they may just acknowledge the other person's point of view and then redirect the conversation subtly bringing in the correct answer without pointing out his or her error. This allows the other person to save face and garner you much more honor and respect than making an outright contradiction.

- **The Conclusion:** At the close of a conversation a leader will do a quick summary of what has been discussed. If you are not the leader but are trying to assert dominance the this would be the perfect time to step up and volunteer for this role. People will begin to see you as someone who can step up and be a good leader.

Assertiveness: It is important that you speak assertively. This means that you won't want to give up or relinquish your right to speak but instead make sure that everyone not only hears you but understands it too. There are several steps to accepting this role.

- **Make sure everyone understands:** As a leader your responsibility is not just to disseminate information but to make sure that all of your subordinates are clear on what is expected. You can verify this by asking questions like, "Are we clear?" "Do you understand?" or "Did you get it?" In some situations, you might ask them to repeat your instructions back to them so you know they fully grasp your expectations.

- **Always Expect an Answer:** In some situations, people will be reluctant to answer a question or concern you have raised. They may switch the subject or they may just pretend they didn't even hear the question. In some cases, they may even dismiss it as unimportant to the conversation. Never accept this. If you find someone who is reluctant or refuses to answer your question either repeat the question with a stronger tone that lets them know that you expect an answer or bring the conversation back around to the point of your discussion. Either way, never accept a non-answer to a direct question.
- **Repeat When Necessary:** If you find you are speaking in a group that may get too loud at times, the temptation is to raise your voice to make sure that you're heard. While this may work you run the risk of being seen as too aggressive rather than assertive. However, if you simply pause when the noise level gets too high and then repeat your message when the noise level drops again, you'll gain more respect.

You can also remind them of your official authority position and let them know that there is no other source for which to get the information you want to share with them. Make sure you have an assertive tone and the inflection reflects the kind of position you claim to have.

- **Avoid Being Verbally Aggressive:** Verbal aggression runs rampant on the political and business front. However, this doesn't mean you have to take that road. There is a difference between asserting your dominance and the use of verbal aggression. A person who is verbally aggressive will speak over people and at times literally rob them of their right to speak for themselves. They will cut people off or force them to be defensive in their remarks. These are strong-arm tactics where you are literally railroading the other person and forcing them into submission. While this will help you to be seen as an authority, you are instilling fear and intimidation to get what you want often even shaming them into accepting your position.

If you find yourself being attacked in this manner, don't go into the defensive mode. Instead, launch your own counterattack by reframing the subject in question or refuting their statements with your own evidence. As soon as you go on the defensive you automatically relinquish your power to them. Instead, stop his attack early on in the conversation. Match their own nastiness by pushing back with equal aggression or denying any accusations they may have made.

The launch your own counterattack, pointing out their hypocrisy or any errors in their argument. Remember, the power they gain from this encounter is only as strong as their accusations against you. Your goal is not to defend your argument but to rob them of their power. Don't take a stance on any position that it would be difficult to defend or prove. Work at showing a side that your opponent doesn't want seen and force him to get back to the truth as soon as possible. Winning a heated debate like that will earn you loads of points you would have to work even harder to achieve.

- **Ignore people:** By ignoring people, you show a lot of dominance. This is an important skill that is of high quality and can prove very valuable. You can prove your dominance by ignoring people's errors or when they take an action you don't approve of. Rather than blatantly pointing out their error, ignoring them is a silent way to show disapproval.

- **Say a lot with fewer words:** The most powerful people in the world are not always full of a lot of rhetoric. They don't mind people noticing them so they are calm in the face of social scrutiny. When they speak, they usually express themselves slowly and don't hesitate to pause to let the silence drive home their point.

When replying to another person, the general rule of thumb is to wait two seconds before speaking. Don't be afraid of the silence, it adds pressure to the other person and they are compelled to fill in the void.

- **Use Power Words:** Your speech should make good use of power words.
    - Listen
    - I don't understand
    - Can you repeat that
    - Yes, that's right
    - No. That not right at all
    - Wrong!
    - You're mistaken.
    - And you're okay with that?
    - Before we continue, I need you to answer my question.
    - I don't want to talk about that now.
    - Tell me something more interesting.
    - Quiet! Silence!
    - The numbers speak for themselves.

Whether you're speaking one on one or in a crowd, asserting dominance is all about projecting the right attitude. It is a very faint line that exists between being aggressive and being assertive, but if you can master these elements in asserting your dominance, you'll not only have a lot of people following you, you'll have earned their respect too.

Dominant Behavior to Show Who's Boss

Showing dominance through behavior can be very similar to using body language. In fact, some of the methods here will overlap with those in how you present yourself physically. Spend some time observing people in power and you'll begin to see what social dominance really looks like.

Take the Lead: Clearly, taking the lead in any given situation can help you to assert your social dominance. Consider the impression you leave in others when you are:

- Walking. If you are going with a group, you'll notice how the more submissive people will begin to look around for someone to take the lead. As a leader, you don't wait, you just start walking. Try it and see just how many people will start to follow you.

  If you are new to a group, don't just jump ahead. Wait and see if they already have an established leader and if no one steps forward, then you can assert your position.

- Look for ways to protect those around you. This is a classic dominant role that exudes power and is deserving of respect. Protecting and caring for others could be simple gestures like offering someone a hand when they are trying to get out of their seat to defending their decision on a business project. This strategy has no downside. A strong leader who exercises care for those in his charge is a healthy way to get any kind of relationship off to a good start.

- Expect people to follow you. If people are not sure you're the leader it will be difficult for them to follow you, but simple gestures can help them along. For example, shaking someone's hand and placing the other on their back helps direct them to move in the direction you want them to go.

- Become a good guide: Take the initiative and invite others to join you whenever possible. Not only is this a powerful way to assert dominance people will automatically see you as a leader.

- Take the lead in small things. If the entire group sits, delay sitting for at least ten seconds before joining them. If you are invited inside, delay entering. You can tell them to take one second to enjoy the view or to answer a phone call. If you are in a position that dictates you must follow, do so in a nonchalant sort of way and avoid making any eye contact with them.

- Assign tasks: Whenever possible, give tasks to others. Delegating is a sign of authority. You will notice some people assign tasks even if they don't have any formal authority. If you are assigned a task, question the command. This will make the assigner have to defend his position. The more your challenge those in authority the more power you take for yourself. However, there will be times when someone does have the authority to give you a task. If this is the case, accept the assignment gracefully but continue to challenge tasks given from those who are not in an authority position to do so.

Exert Social Pressure: Creating tension within a social environment pressures other to comply. At times you can create tension even without a reason for it, just to assert your dominance.
Use intimidation with full frontal body language or loud aggressive tones in your voice to get less important individuals to cower in submission.

Use Fewer Words: Talking too much can be a sign that you are nervous or lack confidence. Rather than expressing every thought on your mind, let your facial expressions and body language communicate for you.

Touching: You can also show dominance through touching. In fact, just the act of touching alone can put you in a more dominant position. Studies have often shown that those who touch others are automatically viewed as more dominant. However, there is the right kind of touching and the wrong kind.
- **The Parental Touch:** Parental touches doesn't necessarily mean they are exclusive to parents and their children. A boss can use a parental touch and automatically push his charges into a more submissive role.
    - Patting them on the head
    - Pinching their cheek
    - Touching their face

    All of these touches indicate who is the parent and who is the child. They are also signaling that they are ready to take care of their subject and are ready to take charge.

Follow the Pattern: There is a distinct pattern of events that can carry you from the submissive one to the more dominant role in any type of relationship. You may start at the bottom rung of the ladder, then you move on to assertion, which will gradually slip you into a dominant role. The most effective role you can take is to follow the natural course of these patterns. The best ones to take an assertive role are those who are very good at handling those who are aggressive.

Part of that journey, however, is learning when to show aggression, punish, or intimidate. People who fall back on these dark habits when not needed usually earn the title of leader but not the respect due them. But there is a place for them in a number of interactions. Here are a few guidelines you need to follow.

- Slapping: This does not have to be a harsh type of slap that will leave your victim's cheeks burning. In fact, a light but threatening slap may be even more intimidating than outright brute force.
- Confiscating property: Picking up or taking another person's property is a very intimidating way to assert dominance. In essence, you are telling them that not only does their property belong to you but they do too. To fight back this approach, you can refuse to let them take your property or you can take theirs putting you both on equal footing.
- Territorial: Everyone feels territorial about something, but submissive people don't stand up for what they know is theirs. To assert your dominance, you will defend property that is your own with a strong sense of confidence.

Command Attention: Exerting a quiet sense of confidence always commands attention. There is no need to be flashy or bold in order to get people to follow you. While you can certainly take that route, just following the natural course of nature will have people gravitating to you with ease. Consider being helpful to those around you. By offering to fix problems, address needs, and protect those you want in your following, you will become a natural leader without too much effort.

Asserting your dominance may not be easy at first, especially if you're used to being in a more submissive position. But, if you continue to practice these simple techniques, you'll be surprised at just how fast you can move up in your role of becoming a master manipulator.

Conclusion

Becoming a master manipulator is not as difficult as it may seem. It will take practice and commitment, and you won't master it overnight. Nothing you do well in life is ever easy, but if you stick with it through to the end you will inevitably yield positive results.

No doubt, you've heard a lot of things about manipulation. It's evil, it's dangerous, and it is demeaning, but there are both good and bad ways to view the practice. We live in a world of manipulators no matter where you look. The reality dictates that if you're not manipulating then there is a really good chance that you are being manipulated so you're going to be on one side of the coin whether you agree with it or not.

The question you really should be asking yourself is what kind of manipulator are you going to be. Parents manipulate their children as they mold them to become mature adults. Teachers manipulate their students to groom them for the future, and employers manipulate their charges to increase productivity. All of us have been manipulated in one way or another and we have all worked our magic on others. If your moral compass is triggered by this thought, then realize it is a matter of choice.

Becoming a master manipulator involves understanding how our thoughts and emotions work together. As your emotional intelligence grows so will our understanding in these areas. We've discussed how to build up our EQ and learn how to use it to identify our own emotions and those in others. This can become a powerful tool in our arsenal. Every master manipulator needs a good EQ. Without it, we will always struggle to get people to recognize us and give us what we want.

You also learned how to choose your target and the qualities that draw people to you. Everyone is not a prime target for manipulation and some can be much harder than others to convince. Especially in the beginning, you want to use the hooks listed in Chapter three to choose those who will be easier to convince. As you gain more experience, you can then try your skills on those harder and more challenging targets.

In Chapter Four we talked a great deal about body language. Learning how to read subtle cues can tell you a lot about a person and what they are thinking. Developing this skill can almost give you the power of mind reading. Learning about microexpressions and the way people walk will tell you much about what to expect and what you can ask from everyone around you.

Then we learned how to use several manipulation tools to help you get what you want. We started simply with some basic tactics that all people use and can easily be recognized. Applying the Six Laws of Persuasion can be very effective if you are well-informed about what they really are. Manipulation is a psychological game and the key to winning knowing where to position yourself to assert dominance over others. These tools are how you navigate this game.

So, whether you're looking to secretly manipulate your boss to do what you want or you're trying seduce someone into a romantic relationship the rules of the game are the same, you're just using different tools to accomplish your goals. Success can only come from asserting your dominance and staying the course.

Through the pages of this book, you have learned a lot about manipulation. No doubt, you will have to read some sections several times in order to get the full sense of them. But as you do, make sure to put them all into practice as soon as possible. This will help you to make faster progress. There will be times when you will fail miserably at your attempts to persuade others to do your bidding, but don't be discouraged; that is just part of the process. If you persist, it is just a matter of time before you can honestly say that you are truly a master manipulator.

Become Your Better Self With Positive Daily Affirmations

Boost Your Self-Esteem, Learn to Love Your Life and Make Everyday Special with Comforting and Motivational Daily Affirmations

TABLE OF CONTENT

INTRODUCTION 157

CHAPTER ONE DAILY POSITIVE AFFIRMATIONS TO START OFF YOUR DAY 159

CHAPTER TWO POSITIVE AFFIRMATIONS FOR LOVE 169

CHAPTER THREE POSITIVE AFFIRMATIONS FOR HEALTH 178

CHAPTER FOUR POSITIVE AFFIRMATIONS FOR FINANCES 187

CHAPTER FIVE POSITIVE AFFIRMATIONS FOR BUSINESS 195

CHAPTER SIX POSITIVE AFFIRMATIONS FOR CONFIDENCE 204

CHAPTER SEVEN POSITIVE AFFIRMATIONS FOR PEACE OF MIND 212

CHAPTER EIGHT POSITIVE AFFIRMATIONS FOR SPIRITUALITY 221

CHAPTER NINE POSITIVE AFFIRMATIONS FOR THE CAREER MINDED 231

CHAPTER TEN POSITIVE AFFIRMATIONS FOR CREATIVITY 242

CHAPTER ELEVEN POSITIVE AFFIRMATIONS FOR WOMEN 249

CHAPTER TWELVE POSITIVE AFFIRMATIONS FOR MEN 259

CHAPTER THIRTEEN POSITIVE AFFIRMATIONS FOR TEENAGERS 268

CHAPTER FOURTEEN POSITIVE AFFIRMATIONS FOR PREGNANCY 276

CHAPTER FIFTEEN POSITIVE AFFIRMATIONS FOR TOUGH TIMES 286

CHAPTER SIXTEEN POSITIVE AFFIRMATIONS FOR WEIGHT LOSS 295

CHAPTER SEVENTEEN POSITIVE AFFIRMATIONS FOR MANIFESTING DESIRES 305

CHAPTER EIGHTEEN POSITIVE AFFIRMATIONS FOR MEDITATIONS 314

CHAPTER NINETEEN POSITIVE AFFIRMATIONS FOR BIRTHDAYS 323

CHAPTER TWENTY POSITIVE AFFIRMATIONS FOR THE TRAVELLER 332

CHAPTER TWENTY-ONE POSITIVE AFFIRMATIONS ABOUT EMOTIONS 338

INTRODUCTION

There is a general saying in life; that you are what you eat. If life has taught me anything, it is the humble knowledge that we are a sum total of our experiences and our experiences are dictated by the words that we speak. Many people would find it difficult to accept this simple truth and this is because most people fall into two spectrums. Those who have resigned themselves to the dictates of fate and those who struggle daily to control their fate.

The first set of people believe that the Universe is solely responsible for whatever we go through in life. And if you question their logic, they have this belief that the Universe is a being of immerse power and strength with little to no care for mankind. This being just does what he or she pleases and acts impulsively to satisfy their whim. Which is why a person would be born into a life of hardship, toil their way to the top and just at the point when they are about to reap the rewards of their labor, the person's life is cut short by a totally random event like a rock falling out of the sky or a quick ailment. In the same way, you have a person born into a completely lavish lifestyle and for the rest of their life, they do not have to toil a single day. The contrasts between these two personalities and the unfairness of it all is what the first group of people use to allude to a supernatural being that is sometimes called the Universe.

The second group of people have a firm grip on their destiny and they refuse to relinquish control to anyone or anything…human or supernatural. Their lives are sequential order of events managed to the point of obsession by time. For them, life happens but they are going to do everything in their power to ensure that life happens the way that they want it. Sometimes, things do not go exactly according to their plan. This can be extremely frustrating for them and if care is not taking, it can cause a deep psychological break down. When that doesn't happen, they piece themselves pack together and attack life with the same tenacious vigor that characterizes everything that they do. The problem with them is that anything that doesn't fit into their plan is quickly brushed aside or thrown under the bus. Their experiences are limited to their plans.

Life is meant to be lived with limitless possibilities. You can't control what happens to you but you can control how you perceive the experiences you have had. In fact, you can go a step further to redefine how your life is shaped by those experiences. The best part of this is that you don't have to appeal to any supreme being or take permission from anyone to live your life to the fullest. By speaking positive words, you attract positive experiences into your life and even when tragedy occurs (because this is life), your words can shape exactly how that tragedy can affect you. It would either shape you or break you. This is a subconscious choice that you must make everyday and without realizing this, we make this choice with the words that we speak. In this book, you would find positive words of affirmations that can be adapted to suit every situation. From sunrise to sunset, through every season in your life, fill your mouth with words that elevate you and deliver to you, experiences that make life worth living.

Be inspired to live better every day!

CHAPTER ONE

DAILY POSITIVE AFFIRMATIONS TO START OFF YOUR DAY

1. Today is going to be a wonderful day
2. I open my heart, my mind and my body to amazing experiences
3. My today is better than my yesterday
4. Every day and in every way, I am getting better and better
5. Today, I am abundantly joyful and happy
6. I am full of gratitude for my life this morning
7. I find beauty and joy in all the things I do today
8. I am clear, untouched, and unharmed by all the negative experiences of yesterday.
9. My life today is a joy. I relax easily and open myself up to delightful surprises
10. I permit myself to live a life that is joyful and filled with love, fun and friendship
11. Right now, I choose love, joy and freedom
12. I open my heart and allow wonderful gifts of life to flow into me
13. Everything in my life is exactly as it should be
14. As the morning glory blossoms in the morning, my life is blossoming in perfection
15. Today, I am radiating with loving kindness and life mirrors this back to me
16. Like the morning sun, I am full of positive life-giving energy.
17. I experience total freedom from the burdens of my past.
18. I refuse to live like a victim this beautiful day
19. Yesterdays experiences has lost its hold on me

20. Today, I live in the consciousness of who I am in this present moment
21. I forgive myself for the mistakes of yesterday and set myself free from guilt.
22. I am abundantly blessed with treasures and gifts that warm my heart
23. I use my gifts and blessings lovingly when I have influence over others
24. I fill my heart positive musings that amplify my zest for life
25. I embrace wisdom, knowledge and understanding today
26. I am a powerful being and I bask in the knowledge of who I am
27. I resist and shut out any negative force that seeks to diminish my light
28. As the world awakens to the brightness of the sun, so do people come to my rising
29. The relationships that I need to thrive are locating me today
30. I welcome love and romance into my life.
31. I feel my center with light and love
32. My life is open to people who reflect the same degree of light and love
33. I am surrounded by loving and supportive relationships
34. I deserve love and I get it in abundance.
35. I am loved, loving and lovable.
36. I am building and nurturing healthy relationships with my family and friends
37. I am blessed with an incredible family and wonderful friends.
38. I give out love and it is returned to me multiplied many folds.
39. Good things are happening throughout today.
40. No matter what happens today, then end result would be joy
41. I am filled with love, hope and confidence about my future
42. I greet each second of today with enthusiasm and hope.
43. I am awake to the opportunities that are present in this day.

44. If I falter, I get positive reminders that my life is filled with joy and love.
45. I do not live in the fear of making mistakes
46. There is a magical element to me, and my life is full of serendipity
47. My thoughts and feelings are positively nourishing.
48. I am present and conscious of every beautiful moment.
49. I see beauty in every person I meet.
50. People treat me with kindness and respect, and I treat them the same.
51. I am surrounded by peaceful people.
52. I bring peace to the people who encounter me today
53. My environment is calm and supportive.
54. I am the architect of my life. I am the creator of my reality.
55. I envelop myself in self-acceptance today
56. I choose to believe that I am supported and loved by the Universe
57. I am surrounded by abundance.
58. I am healthy, energetic and optimistic.
59. I am overflowing with happiness, joy and satisfaction
60. I transcend every form of negativity.
61. I proclaim that I can, and I will achieve greatness today
62. I know that everything happens for a reason; everything leads to something positive.
63. I let go of any grudges I am holding against myself or another person.
64. I am forgiving. My compassion replaces anger with love
65. I am at peace with my past.
66. I make the choice to reflect love, happiness, grace and positivity
67. I am patient, diplomatic and tolerant.
68. I am grateful for the miracles in my life.
69. No matter what, the universe supports me in every possible way.

Positive Daily Affirmations

70. The experiences in my life today helps me to grow.
71. Today I lay the foundation for a wonderful future.
72. I am sowing seeds with fruitful dividends
73. I am safe and protected by divinity in all my goings and comings
74. Danger and harm are not featured in my day
75. All the resources I need to thrive are made available to me
76. Everything I seek can be found within.
77. I set myself free from and anxiety and fears about the future
78. I am significant. I contribute to the advancement of humankind.
79. Today, my footprints in the sands of time are etched deeper.
80. This day will bring me nothing absolute joy, fulfillment and happiness.
81. I have all it takes to make this day relevant and memorable
82. I face any difficulties in this day with courage and endurance.
83. I am excited to witness the making of the best years of my life.
84. I am excited about the amazing journeys I am going to take today.
85. I am mentally and emotionally prepared for the challenges of the day.
86. Today I fill myself with positive energy.
87. I am calm and patient in the face of any crisis today
88. I am filled with confidence and positivity at the thought of facing today
89. The blessings of this new day energize me.
90. This morning, I make the conscious choice to be happy
91. The potential in my day is not lost to me
92. Today is a blessing and a gift that I will not waste.
93. I trust my inner wisdom to guide me throughout my day.
94. I avoid self-doubt today by not comparing myself to others.
95. I am full of potential and today, I recognize it

96. I receive the people I meet today with an open heart and an open mind.
97. I will not compare myself to others.
98. Today I feel healthy and strong, physically, emotionally, and mentally.
99. Today I will accomplish greater things than I did yesterday
100. Today, I am triumphant in my dealings

ACTIONABLE AFFIRMATIONS FOR YOUR DAY

1. Happiness is my birthright. This morning, I am using happiness as my default setting.
2. I free myself from greed and choose instead to feel joy and contentment at this moment right now.
3. I am not sad or depressed, instead, I am feeling happy and enthusiastic about life.
4. I can tap into a wellspring of inner happiness today I wish therefore I am optimistic.
5. I inspire others to be happy as well by allowing myself to be happy
6. I have fun with all my endeavors, even the most mundane activity brings me joy.
7. I look at the world around me and can't help but smile and feel joy.
8. I find joy and pleasure in the simplest things in life.
9. My sense of humor is active, and I love to share this to bring laughter to others.
10. My heart is overflowing with joy, nothing threatens my joy today/
11. Life is happening in this moment and I choose to live in the consciousness of this
12. I will not falter today because trust myself and know my inner wisdom is my best guide.
13. My name has value because I have integrity. I am totally reliable. I do what I say.

14. Today, I put aside all irrational thoughts. I act from a place of personal security.
15. Today I will not settle for less because I fully accept myself and know that I am worthy of great things in life.
16. I will not wallow in poor opinion of myself. I boldly choose to be proud of myself.
17. I am not afraid of what today holds as I am willing to accept and embrace all experiences, even unpleasant ones.
18. I remove any dark clouds hanging over me and fill my mind with positive and nourishing thoughts.
19. At the end of today, I will I rest in happiness when I go to sleep, knowing with my entire being that all is well in my world.
20. I choose to use my time better by assessing/ myself and my actions rather than judging the deeds or misdeeds or other people in my life
21. I am making bold choices without fear today. Choices that reflect the beauty and light that resides within me.
22. This morning, I embrace the chance to be better than I was yesterday. I am making only the best decisions for my life today.
23. I am choosing to maintain a positive attitude today despite any hurdles that come my way because I know that I have what it takes to succeed.
24. In this moment, I am exactly where I need to be in life. I welcome the challenges and opportunities that I am facing today, and I choose to learn and grow.
25. To harvest a better tomorrow, I only plant positive seeds in the world today. I do not waste one precious moment in anger, hatred, or envy.
26. I am not living my life passively with no purpose. I am on earth for a reason, and I am committed to living a positive life and being a positive influence on others.

27. I choose to take responsibility for my own happiness today. I do not allow anyone else to have the power over how I feel because I am in control.
28. I see my true nature. I am beautiful and I look and feel radiant both inside and outside.
29. I recognize the talent that I have and knowing I have so much to offer the world, I refuse to be mediocre.
30. I refuse to waste my talent today. I am a person of excellence therefore, I am putting my 100% in all I do
31. I keep the energy revitalizing today therefore I will not be engaging in activities like that drain me emotionally like gossiping, bullying and so on.
32. I have a winning mentality so even if I fail at something today, I choose not to be defined by it
33. My path to the life that I hope for is revealed to me and I do not have to hurt or harm anyone to get to my destination
34. My vision for my life today is as clear as the sun, I am not stumbling around in the dark to achieve my goals today
35. I trust in the provisions made available by the universe therefore I do not live in fear for the security of my life, my family and my properties.
36. Today, I make enlightened decisions about my life and I no longer fear for the consequences of my actions because I am sowing the right seeds
37. The words that I speak today are graceful and pleasing to the ear so that even in anger, my words remain pleasant and nurturing
38. As clear as clouds are on a sunny day, so are my thoughts. I am not confused or double minded about the choices I make
39. This light that burns brightly on the inside of me will not be hidden from the world. I choose to shine brightly for the world to see

40. I love myself and like myself. I choose to focus on my positive qualities and how I can use them to improve myself and the world.
41. I am living my own version of happiness today. My joy is sourced from within and has nothing to do with anyone else. I am happy for anyone else who is happy and other people are happy for me.
42. I accept that I am not perfect. And if I do something wrong, I will go back and find another way. I create a new course of action. I do not stop.
43. Today, I am ready to commit to the life that I dream of, and the world works along with me to help attain my vision.
44. Today, I take the first of many steps towards attaining my goals and the rest comes naturally.
45. Today, I choose to use the time I have in a way that is in line with my values and goals. Rather than complaining about not having enough time today
46. I refuse to be idle this wonderful day. I am making a conscious effort to make the best of every moment I am given today.
47. I trust my own wisdom and intuition to guide me in my productive endeavors. I know what is best for me and I surround myself with people who want the best for me.
48. On this day of blessings and abundance, I refuse to believe that my options are limited. The opportunities coming my way are limitless.
49. Today, I am ready to create more success in my life and I refuse to entertain any excuses that will slow me down. I am productive and focused on attaining results.
50. Today I am elevated to greater heights

AFFIRMATIONS FOR THE SUCCESS OF THE DAY
51. I am setting up my mind for greatness today

Positive Daily Affirmations

52. The light of the sun touches every area of my life that has been experiencing darkness
53. I feel the pulse of the universe as I set out today
54. I am pulsating with positive energy for greatness
55. I do not have a mentality of failure today. I have blessings and lessons
56. The winds and the atmosphere are favorable for me today
57. I am alive to the goodness of this day
58. I tap into the source of happiness to get me through this day
59. I will not be hindered by the failures of others
60. I welcome blessings in unexpected places
61. I am revitalized from the inside out for the day ahead
62. My way has been made straight for me, so I sail through the day effortlessly
63. I am resourceful
64. I am determined
65. I am succeeding without any restrictions
66. I am breaking glass ceilings without fear or hesitation
67. I am accomplishing something great today
68. I have ordained this morning as the birthing point of my glory
69. Life is so much easier for me today
70. Today, I refuse to be invisible. My feelings and efforts are recognized
71. Today is the day that I will be celebrated by my peers
72. There is a restoration of broken relationships today
73. I know the right thing to say and do at any point in time
74. Today, I am delivered into a joyful experience that uplifts me
75. The seeds that bring about the permanence of happiness in my life are planted today
76. Just as the night transforms to daytime, I am radically transformed into greatness

77. I refuse to ponder on the things that I lack or do not have
78. Today, my joy knows no bounds
79. As I speak these words of affirmation, I feel the light radiating throughout my entire being
80. I am truly delighted about the changes that are coming today
81. I speak order and organization into this day
82. There will be no chaos in this day and even when chaos presents itself, I will make order out of it
83. I am accomplishing great feats today
84. I do not have the words to describe how amazing the gift of today is to me
85. The environment that I live and conduct all of my affairs is conducive enough for me to thrive
86. Today, I rise out of the ashes of the past
87. I am taking on my day from a place of comfort and wisdom
88. I am capable of handling everything that comes my way today
89. I do not falter under the weight of the events of today
90. I am constantly reminded of the greatness within at different points throughout today
91. Today, I experience the freedom to create my ideal reality for the future I desire. I have a choice in every situation that I face. There is nothing that can get between me and my best self.

CHAPTER TWO

POSITIVE AFFIRMATIONS FOR LOVE

1. I feel pure love within me - and all around me
2. I embrace the blessings of love and romance into my life.
3. The relationship that I am in is loving and supportive
4. I am made for love and I get it in abundance.
5. I am truly loved, very loving and 100% lovable.
6. I have been blessed with an incredible family and wonderful friends.
7. I give out genuine love and the universe returns this to me multiplied many folds.
8. I am constantly radiating love and other person reflects love back to me.
9. I love myself enough to recognize healthy love when I receive it
10. My romantic relationship is healthy, long-lasting and full of love.
11. My partner is kind, compassionate and understanding in our relationship
12. My partner is very physically, emotionally, sexually and spiritually attracted to me.
13. I am with my ideal partner and we share a life full of love.
14. My life is full of love and I find it everywhere I go.
15. My relationship is rooted in love, and my partner and I are perfectly matched.
16. There is a deep understanding between my partner and me.
17. Forgiveness and compassion are the foundation of my romantic relationship.
18. My words towards others are always kind and loving, and in return, I hear kindness and love from others.
19. Every day of my life is filled with genuine love.

20. All forms of communication between my partner and I are established in love.
21. I know I am amazing, and I am worthy of true love.
22. My personality attracts the right kind of person for me
23. I know that I face each day with the support and love of my partner and the people who love me
24. All my relationships are nurturing and healthy because they are based in love and compassion.
25. I attract love and light into my life because I am a beacon of love and compassion.
26. I have a vibrant personality, and everyone sees how much joy and love I have for life.
27. I experience positivity in all my relationships as they are filled with love and compassion.
28. I see the good in other people and I acknowledge their efforts to be their best.
29. I always find opportunities to be kind and caring at every turn.
30. I am genuinely in love with myself and feel great about myself.
31. I accept myself and the love I have for myself is unconditional.
32. My heart is always open to forging new relationships. I am kind to every person I meet.
33. I surround myself with love, so I attract kind people.
34. I love people unconditionally and I do so without hesitation.
35. I dwell in love. I do good deeds and my efforts are appreciated by those around me.
36. I am accompanied by love everywhere I go.
37. Love, forgiveness and understanding is the very foundation of my relationships.
38. I have the capacity to give and receive love equally.
39. I accept my partner wholesomely and unconditionally.
40. I am treasured for who I really am in my relationships

Positive Daily Affirmations

41. My marriage/relationship is waxes stronger, deeper and more loving with every single day.
42. My friendships are meaningful, supportive and rewarding to me and the people involved
43. My friends know and love me for who I am.
44. I am accepting of others and it helps me to establish long-lasting friendships.
45. I attract positive people into with whom I quickly forge lifetime bonds.
46. I surround myself with friends who genuinely care about my wellbeing and treat me well
47. My partner and I share a deep and powerful love for each other that keeps us connected.
48. I wholly trust, respect and admire my partner and I see the best in him/her.
49. I love my partner exactly how he/she is and enjoy his/her unique qualities without conditions.
50. My partner and I share emotional intimacy daily through activities we both enjoy.
51. I have healthy boundaries with my partner, and they respect it.
52. My partner and I have fun together and find new ways to enjoy our time together.
53. My partner and I communicate openly and resolve conflict peacefully and respectfully.
54. I am the most authentic version of myself in my love relationship.
55. I am able to communicate my desires and needs clearly and share with my partner.
56. I want the best for my partner and my actions reflect my desire for my partner
57. I easily go out of my way to support my partner to achieve their goals
58. I am grounded in love and empathy

59. I am worthy of love and trust in my relationships and friendships.
60. I actively nurture healthy relationships with the people I love.
61. I bring joy to those around me.
62. I am grateful for all who love and care for me.
63. My friendships are important to me.
64. My love and loyalty are not called to question at any point
65. I know how important it is to just listen to others.
66. My friends love and respect me.
67. My relationships bring me joy.
68. I have an inner fountain of love that I continuously draw from
69. My love tank is consistently replenished
70. Love is not a foreign concept to me
71. I have learned how to speak the love language of my partner fluently
72. I am not confounded by the actions or inactions of others in my relationship
73. The love that I give is not dependent on any external source
74. I have the ability to recognize genuine love
75. I do not love people to the point of obsession
76. My partner does not feel caged by the love that I show them
77. The love that I give is strong and healthy
78. I am capable of loving people past their flaws and errors
79. The negative love experiences of my past do not define my present relationships
80. My heart is big enough to embrace the people in my circle and beyond
81. I am compassionate and giving in the way that I love
82. I recognize the worth of the people in my love
83. I open up myself to communicate effective in my relationships
84. I do not shut out my partner or the people that genuinely care about me

85. I appreciate the love that I receive, and I show my appreciation appropriately
86. The love that I have is not a bargaining chip in any of my relationships
87. I have a unique insight into the needs of my partner
88. I do not betray my partner at any point in our relationship
89. I do not expect perfection from my partner, but I love him/her perfectly
90. The love that I give is rooted in the right things
91. I am secure in the love of my partner and vice versa
92. I fall in love with myself each passing day
93. My expression of love is not limited by my experiences
94. I have no desire to validate the love I feel to anyone but me
95. I love myself enough to leave toxic relationships
96. I embrace the differences between myself and my partner
97. My love for my partner is consistently renewed in committed relationships
98. I am ready to put in the work that it takes to keep my relationships alive
99. I do not speak words that destroy people
100. I am a nurturer and my love cause people to blossom
101. I am patient, kind and understanding
102. I do not make assertions people without verifying the authenticity of that statement
103. I give of myself freely without conditions or expectations
104. My love is not dependent on the circumstances surrounding me
105. I am capable of loving the people in my life through good and bad times
106. My relationship is built on shared principles that provide a solid foundation
107. I have a shared intimacy with my partner that is deep
108. I do not hold grudges or hold past sins against my partner
109. My expectation of love is rooted in tangible principles

Positive Daily Affirmations

110. I value loyalty and therefore, I am a loyal friend
111. I have the courage to apologize when I have wronged the people, I care about
112. I completely forgive people who have wronged me in turn
113. I am discreet about the personal details that people confide in me
114. I do not betray the trust of my friend, partner or family
115. With each passing day, I am presented with an opportunity to grow in my relationship
116. The love that I share with my partner in marriage is divine
117. I am not a loner, I have the ability to make good friends
118. I am an appreciative person
119. There is enough room in my heart for love
120. I am selfless but that does not mean that I love myself less
121. I hold myself accountable for the relationships that I have
122. In times of disagreement, I communicate without humiliating
123. My partner and I grow together. We do not grow apart
124. There is room for positive growth in all my relationships
125. In my marriage, my partner and I aspire for attainable things
126. I am very content in this relationship
127. My relationships are characterized by love, happiness and genuine affection
128. I am moved by the pains of my partner and I actively try to stop the hurt
129. I am not vindictive in any of my relationships
130. There are no dangerous secrets between me and my partner
131. The environment in my marriage makes it easy to talk about everything
132. My partner's happiness is independent of me and vice versa
133. My marriage is set up for the long haul
134. My relationship is a haven for me, and I find peace in it

135. I am mentally and emotionally strong to weather the tides and seasons of my marriage
136. My partner is mentally and emotionally strong to weather the times and seasons of this marriage
137. I distance myself from toxic people and toxic relationships
138. I am supportive and progressive in all of my relationships
139. My love is not restricted to a few but welcoming to all
140. My partner and I age gracefully but our love remains new
141. My marriage is everything my partner and I envisioned for ourselves
142. I am articulate without being hurtful in my communication with my partner
143. My partner and I are on the same page emotionally, financially and spiritually
144. My home is a harbor from the outside world that is full of peace, love and harmony
145. I am comfortable in my relationship
146. I am deeply connected to my partner in the ways that matter
147. Love is not an elusive concept for me
148. I am unwavering in the trust I have for my partner
149. My partner gives me no reason to question the trust I have for them
150. I am completely open to my partner. I do not hide parts of myself from them
151. There is order in my relationship
152. Regret is a foreign concept in all my relationships
153. I deal with loss in a healthy manner
154. If I experience loss, I do not hide from the grief but I am not overwhelmed by it
155. This union is a successful and progressive union
156. I fall in love with my partner every single day
157. I am fervent and consistent in my affirmations of love

158. I never miss the chance to tell my partner how much I love them
159. I never miss the chance to declare my affections for the people I love
160. I belong wholly to my beloved as my beloved is mine
161. I prioritize the relationships that I have
162. I do not take the people that I care about for granted
163. I do not sit by and watch another human suffer
164. I show empathy and compassion when they are needed
165. I am reliable and dependable in relationships
166. I am moved to show acts of kindness on a daily basis
167. I am not discriminatory in my relationships
168. My friends find it very easy to confide in me because they know that I am discreet
169. I have genuine respect and love for the people in my life
170. I do not feel bitter or jealous about the successes of my friends
171. I am letting go of bad habits that influence my love negatively
172. I am embracing good habits that nurture and grow my love
173. I am a blessing to the people in my world
174. I don't try to impress people with my love. I simply express it
175. I work in the consciousness of the divine love that I have within
176. I instinctively know how to love the people I come in contact with
177. The in my heart for my partner is not something I have to labor painfully for
178. Love comes into my life effortlessly
179. My love is like the stars at night. Even in the darkness of life it shines through
180. I am not unreasonable in love. My head and heart are involved

181. My love does not discriminate but it is not blind either
182. Every good thing that has been said about love is a daily experience for me
183. I conquer every negative stereotype about love and transcend any unhealthy expectation concerning love
184. My self-love game is top notch. I love myself in the most beautiful ways
185. I surround myself with the good kind of love, but I can always look inward and find the love I need
186. The size of my wallet does not determine the degree of my love
187. I always find creative and positive ways to express my love
188. I will always feel loved no matter what
189. I do my part in making the world a more loving and forgiving place
190. The love I have for humans is extended to the world as a whole
191. I care for and love the plants and animals that I have been blessed to know and nurture
192. I am not unkind to people regardless of station or status
193. I surround myself with people I love, and care about, but also take time to nurture my relationship with myself.

CHAPTER THREE

POSITIVE AFFIRMATIONS FOR HEALTH

1. I deserve to be healthy and feel good about myself
2. I am full of energy and vitality and my mind is calm and peaceful.
3. Every day, I am getting healthier and stronger.
4. I honor my body by treating myself to healthy meals
5. I attend to the needs of my body; trusting the signals that it sends me.
6. I manifest perfect health by consciously making smart choices.
7. I engage in healthy stimulation throughout my day.
8. I eat healthy, nutritious food during my lunch break and my body is grateful, granting me energy and good health in return.
9. I radiate success and health.
10. I develop healthy habits that support my health journey
11. I wake up in good health daily
12. I am grateful for how effectively and efficiently my body works.
13. I embrace the shape of my body and I find it beautiful and appealing.
14. I only make healthy and nourishing eating choices.
15. I take care of my body and exercise every day.
16. My body is healthy and full of energy.
17. My body is a constant marvel to me
18. My body is filled with healing energy every time I inhale.
19. I amazed by the things I can accomplish with my body
20. I am very grateful and happy that I weigh ___ (fill in with desired weight).
21. I crave healthy, nutritious foods.

Positive Daily Affirmations

22. I am surrounded by people who positively motivate my health choices
23. I love the taste of fruits and vegetables.
24. I am in love with every curve in my body.
25. Every organ in my body is working the way it was designed to work
26. I am grateful for the life force and energy that runs through my body.
27. Everything I think, say and do makes me healthier.
28. I feel safe and comfortable in my body.
29. No food is off limits to me. However, I eat in moderation
30. Everything I do is fun, healthy and exciting.
31. I crave new but healthy experiences.
32. I eat the foods that I desire but I practice portion control
33. Every day I'm getting healthier.
34. I am full of vitality.
35. Every meal that I take is consciously prepared with the needs of my body in mind
36. I take good care of my body and eat a healthy, well-balanced diet.
37. My body is a holy temple. I keep it clean and maintain its functionality.
38. I exercise regularly and strengthen my body.
39. Every cell in my body vibrates with energy and health.
40. I observe my emotions without getting physically affected by them
41. I nourish my body with healthy food.
42. All of my body systems are functioning perfectly.
43. Every single cell in my body is working as it was designed to
44. My body is healing, and I feel better and better every day.
45. I enjoy exercising my body and strengthening my muscles.
46. With every breath out, I release stress out of my body.
47. I indulge in practices that promote healing
48. I send love and healing to every organ of my body.

Positive Daily Affirmations

49. I breathe deeply, exercise regularly and feed only good nutritious food to my body.
50. I pay attention and listen to what my body needs for health and vitality.
51. I sleep soundly and peacefully and awaken feeling rested and energetic.
52. I am surrounded by people who encourage and support healthy choices.
53. I approve of myself and love myself deeply and completely.
54. My confidence, self-esteem and inner wisdom are increasing with each day.
55. I have sound health teachers all around me
56. I have peace of mind concerning my health
57. My body may not meet the worldly standard for beauty, but I am beautiful
58. I don't engage in exercises or activities that jeopardize my health
59. My body is a constantly enjoying daily health benefits
60. I have the resources needed to stay healthy and in good shape
61. I have the right kind of health information to stay in peak performance
62. The aging of my body occurs slowly so that I look younger than my actual age
63. Despite my genetic history, I am a picture of perfect health
64. I am not plagued by the medical history of those who came before me
65. I will not be shamed into making choices that do not reflect my health decisions
66. I am constantly alert to my body and I listen to its needs
67. I do not take short cuts to attaining the healthy lifestyle that I desire
68. I am a vision of health in motion
69. I am confident that I am always in a state of good health
70. I enjoy the daily benefits of being healthy

71. I am not worried about my health as the universe works to ensure that I am fine
72. I take delight in health focused activities
73. There is no lack of vital health information to me
74. I intuitively know the things that are good for my body and I take the steps to follow through on those things
75. My eyes are open to the daily benefits that surround me
76. I am grateful and appreciative of the good health that I have
77. I am programmed to engage in activities that are beneficial to my health
78. I do not fall for the gimmicks of fake health experts
79. I successfully stay on track with all my health goals
80. My vibrancy is not diminished by the day
81. My heart is strong enough to support the needs of my body
82. My lungs take in the right amount of air needed to replenish my body
83. I am revitalized from the inside out
84. When it comes to my health I don't just live, I thrive
85. My health is getting better and better
86. My family would not receive any negative news concerning my health
87. I am an example of picture-perfect health
88. My bones are strong enough to support the weight of my body
89. I refuse to procrastinate about the healthy needs of my body
90. I avoid people or situations that compromise my overall health
91. The state of my health transcends the physical
92. I am emotionally and mentally healthy too
93. I have healthier ways to cope with stress
94. I do not eat my feelings, instead, I discover healthier outlets for them
95. I know my health triggers and I take conscious steps to avoid them

96. I do not live in the shadow of whatever medical condition ails me
97. I am proactive about the choices that I make
98. I make health goals that are critical but attainable
99. I have the right kind of support needed to keep me on track with my health goals
100. I am not fazed by the prospects of tomorrow. Things are good
101. All the organs and systems in my body are working in unison for the betterment of my body
102. There is no shortage of ideas on how to keep me healthy
103. I take my health and its care seriously
104. My health providers are heaven sent and they go above and beyond duty to keep me in good shape
105. The science needed to keep me healthy has been invented
106. In the event of frailty, my body's healing process is fast tracked
107. There are no limitations to what I can achieve with my body
108. What was meant to be a disability for me is channeled into laying the foundation for my strength
109. I am a multi-purpose being. All my senses are engaged therefore, the shutting down of one part does not mean I lose that function completely
110. Accidents happen, but I am in complete control of what happens afterwards
111. I expect good news concerning my health today
112. Any cell growth that is contrary to the norm and has the potential to compromise my health, I stop it right now
113. Everything in my body is as it should be
114. My paths will never cross with that of anyone who seeks to profit off my health needs at my expense without proffering real solutions

115. I am mentally competent to make decisions regarding my health
116. I am physically fit and mentally strong
117. I am proactive in anything that has to do with my health
118. My health is stable
119. I find fun and innovative ways to include a balanced diet and exercise into my daily routine
120. I am mastering the art of living healthy daily
121. My kitchen and fridge are a reflection of the healthy choices I have decided to make
122. My body is weaned off those harmful things that I crave
123. The state of my health is not defined by my age
124. I am constantly doing the best to stay in shape, and I do this effortlessly
125. Any addiction I have that compromises my health is stopped today
126. I am better today than I was yesterday
127. My commitment to staying in good health is displayed in my actions
128. I hold myself accountable for my health and I do not wait on other people to attain my health goals
129. I deliberately surround myself with people who share the same goals with me
130. There is no shortage of new and exciting ways to remain in good health
131. I am willing to invest in my health
132. The laws of the land and the laws of the universe are aligning together to work in favor of my wellbeing
133. The health policies that are being formulated are in my favor
134. I get the help that I need exactly when I need it
135. I am daily inspired and motivated to be healthy
136. My thoughts are centered on healthy
137. I am thinking of vitality in my waking moments

138. I do not accept any condition that does not reflect good health
139. The divine plan is for me to be in good health and I align my thoughts with this
140. My words, my thoughts and actions are a reflect of the perfect state of my health
141. I possess and claim the healing power that my body needs to thrive
142. My body is conditioned to be in good health
143. I am conscious of the vitality of my body
144. Good health is my birthright and I claim it
145. There is no limit to the abundant healing power that is flowing in my body
146. I do not accept any diagnosis of "incurable" disease
147. There is a solution for whatever my body is going through
148. I am perfectly whole and healthy
149. My physical stamina today is getting stronger
150. In areas where my body is ailing, I speak healing to those parts
151. Divine healing finds expression in my body
152. I am not held captive or hostage by any ailment
153. My body conforms to the words that I speak over it
154. I always speak positively concerning my health
155. I am completely healthy in body, mind and spirit
156. Wherever there is a disconnection or malfunction of an organ, cell or system in my body, I speak restoration over it
157. My body is strong. My body is agile. My body is a power house
158. I constantly defy medical expectations in a good way
159. I enjoy the pleasures of good food and food has always been good to my body
160. I have a positive attitude towards my body
161. My body is positively exceptional
162. I don't push my body beyond its limits

163. I eat and enjoy all types of food
164. Every exchange of breath restores vitality to my body
165. The cells in my body intelligently work together to revitalize my body
166. I develop the right partnerships that help promote my health
167. Anything that will compromise my health is positioned far away from me
168. Everything is working together for my wellbeing
169. Healing is my daily portion in life
170. Good health is a constant presence in my life
171. I am not moved by the diagnosis of doctors and physicians, I know that I am healthy
172. I am a manifestation of the divine healing power within
173. My intuition guides me on the right choice to make pertaining to my health
174. My home is a hub of vitality and goodness
175. When I close my eyes to sleep, my body's self-healing system is reactivated
176. I wake up refreshed, revitalized and fully restored
177. The words that I speak over my body are filled with life
178. Pain and disease are a rarity for me
179. I always have good news about my health
180. I am immune to any air, water or food borne virus that compromises my health
181. My immune system is in excellent condition
182. I do not fall victim to any plague or virus
183. My health is divine, and it is not conditioned by what is going on around me
184. I have peace of mind regarding my health
185. I am undoing any harm brought on my body by years of bad habits
186. I receive positive feedback for the efforts I put into staying healthy

187. My immune system is very strong and can deal with any kind of bacteria, germs, and viruses.
188. I outgrow any childhood illnesses or inherited genetic disorders
189. I speak order to the chaos in any part of my body
190. My body is youthful, and time does not influence this fact
191. My health is always going to be remain stable

CHAPTER FOUR

POSITIVE AFFIRMATIONS FOR FINANCES

1. Money comes to me easily and effortlessly.
2. I constantly attract opportunities that create more money.
3. I am worthy of making more money.
4. I am open and receptive to all the wealth life offers me.
5. My actions create constant prosperity.
6. Money and spirituality co-exist harmoniously in my life
7. I attract money effortlessly and easily.
8. I continuously discover new avenues of income.
9. I am open to all the wealth life has to offer.
10. I use money to better other people's lives.
11. I attract lucrative opportunities to create money.
12. I see abundance everywhere.
13. I am becoming more and more prosperous with every day.
14. Life takes care of all my needs.
15. My life is full of prosperity.
16. I deserve abundance and prosperity.
17. Money spent comes back to me multiplied.
18. I have all the power I need to create the success I desire.
19. The universe provides bountiful opportunities for my success.
20. I refuse to be distracted from my goals and vision.
21. Every day is filled with new ideas and new possibilities.
22. Being successful comes easily to me.
23. I am worthy of financial stability.
24. I am open-minded and willing to explore any path to success.
25. Limiting beliefs have no power over me. I am optimistic and open-minded.
26. I expect to be successful in all of my endeavors. Success is my natural state.

27. I easily find solutions to challenges and roadblocks and move past them quickly.
28. Mistakes and setbacks are stepping stones to my success because I learn from them.
29. Every day in every way, I am becoming more and more successful.
30. I feel successful in my life right now, even as I work toward future success.
31. I know exactly what I need to do to achieve success.
32. I see fear as the fuel for my success and take bold action in spite of fear.
33. I feel powerful, capable, confident, energetic, and on top of the world.
34. I have an intention for success and know it is a reality awaiting my arrival.
35. I have now reached my goal and feel the excitement of my achievement.
36. I am attaining my financial goals from a place of contentment
37. Money comes to me effortlessly
38. I am a powerful money house
39. I do not owe people as I always fulfill my debts
40. I have all the resources I need to fulfill my financial obligations
41. I do not work for money. Money works for me
42. I have the intellectual resources to create wealth
43. I have the wisdom to make smart decisions about money
44. I enjoy the wealth that comes to me
45. Money is not a problem for me
46. I am a money magnet
47. I come up with innovative ideas that build wealth
48. I am a wealth creator
49. My actions are not governed by greed
50. As I apply myself in the pursuit of wealth, I do so legally
51. I have the right connections to get me to my financial goals

Positive Daily Affirmations

52. I control a conglomerate of wealth
53. My wealth is inexhaustible
54. I am able to provide for my family even on to the fifth generation
55. I break every limitation over my attaining wealth
56. I am prosperous in all of my endeavors
57. I am rich in every currency of the world
58. Poverty is far away from me
59. As I accumulate wealth, I am generous to the people around me
60. The works of my hands are blessed to consistently produce fruits
61. I eat the fruit of my labors
62. I am wealthy
63. I am rich
64. I am surrounded by abundance everywhere I go
65. There is no such thing as lack for me
66. I have the ability to buy everything I want
67. I am not foolish in the matters of wealth
68. I am plugged in to the source of wealth in the universe
69. All the elements I need to create and sustain wealth are available to me
70. Money is attracted to my endeavors
71. My wallet and bank accounts are never empty
72. I shall never be financially stranded
73. I have a positive attitude towards money
74. I breathe, eat and sleep in wealth
75. I have grossly exceeded my financial expectations this year
76. I am not a stranger to wealth
77. I break any hold that poverty has over my family
78. I develop money habits
79. I am making money throughout the day
80. I am making money when I am asleep and when I am awake

81. I have the foresight to anticipate potential money-making moves
82. I am well versed on the art of creating wealth
83. The wealth that I create is sustainable
84. The doors of opportunities that lead to wealth creation are open to me
85. Money for me is as abundant as the air that I breathe
86. I can never be poor in this life
87. I can never be broke in the life
88. I reject the seeds of poverty in my life
89. I surround myself with wealth creators
90. I am relating with some of the world's biggest financial influencers
91. I do not inherit the debt of my father and his father before him
92. I am financially equipped to meet the needs of my family
93. I am setting smart financial goals this year
94. The margin for failure in my life is next to none
95. I dwell in riches and wealth
96. I am an epitome of success and financial wealth
97. I enjoy my wealth
98. I am unfazed by the economic climate of the present times
99. My wealth is independent of what is going on in the world today
100. I make wise investment decisions
101. I make money moves that bring in rich dividends
102. I am a partaker in the divine wealth of the universe
103. I have been programmed for success
104. There is no such thing as limitation when it comes to making money
105. I speak the language of wealth creation fluently
106. The money in my account is abundant
107. At any point in time, I have the right resources to make a profitable transaction
108. I can never be poor in my life

109. I have an aversion to poverty
110. I think rich and wealthy thoughts
111. I am success on the move
112. Things don't happen to me in the world of finance, I happen to things
113. I am the boss of money, I tell money what to do
114. I am consistently creating wealth
115. I am dogged in my determination to remain wealthy
116. I am not appalled by wealth
117. I rule over money in my life
118. Success is not in the quote that I hang up on my wall, it is my experience
119. I walk in financial freedom daily
120. I am making good financial transactions everyday
121. My desire for wealth is not motivated by greed
122. I do not engage in any unlawful activity to build my wealth
123. The wealth that I possess is borne from intense hard work
124. I can never work in vain
125. Success and wealth are the rewards for my efforts
126. Wealth is a constant companion in my life
127. Being wealthy is my fundamental right and divine heritage
128. I am constantly making progress
129. Every minute of my day brings in wealth for me
130. My life is characterized by financial abundance
131. I am not ashamed of creating wealth
132. Any religious programming that shames me for being wealthy is deactivated
133. I was born to reign triumphantly in this life
134. I was created to be wealthy
135. I will not be defeated or defined by failed endeavors
136. The lessons that I learn in life empower me to be greater
137. I always win financially
138. My wealth is not just for display. I use it to actively transform my community positively

139. My wealth is protected from financial locusts
140. Because I am connected to the universal source of wealth, I can never run dry
141. Even in abundance, I know how to spend money wisely
142. My journey to greater success and wealth begins today
143. My financial expectations are not cut off
144. I am forging bonds with the right people to bring about the manifestation of my financial goals
145. I have total peace of mind concerning wealth
146. This is very little that I cannot accomplish financially
147. I have allies in the right places
148. Wealth is not a foreign concept to me
149. I am not defined by wealth, but my life is characterized by it
150. My mind is constantly working on innovative ways to create wealth
151. I move on own timeline for wealth actualization
152. I do not compare my financial journey to others
153. I will arrive at my financial destination on time regardless of circumstances
154. My journey to wealth is filled with excitement and joy
155. As I work towards my success goals, I release myself from worry and trepidation
156. I have access to treasures in hidden places
157. The knowledge of the hidden wealth of this world is mine
158. I have obtained divine favor to succeed in my financial endeavors
159. The creation of wealth is an effortless process for me
160. I excel in everything that I do
161. My wealth is like the leaves of an evergreen tree; it is renewed with each season and it never runs dry
162. I am divinely ordained to be a successful wealth creator
163. The economic policies of the world are working in my favor

164. Even when the world is in a season of loss, I am creating wealth
165. There nothing that is adequately equipped to stop me from being successful in life
166. Even I cannot sabotage my efforts to be successful
167. I am swimming in oceans of wealth
168. My financial motivations are not rooted in fear or greed
169. My biggest failure in life is not enough to stop me from prospering
170. Just like the phoenix, the ashes of my failure is a launch pad for my success
171. I am elevated above poverty
172. I am ridding myself of any poverty mentality that is holding me back from making progress in life
173. If I am sabotaging my own success with my hands, I am making the choice right now to put a stop to it
174. Money has a name and it responds to me when I call it
175. My wealth causes me to be a financial blessing to my world and the people in it
176. I elevate people with my wealth as I am not selfish
177. I feed myself with thoughts that motivate and excite the wealth creator in me
178. The wealth that I possess is not limited or restricted by any border
179. I am equipped to enjoy the wealth that I have created
180. I have the mindset of a wealth creator
181. My financial situation can never be hopeless
182. My mind is a wealth of ideas that I consistently mine for productive results
183. It is impossible for me to run out of money because the source of my wealth is within. As long as I am alive, I am making money
184. My financial future is consistently in an upward drive

185. I experience a consistent progression in the wealth that I create annually
186. I was borne to live a life of success
187. Every day, I am climbing from one level of success to another
188. I do not stand in the way of the successes of other people
189. I have a clear vision of the life that I want
190. I pursue my financial goals with renewed vigor each day
191. Today I am successful. Tomorrow I will be successful. Every day I am successful

CHAPTER FIVE

POSITIVE AFFIRMATIONS FOR BUSINESS

1. I am running one of the most successful businesses in the world
2. I easily accomplish all my business goals.
3. I only desire things that are in line with my business goals
4. I instantly manifest my desires.
5. The business that I run is not just making money. It is making a difference
6. I can achieve whatever I desire.
7. I can conquer all the challenges I am confronted with.
8. I am becoming more confident and stronger each day in the choices I make.
9. My potential to succeed is infinite.
10. In this business, I am becoming more knowledgeable and wiser with each day.
11. I am creative and bursting with brilliant ideas.
12. I am courageous and overcome my fears by confronting them.
13. Challenges bring out the best in me.
14. I have confidence in my abilities and skills.
15. I make sound financial decisions.
16. I am bold and courageous in pursuing my business goals.
17. I face difficulties associated with running a business with courage.
18. My business makes a profound difference in this world.
19. I am building a successful business for global impact.
20. I create value with my service. My business is a gift to this world.
21. I am savvy about business.
22. Each failure has made me a better businessman/businesswoman.

Positive Daily Affirmations

23. I am successful in whatever I do.
24. Failure teaches me how I can become successful in life.
25. I leave no stone unturned in my journey to become successful.
26. I attract divine success.
27. I am pursuing my own definition of success
28. Everything will work out for me.
29. I am a winner.
30. The tools I need to succeed are in my possession.
31. There is nobody better to get the job done than me.
32. I have faith in my business ideas
33. I am grateful for the things I have.
34. I will achieve all of my goals.
35. My goals are simple and uncomplicated
36. Clients will flock to me from different parts of the world
37. My goals are getting closer to completion every day.
38. I set clear goals and work to complete them every day.
39. I have a plan of action to achieve my desires.
40. My priorities are clear. I work to finish my most important tasks first.
41. My goals are my focus.
42. I only set goals that matter.
43. My focus on success is unwavering
44. When my need is strong enough, I will find a way.
45. I am committed to becoming the person I will become.
46. My mind is like water. I will change and adjust as needed in business.
47. Success is in the future of my business
48. I will master distractions and keep my focus on my goals.
49. I must rely upon myself.
50. Blame for failure rests upon my shoulders but it would not hold me down.
51. I am my own best chance for success.
52. I will accept nothing but the best.

Positive Daily Affirmations

53. Success is in my future.
54. I am constantly improving.
55. I desire to learn new things.
56. Where others see a challenge, I see new opportunities.
57. I have a growth mindset.
58. Time is my friend. I finish all the tasks I need to finish.
59. My life is made for joy. I will build my business with exuberance.
60. I will be proactive in discovering obstacles to my accomplishments.
61. Mindfulness will help me get the most from my time.
62. I take responsibility for my successes and my failures.
63. I am not dependent on anyone else.
64. I follow my dreams with vigor.
65. The little things in life make all the difference.
66. I enjoy being surrounded by the people I work with
67. My fear diminishes as I live my life with courage.
68. A successful business man/woman lives within me, and today that woman/man is running my business.
69. I am confident and calm.
70. Doors of opportunity and abundance open to me today.
71. New opportunities come easily to me.
72. There are no limits to what I can achieve.
73. Today I am optimistic. I think positively and surround myself with positive energy.
74. I feel strong, excited, and powerful about the future of my business.
75. I regularly add income to my business.
76. Today I will move my business forward.
77. Amazing opportunities are constantly coming my way.
78. I attract positive customers and team members to my business.
79. There are no limits to what I can and will achieve today.
80. I can and I will do this! There is nothing stopping me.

Positive Daily Affirmations

81. I will work smarter, not harder.
82. I am a positive influence, and I surround myself with others like me.
83. Time is my most valuable asset. I guard my time carefully.
84. Balance is key. I will mix self-care with effort.
85. My progress is always moving forward.
86. I feel free to give myself the TLC I need.
87. Positive energy surrounds me.
88. I am a wonderful employer. My employees are lucky to have me.
89. My business goals will manifest as just as it is in my dreams.
90. When I say "no" to the wrong project, I move that much closer to the peace of mind I need in business and I understand this.
91. My new business income will continue to increase.
92. I am calm and confident in running the affairs of my business.
93. New opportunities come easily to me.
94. I will attract positive customers.
95. When business opportunities knock, I am more than prepared to answer the door.
96. Organization comes naturally to me.
97. I control my day; I will not let my day control me.
98. My passion for business brings tangible results.
99. I will not let others impose their limitations on me.
100. I am fully committed to achieving success in my life.
101. My only limit is myself.
102. My intuition and wisdom guide me in the right direction.
103. I have faith in myself.
104. I am able to meet the best decision possible for my business daily
105. I have confidence in my decisions as I intuitively know what is right for business
106. Even if I meet the wrong decision, it will always lead me somewhere positive.

107. I make responsible business decisions and consider how they affect other people.
108. . I reach any business goal I set my mind to. If I dream it, I can do it. No goal is out of reach.
109. I never stop learning and see opportunities for growth everywhere. I improve every day for the rest of my life.
110. My business today is better than it was at this point last year, and it is becoming better and better with each passing day.
111. I am programmed to hire the right kind of people in my business
112. I am patient with myself as I pursue my business goals and accept that positive changes may take some time. But different elements of my vision for my business is emerging every day.
113. My employees are passionate about the positive outcome of my business just as I am
114. I release my attachment to anything that does not serve me in pursuant of my business goals. I don't let anything, or anybody hold me back. I am finished with negativity in my life.
115. I have found a way to effectively communicate my business ideas to the people would assist me in making it a reality
116. I ask for what I want because I deserve it. I honor my desires today and always.
117. I do not fear for the future of my business as I have successfully mapped out the pathway to success and I have mitigated any possible threat to the success of that business
118. Regardless of any situation that confronts me, I am blessed. I am blessed with every lesson I learn from hardships I face. I continue to grow in light of all of the positive and negative things that come my way.

119. I am consciously making the effort to remain excited about business
120. I reach my goals even if I make mistakes because I know there is nothing to stop me from getting what I want.
121. If I reach a point where I am struggling with growth in business, I get divine inspiration on how to take things to the next level
122. I do not allow other people to hold me back from achieving my goals. I give myself permission to walk my own path and allow other people to do the same.
123. I am built to handle the success capacity of my business so that I do not get overwhelmed by it at any point
124. The success capacity of my business exceeds my personal expectations and the projection of others
125. I forgive the people who have hurt me in business to release myself from any past pain. As I forgive, I experience freedom. I am leaving the past errors in the past, and I am only living for the present and the future.
126. I know what I want, and I know I deserve it. I take responsibility for everything I have brought into my business.
127. My business motivation comes from a place of peace
128. I am hungry to drive the vision that I have for my business forward
129. I am not hesitant execute the brilliant business strategies that I have
130. The road to my success is exciting and full of delight
131. I find fulfillment in the success of my business
132. My business is able to satisfy the needs of my clients
133. I am building sustainable solutions with my business
134. My business is the answer to the needs of my client
135. At any point in time, the word "no" does not define the outcome of my business
136. I get more yeses than no

137. People may try to copy my business but the uniqueness of my business model and ideas make my business to stand out
138. I make fair and rational decisions in business
139. My business competes favorably in the global market
140. I am awarded contracts that positively impacts my business
141. Every job assigned to my company is an opportunity to shine and I am always eager to execute them
142. I do not take anything that happens to me in business for granted
143. My company is an exciting place for employees to work in
144. The best hands in the business are always eager to come and work for me
145. The team spirit in my company is such that we feel like a family unit
146. I have created a conducive work atmosphere for both clients and workers
147. Every negative and disruptive force is repelled from me or my business today
148. I have the right kind of attitude towards a successful business
149. I have all the resources need to take my business from where it is right now to where I would like it to be tomorrow
150. There are no restrictions or limitations to the kind of success that my business attains
151. My business is an extension of my dreams and through it, I am able to achieve the other dreams that I have
152. The atmosphere above, around and within my business is positive
153. My business is always relevant
154. The business that I build is a legacy that will be inherited by the generations to come
155. I am moving forward, and the success of this business is in an upward projectile
156. My business is success in motion

157. The foundations I have laid for this business is strong enough to enable it weather whatever economic climate it finds itself in
158. I am attracting the right kind of investors for my business
159. I leave nothing to chance in the affairs of my business
160. I find favor and grace in all of my business dealings
161. I have a strong and supporting base and this gives me confidence
162. I do not lose sight of my goals or objectives at any point
163. I am daily inspired to be excellent
164. I refuse to operate my business at the level of mediocrity
165. I employ sound business principles that deliver profitable results
166. My business world is on a global stage and I thrive in it
167. I am employing the right kind of talent needed for my business to take it to the next level
168. My business net worth is vastly impacted by my network as I am making the right kind of connections
169. I never fail in business as I am always winning or learning. The failures that come as lessons are my launch pad for greater things
170. The future for my business is bright. All dark clouds have dissipated
171. I do not run my business on debt. I am sufficiently able to keep my investors happy
172. As I make good financial decisions, I am also making sound social, political and environmental choices
173. I am able to run my business and still lead a life that is fun and fulfilling
174. The contracts that I sign in my business are in my favor
175. My business is protected against the vices of economic devourers that have led to the sudden demise of many businesses

176. Money is not the main objective of my business. I am dominating in my field
177. There is no challenge that is insurmountable for me in business
178. I have the right people in my corner, so my business is in the right hands
179. My business advisers have my best interest at heart
180. I do not lose money to theft, carelessness or by accidents
181. In the case of an accident, I have the wisdom to put the right steps in place to mitigate against such
182. There is order and thorough organization in my business
183. My business is a source of joy to me and many people
184. Through me and my business, the lives of many people have been impacted positively
185. I am breaking the mold and creating new pathways in business
186. My business stands out as a shining example of how businesses should be done
187. My business is winning global awards in different fronts for excellence
188. My business is associated with quality, superiority, excellence and innovation
189. I have a very happy customer base
190. Through my business, I am meeting with world leaders and global influencers
191. I am made to run a successful business and this business is going to e a lasting legacy that will stand the test of time.
192. There is nothing stopping me from growing. I seize opportunities and make things happen.

CHAPTER SIX

POSITIVE AFFIRMATIONS FOR CONFIDENCE

1. I remember myself as the master that I am, the master I have always been.
2. I know I have mastery over my life by how still I can keep my mind and how alert I am in the now.
3. I use my power lovingly when I have influence over others
4. I am connected to divine love and wisdom.
5. I am clear, untainted, and unharmed by any negative that I have experienced in my life.
6. I trust in the process of life
7. My possibilities are endless.
8. I am worthy of my dreams.
9. I am enough.
10. It is easy for me to look in the mirror and say, "I love you."
11. I am attractive.
12. My partner finds my sexy because (he/she) is attracted to every part of me.
13. I love everything about my body.
14. I radiate confidence and others respect me.
15. Others find me sexy and desirable.
16. I am filled with excitement when I look in the mirror.
17. I am rewarded for doing my best.
18. Every action I take increases my confidence.
19. I see problems as interesting challenges.
20. I radiate confidence.
21. I am worthy of happiness and love.
22. I feel relaxed and comfortable around other people.

Positive Daily Affirmations

23. I enjoy meeting new people. I even seek out others.
24. I am outgoing. I can enrich other people's lives.
25. I am easy to talk to. I am confident when I am around others
26. I get better with each day. Practice helps me to attain greatness.
27. I believe in my ability to overcome drawbacks.
28. I replace every unconstructive criticism with encouraging support.
29. Perfection can be found in all my flaws.
30. I always give my best and am a good-hearted person.
31. Other people will not take advantage of me.
32. I have confidence in my skills.
33. I am not afraid to be wrong.
34. Happiness is within my grasp.
35. I am confident in the presence of others.
36. Success will be my driving force.
37. The success of others will not make me jealous. My time will come.
38. I will speak with confidence and self-assurance.
39. I will say "No" when I do not have the time or inclination to act.
40. The only person who can defeat me is myself.
41. I dare to be different.
42. My every desire is achievable.
43. Even outside my comfort zone, I will be comfortable in my own skin.
44. If I fail, I will fail forward.
45. My confidence knows no limits.
46. I do not need other people for happiness.
47. I choose hope over fear.
48. Positivity is a choice that I choose to make.
49. I will not take another person's negativity personally.
50. My commitment to myself is real
51. I believe in me.

Positive Daily Affirmations

52. I acknowledge my self-worth–my confidence is soaring.
53. I am not my mistakes.
54. I accept myself unconditionally.
55. I am proud of myself and all that I have accomplished.
56. I am successful.
57. I am a beautiful person.
58. I deserve love, compassion, and empathy.
59. I believe in the person I dream of becoming.
60. I choose to be happy and completely love myself today.
61. I honor my commitments to myself.
62. There is no wrong decision.
63. I am now creating my life exactly as I want it.
64. Positivity is a choice; I choose to be positive.
65. I am free of worry and am at peace with who I am.
66. I matter. I am allowed to say "no" to others and "yes to myself.
67. What I give is what I receive.
68. I choose not to take it personally.
69. I will stop apologizing for being myself.
70. Negative self-talk has no place in my life.
71. I do not bow to my fears.
72. My mind, body, and soul are fit and strong.
73. When I breathe, I inhale confidence and exhale timidity.
74. I love meeting strangers and approach them with boldness and enthusiasm.
75. I live in the present and am confident of the future.
76. My personality exudes confidence. I am bold and outgoing.
77. I am self-reliant, creative and persistent in whatever I do.
78. I am energetic and enthusiastic. Confidence is my second nature.
79. I always attract only the best of circumstances and the best positive people in my life.
80. I am a problem solver. I focus on solutions and always find the best solution.

Positive Daily Affirmations

81. I love change and easily adjust myself to new situations.
82. I am well groomed, healthy and full of confidence. My outer self is matched by my inner well-being.
83. Self-confidence is what I thrive on. Nothing is impossible and life is great.
84. I face difficult situations with courage and conviction. I always find a way out of such situations.
85. I always see only the good in others. I attract only positive confident people
86. I use my emotions, thoughts and challenges to lead me to deeper, more interesting places within myself.
87. I am grateful for all that I am
88. I am grateful to be alive. It is my joy and pleasure to live another wonderful day.
89. Happiness is my birth right. I choose to be happy and I deserve to be happy.
90. Being happy comes easy to me. Happiness is my second nature.
91. I am deeply fulfilled by what I do.
92. I love my face and all my features and see my imperfections as signs of a life well-lived.
93. I am a source of knowledge that people seek out when they need information.
94. I am constantly amazed by my body and its abilities.
95. I exude confidence when I go out in the world and others see it in me.
96. I hold my head up high and put a smile on my face every day.
97. I let go of my need to impress other people. There is nothing that I need to prove. I accept myself just as I am.
98. I am excited to show the world who I am and everything I have to offer. No one can stop me from meeting my goals.
99. I am brave and willing to embrace my full power. I have complete control over my actions and my life.

100. I am the president of my life and no one else can take that role. I trust myself to make the best decisions for my life.
101. I have infinite possibilities today. I love life and I am ready to take inspired and motivated action on my goals.
102. I don't have to wait until I feel ready to act on my goals. The timing will never be right. I'm ready now.
103. I will take action despite any fear of failure. No matter what, I am proud of myself for trying.
104. I am not afraid of the unknown because I know I can overcome all the challenges that come my way.
105. I embrace my full potential, even if it makes other people uncomfortable. I do not play small. I am supposed to do big things.
106. I radiate respect and love and I get it in return.
107. I am enough. Always.
108. I am love.
109. I am loving.
110. I am loved.
111. I trust in the person I am.
112. I am kind to myself.
113. I make time to look after myself.
114. I deserve love and respect.
115. I am strong and capable.
116. I have a lot to offer the world.
117. I am sunshine.
118. I have a beautiful laugh.
119. My smile makes others smile.
120. I exude warmth and kindness.
121. My heart is full of love for who I am.
122. Love is what I believe in most of all.
123. My hugs are full of love and warmth.
124. I bring joy to the world.
125. I rock at being me!

126. I am proud of the person I am today, and the person I will be tomorrow.
127. I work hard and know my worth.
128. I have many skills to offer.
129. I place value on the experience I have, and my ability to learn and grow more.
130. I have the inner strength to navigate challenges at work.
131. I have my own definition of success.
132. I take pride in the work I do.
133. Work is an important part of my life but it is not my sole purpose or passion.
134. When I work, I apply myself with focus and positivity.
135. I take time to rest after working hard.
136. I am reliable, responsible and respected at work.
137. I am a creative person.
138. There is always a place in the world for my creativity.
139. I share what I create with pride and grace.
140. The world wants more of what I have to offer.
141. There is always a place in the world for what I create and make.
142. I am passionate about my creativity.
143. My creativity has a purpose in my life and in the world.
144. My life is fuller when I make time and space for my creativity.
145. I keep my eyes, ears and heart open for creative inspiration.
146. I focus on what I can control, and I let go of what I can't.
147. I love my beautiful mind.
148. I invest in myself through big and small acts of self-care and self-love.
149. My inner strength knows no bounds.
150. I breathe in energy and love, I exhale negativity and doubt.
151. I take time to know my needs, limits and boundaries better.

152. I know that good mental health is a journey, not a destination.
153. My mental health is just as important as my physical health.
154. I'm not ashamed or alone in having mental health struggles.
155. I look after my mental health because it deserves my love.
156. I am always stronger than I look and feel.
157. The joy that I feel today resonates throughout my body
158. I am full of positive energy
159. I am in a safe space mentally, emotionally and physically
160. I recognise the divinity that lives within me and I pay homage to my greatness
161. I have a winning mentality in everything that I apply myself to do
162. I am strong. I cannot be crippled by my circumstances
163. My mind is a safe haven for all my insecurities
164. I am perfect in all my imperfections
165. My failures or mistakes do not define my personality. I am a winner
166. I am a success going into the world to happen
167. I am a person of excellence. I do not deal in mediocrity
168. I have overcome the hurdles of today to become better than I was yesterday
169. I rise above challenges and limiting circumstances
170. I have defeated the traumas of my past and I am no longer defined by my history
171. I am getting better in every way
172. My strengths have compensated for my weaknesses and I am better for it
173. Today, I choose to be a victor and not a victim
174. I have been emotionally and mentally programmed to be a success. Nothing can stand in my way

175. I will not be intimidated by the circumstances or challenges in my life
176. This is my appointed time for greatness and I will rise to the occasion
177. Today I have the courage to advocate for my peace and happiness
178. I refuse to be bullied or silenced into accepting situations that are not good for me
179. I have the courage to prioritize my needs and wants above others
180. I am not a selfish person but I do not think less of myself either
181. I engage in activities that promote my happiness and joy
182. I will not sabotage my own happiness today because I am aware and I believe that I deserve it
183. The only person I am in a competition with is myself and i strive to be better
184. Because I am aware of my self-worth, I refuse to give up on myself
185. I have a sound mind and I am making strategic decisions that will work in my favour
186. I am not afraid to fail that because I am aware that failure cannot hold me down
187. I am not ordinary. I am an extraordinary human being
188. I am not afraid to take calculated risks because I am bold
189. I am bold. I am gold and I am exceptionally blessed
190. I walk tall and am proud of who I am.
191. I am the author of my own story, therefore, I do not live according to the script of other people. I am the leading character in my life

CHAPTER SEVEN

POSITIVE AFFIRMATIONS FOR PEACE OF MIND

1. I am at peace.
2. As I become more and more aware of myself as eternal consciousness, I become more peaceful and at ease with all that happens in my life.
3. Physical reality reflects this peace back to me.
4. My relationships are loving and harmonious
5. I am a channel for loving peaceful energy
6. I am harmonious and at peace regardless of my surroundings
7. My body is relaxed. My soul is at peace. My mind is calm
8. My intuition and inner wisdom guide me in every situation
9. Life always wants the best for me.
10. The challenges I'm confronted with are opportunities for growth.
11. Every time I exhale, I breathe out tensions and anxieties.
12. Every situation serves my highest good.
13. I am calm, patient, and in control of my emotions.
14. The more I give, the more I will receive.
15. My negative thoughts and self-images are gone.
16. My strength is stronger than my anxiety.
17. I move beyond stress to peace.
18. My thoughts are positive and full of joy.
19. I am safe. I trust life, and I trust in myself.
20. I feel wonderfully peaceful and relaxed.
21. I let go of everything that worries me. I will confront these challenges tomorrow.
22. My mind is at peace.
23. My world is a peaceful, loving, and joy-filled place to live.

24. I sow the seeds of peace wherever I go.
25. I surround myself with peaceful people.
26. My work environment is calm and peaceful.
27. I breathe in peace, I breathe out chaos and disorder.
28. My home is a peaceful sanctuary where I feel safe and happy.
29. In all that I say and do, I choose peace.
30. I release past anger and hurts and fill myself with serenity and peaceful thoughts.
31. Peace descends all around me now and always.
32. I send peace from myself into the world.
33. I respond peacefully in all situations.
34. I am grounded in the experience of the present moment.
35. I am focused and engaged in the task at hand.
36. I am conscious that all is well right now.
37. **I am grateful** for this moment and find joy in it.
38. I am free of anxiety, and a calm inner peace fills my mind and body.
39. I am not my thoughts and pay attention to my actions without judging them.
40. I am fully present in all of my relationships.
41. I am unique. I feel good about being alive and being me.
42. I find deep inner peace within myself as I am.
43. I am completely pain-free, and my body is full of energy.
44. Every day I am more and more at ease.
45. I am in the present moment and release the past to live fully now
46. I have a peaceful aura around me and I influences those around me
47. Calmness washes over me with every deep breath I take.
48. I meditate easily without resistance or anxiety.
49. Being calm and relaxed energizes my whole being.
50. All the muscles in my body are releasing and relaxing.
51. All negativity and stress are evaporating from my body and my mind.

52. I breathe in relaxation. I breathe out stress.
53. Even when there is chaos around me, I remain calm and centered.
54. I transcend stress of any kind. I live in peace.
55. I gently and easily return to the present moment.
56. All is well in my world. I am calm, happy, and content.
57. I fall into a deep and relaxing sleep.
58. I am deliberate in my pursuit of peace
59. Every encounter or interaction with me can be described as peaceful
60. I actively pursue peace with myself as well as peace with the people around me
61. I engage in activities that bring about a peaceful and clear state of mind
62. I have made peace with mistakes I made in the last. I refused to be consumed by guilt for those actions
63. I take out time throughout the day to cultivate thoughts and words that promote the peace of my mind
64. I cancel out any negative vibes that threatens the piece of my mind
65. I have found my happy space and I guard it zealously
66. I feel blessed to live the life that I live today
67. I stay in the moment and I am not worried or anxious about what will happen tomorrow
68. I release myself from any negative emotion that is stressing me out
69. Even in the eye of the storm I remain calm
70. I am as grounded as the Earth therefore I remain unshakeable in the face of trials
71. I understand that life is a cycle of ups and downs. I may be down today but there is definitely an up tomorrow and I am calm in this knowledge
72. I am rooted in the reality of the knowledge that this too will pass

Positive Daily Affirmations

73. My mind is like a slow running brook on a sunny day. It is clear, clean and calm
74. My body reacts positively to stress.
75. I recognize the stressors in my environment and I wisely avoid them
76. I surround myself with people who are interested in keeping the peace
77. I have the mental foresight to plan ahead and save myself from unnecessary stress
78. I am an embodiment of calm and rational living
79. I am not troubled by the expectations of other people
80. I do not wallow in fear of what might or might not happen tomorrow
81. I have the courage to accept the things that I cannot change in my life
82. I have successfully created an atmosphere that is calm amd serene every where I go
83. Situations that usually stirred panic and anxiety have lost their hold over me
84. I distance myself from people who are bent on robbing me of my peace
85. The peace that I experience daily is not a fickle thing. It is as solid as a rock
86. Today, I choose to experience peace
87. I am a conduit for peace and harmony in my world
88. I acknowledge and accept my responsibility as a peacemaker
89. I make the effort to ensure that in all my relationships, peace is maintained
90. The decisions I am taking in my life today bring peace to my mind and my soul
91. I rise above the trials in my life that cause me to be anxious and take solace in the joy that is promised tomorrow
92. When trouble arises I am not swallowed up in panic

93. My actions are not motivated by fear. Rather I come from a place of clear thinking
94. I have a sound mind. I refuse to be afraid
95. The events in my life today would release an outpouring of peace and serenity
96. The universe is collaborating with every positive force in my life to ensure that my peace of mind is retained
97. I am aware of the benefits of dwelling in this place of serenity and I do everything within my power to protect it
98. The events of this day cannot compromise the peace that I know
99. Peace flows into my life today like an endless stream of water
100. I have a clear sound mind
101. I am at peace with everyone including people who consider themselves my enemies
102. The peace that I experience is rooted in sources beyond my circumstances
103. I am able to recognize healthy relationships in my life through the peace of mind that I experience in them
104. I surround my heart and my mind with a hedge that protects it from negative thoughts or emotions
105. I am consistent in participating in practices that promote my peace of mind
106. Today, I refuse to be anxious
107. Everyday, I am making the choice to consciously engage in emotions that are more productive than worry and anxiety
108. Today, I refuse to worry about things that I have absolutely no control over
109. I am replacing the burdens of my fears with the consistent flow of peace into my life
110. I do not dwell on the fears of tomorrow but rather, I live in the joy of the moment
111. I am making a conscious effort not to postpone my happiness because of fears and worries

112. I speak peace into my day
113. I am an ambassador for peace
114. I have learned to avoid situations that rob me of my peace
115. Every breath that I take draws in peace and restores serenity of mind while every breath that I release lets go of every feeling of fear and anxiety
116. As I control my breathing, I am able to control any emotion that stirs up panic and anxiety inside of me
117. I am well-versed in practices, affirmations and actions that calm me in the event of a panic attack
118. My mind is a healthy place that is rich in peace and happiness
119. I have all the resources I need to create a peaceful ambiance and atmosphere in my home
120. My home is imbued with so much peace and serenity that people forget their troubles the moment they step inside it
121. I have overcome my fears and found solace in the voice within
122. Even when darkness comes I am able to find peace
123. The pains and anxieties I have struggled with in the past no longer control my state of mind
124. I plug the peace of mind that I enjoy today into the universal source of peace
125. My mind is not like a ship that is beaten and tossed about on the sea with every wave or tempest that comes. Instead, I stand like a mountain...unwavering and unshaken
126. The peace of mind that I experience is genuine
127. The affairs of life cannot stop me from experiencing happiness
128. My happiness and peace go hand-in-hand as I do not experience one without experiencing the other
129. I have chosen this day to own my peace of mind because I deserve to be happy

130. There is so much peace and happiness embedded within that I do not need to look outside for happiness
131. I am no longer disappointed by the actions of other people as I have chosen to place a higher value on my happiness and where it comes from
132. My life is a constant parade of joy, happiness, peace and wellness and I am at the centre of it all
133. I do not live my life in regrets. I have made the decisions I have made, and taken the actions I have taken. And today, I have made peace with all of them
134. I am taking the deliberate step to sow seeds today that will yield profitable returns in my future tomorrow giving me a platform to rid myself of anxiety
135. The peace and calmness that I experience is contagious. People who come in contact with me immediately reflect the calmness that I feel
136. I have a vivid vision of the future that I desire, therefore, even dark circumstances cannot shake me
137. I know my place in the universe and I have come to a place of acceptance of it
138. I have a very good understanding of my purpose in life so I am not anxious about it
139. I am not afraid of the challenges that lie ahead
140. I know that I have a triumphant victory awaiting me so, even this present failure cannot hold me down
141. I am wise enough to know that giving into my fears is coming into acceptance of a possible outcome that is yet to be determined
142. Today, I am choosing to accept the possibility that all will be well with me
143. I have successfully trained the lions that prowl in my nightmares and successfully converted my fears into a podium for triumph

144. Worrying is pointless so I have chosen to not waste my time on it
145. I am a peaceful force to be reckoned with nothing can hold me down
146. I am calm and serene in the face of troubles
147. I am capable of consistently making rational decisions because I do not operate from a place of chaos
148. I am a reliable, capable and strong partner in a time of crisis because I am always calm
149. I am capable of sieving through the rubble in order to make a clear and concise decision
150. My life right now is a constant manifestation of peace and happiness
151. Even in the darkest night, I am able to see the light at the end of the tunnel
152. I let go of anxiety and embrace calmness
153. I let go of fear and embrace courage
154. I let go of worry and embrace confidence
155. I let go of panic and embrace stillness
156. I let go of chaos and embrace order
157. I let go of pain and embrace healing
158. I let go of grief and embrace the blessed memories
159. I let go of sadness and embrace joy
160. I let go of heartbreak and embrace love
161. I let go of guilt and embrace freedom
162. I let go of hatred and embrace acceptance
163. I let go of greed and embrace contentment
164. I let go of darkness and embrace the light
165. I let go of self-hate and embrace self-love
166. I let go of fakeness and embrace authenticity
167. I let go of expectations and embrace possibilities
168. I let go of losses and embrace recovery
169. I let go of past glory and embrace my future journeys
170. I let go of mistakes and embrace prospects

171. I let go of overindulgence and embrace moderation
172. I let go of jealousy and embrace trust
173. I let go of anger and embrace remorse
174. I let go of failures and embrace lessons
175. I let go of apprehension and embrace beautiful surprises
176. I let go of distractions and embrace things that interests me
177. I let go of aggression and embrace cohesion
178. I let go of pensiveness and embrace optimism
179. I let go of excuses and embrace accomplishments
180. I let go of bitter thoughts and embrace positive memories
181. I let go of shame and embrace my uniqueness
182. I let go of poor self-esteem and embrace the power within
183. I let go of disapproval and embrace my awesomeness
184. I let go of control and embrace fluidity
185. I let go of pride and embrace humility
186. I let go of confusion and embrace soundness of mind
187. I let go of criticisms and embrace self-affirmations
188. All I need to do right now is breathe
189. I am in a safe space and a warm, positive energy surrounds me
190. I let go of any burden that has affected my sleep
191. I go to bed knowing that all is well with my world.
192. I am at peace and feeling very sleepy. I am ready to fall asleep.

CHAPTER EIGHT

POSITIVE AFFIRMATIONS FOR SPIRITUALITY

1. The divine guides all my actions.
2. I am a spiritual being that is divinely guided.
3. I am in alignment with the universe.
4. God's grace and love is working through me.
5. I emanate love and joy, complete presence and openness, toward all beings.
6. All problems are illusions of the mind and I am enlightened enough to recognize this
7. I am a bring of light. I do not pollute my beautiful, radiant Inner Being, nor the Earth, with negativity. I do not give unhappiness, in any form, whatsoever, a dwelling place inside me.
8. My peace is so vast and so deep and rooted in the supernatural, that anything that is not peace, disappears into it, as if it had never existed.
9. I am spiritual enough to find creative express for myself.
10. No negative deed that was ever done to me, or which I did to others, can touch, even in the slightest way, the radiant essence of who I really am.
11. I am a Divine creation, a vital piece of God. Therefore, I cannot be undeserving.
12. I am empathetic and compassionate. I perceive the experiences of others just as acutely as I feel mine
13. Because I am spiritually attuned, I am powerful enough to overcome negativity.
14. I am connected to an unlimited source of abundance.

Positive Daily Affirmations

15. I have the ability to accomplish any task I set my mind to with ease and comfort.
16. My focus is not on the million things I may have to do at some future time, but on the one thing I can do right now
17. I have access to unlimited assistance. My strength comes from my connection to my Source of being.
18. I am content with what I have. I rejoice in the way things are because I have the spiritual foresight to know that everything I working out in my favor.
19. I relax and cast aside all of my burdens, allowing God to express through me His perfect love, peace, and wisdom.
20. I realize that there is nothing lacking. The whole world belongs to me.
21. God is within and around me, protecting me; so I will banish the fear that shuts out His guiding light.
22. I am an infinite being. The age of my body has no bearing on what I do or who I am.
23. The healing power of Spirit is flowing through all the cells of my body.
24. In all my cells, the healing light of God is shining. My cells are entirely well, for His perfection is in them.
25. God's perfect health permeates the dark nooks of my bodily sickness.
26. As I unclutter my life, I free myself to answer the callings of my soul.
27. Daily I will seek happiness more and more within my mind, and less and less through material pleasures.
28. I have infinite patience when it comes to fulfilling my destiny as ordained by God
29. I am constantly submerged in eternal light.
30. I live in the present moment by being grateful for all of my life experiences as a child.
31. I am made of the one universal God-substance.

Positive Daily Affirmations

32. Being myself as I was created involves no risks. It's my ultimate truth, and I live fearlessly in it
33. With the sword of devotion to the God I serve fervently, I sever all heart-strings that tie me to any delusions about my true essence
34. I will purify my mind empty myself of fear with the thought that God is guiding my every move.
35. The light of the Universe permeates every particle of my being.
36. I am with God and God is with me always.
37. With a deep and sincere love, I lay my heart at the feet of the Omnipresent one.
38. God's love is working through me now and always
39. I am an extension of God's love
40. I will always endeavor to help people who are weeping to smile, by smiling myself, even when it is difficult to do so.
41. The Divine Spirit is omnipresent. I fell it all around me and I am guided at every step of this journey called life
42. I am living in that light. The Divine Spirit fills me within and without
43. All my thoughts, words and actions are divinely guided.
44. God is the shepherd of my restless thoughts. He will lead them to His abode of peace.
45. The Universe naturally and freely provides for all my needs. So, I am unbothered.
46. I am strong in my faith and in my beliefs
47. I am a spiritual being having a human experience.
48. My mind and body are in complete alignment with the Universe and I am always in the flow.
49. My spirituality boldly expresses my faith in my God
50. My faith and beliefs are alive to me
51. I am responsible for my own spiritual growth.
52. I am bold in the knowledge of the divine power and love that is awake within me

53. I give gratitude to the divinity I have chosen to acknowledge
54. The words that feed my spiritual growth comes alive to me in all areas of my life
55. I trust that everything in my life is working for my highest good and I am receiving all that I am meant to have.
56. My faith and spirituality remain unshakable.
57. My faith in the divine keeps me humble
58. I am a divine expression of a loving God.
59. I give gratitude and praise to God in the highest
60. My life is characterized by an expression of God's divinity
61. I am grounded in the principles that guide my faith
I let go of fear. I let go of pain. I live in love.
62. I grow stronger and stronger in my faith everyday
63. My spirituality is drawn from a deep Faith in God and all things divine
64. My faith surrounds me and makes me whole
65. The people I encounter recognize my faith and are inspired by it
66. I am a loving, kind and forgiving person, in accordance with my spiritual nature.
67. My faith in God gives me courage and confidence.
68. I pay just as much attention to my spiritual health as I do my mental and physical health
69. I know that I can master anything, with divine guidance
70. I am guided by a force greater than myself
71. The love of God flows through me. I am His, He is mine.
72. The love of God radiate through me
73. God loves me completely and wholesomely
74. I am love personified
75. The universal plan for my life is full of love, peace and joy
76. My home is full of Gods love
77. I surrender to God. He is always with me. I do only his bidding.
78. I channel the energy and love of the infinite

Positive Daily Affirmations

79. I ask for forgiveness from all those whom I may have wronged and forgive all those who may have wronged me..
80. My faith in God lifts up those around me
81. My faith in a higher spirit keeps me grounded
82. Religion to me is a way of life. It is a way of living a morally and ethically correct life.
83. My Faith is the foundation of my Life and I live my Life according to my Faith in God
84. I am committed to God and naturally, God is committed to me too
85. I am surrounded by the love of God
86. My higher spirit guides me in the direction of my dreams.
87. When I love people more, I receive even more love from the universe in return.
88. My relationship with God is a powerful relationship
89. My faith in God sets me free from all worry, anxiety and doubt.
90. All is well
91. I let go and put my life in God's hands to guide and lead me
92. When my intentions are clear, the Universe cooperates with me and I can accomplish anything.
93. I think of only positive things and the universe ensures positive things happen in my life.
94. I feel a spiritual essence that is always with me, guiding me.
95. My faith lifts me above my fears
96. I am together with the Divine, here and now.
97. I breath in my spiritual vitality and feel alive everyday
98. I am aligned with my higher purpose.
99. I believe Gods path for me is abundant and joyous
100. All things are possible in the name of God, our father
101. I trust that all the events in my life are unfolding as they are meant to be.
102. As I abide in love for all creatures, they have cone to abide in love for me.

103. I love with the perfect Love of God. I see with the perfect eyes of God.
104. I respectfully ask for Divine guidance in all areas of my life.
105. The divine Spirit is now guiding my steps and all is unfolding for my good.
106. I am strong in my faith of a higher power
107. I am guided by the Universe and part of a bigger plan.
108. I create the perfect plan for my life by choosing the perfect thoughts.
109. My life experiences lead me to be closer to God. God knows what is the best possible gift for me at any moment.
110. I am a perfect, open channel for divine Peace, divine Love, divine Abundance, and divine Inspiration.
111. The entirety of creation is now conspiring for my good.
112. I am a winner and I attract only success through the power of my faith.
113. I am a magnet for the unlimited good things of God and I attract it effortlessly and easily.
114. I open my mind and heart to the perfect love of God.
115. I gratefully accept the totality and wholesomeness of all my good benefits
116. Today, as God opens the windows of heaven and pours me out a blessing, I make room to receive it.
117. The divine ruler of the universe gives me all that I want and need
118. I pursue an authentic relationship with God.
119. I know that my light shines because the Divine Light within me is always shining brightly.
120. I put my life in the hands of Infinite Love and Divine Wisdom.
121. The secrets of eternity are now revealed to me and they have become my reality

122. Infinite Love flows through me, in me, as me.
123. I am a manifestation of the divine presence
124. I am now attracting everything I need, effortlessly and easily.
125. My Faith makes me feel whole in spirit, soul and body.
126. Everything I seek is now seeking me.
127. I lift God up on high and he lifts me up
128. I am part of a spiritually enchanted world filled with exciting opportunities and ideas.
129. My every spiritual experience is filled with joy.
130. In every moment, I know exactly what to do and how to do it. I am spiritually wise and attuned
131. I embrace the glorious mess that my life may seem now, and offer it up as a prayer in gratitude.
132. My life belongs to God
133. I open the doors the lead to my good benefits and lay claim on my Divine inheritance.
134. Every cell in my body is now functioning in perfect Divine order.
135. The world around me is my playground, and I find joy in every experience.
136. I am proud to be part of nature. My world is filled with oceans of love and mountains of courage.
137. My faith and spiritual insight creates my reality
138. I have many strengths and talents inspired by nature. Nature helps me understand I am part of an infinite world with no end.
139. I am now enveloped by the Divine, embraced and cherished, nurtured and protected.
140. I am the expression of a loving God
141. The divine Spirit is around me, always.
142. I am perfect in the eyes of the divine.
143. I abide in the perfect wholeness of creation.
144. I am where the universe wants me to be.

145. I delight in the grace and mercy of God.
146. I am an eternal being with infinite possibilities surrounding me.
147. I excel at the perfect living of Life as designed by the divine
148. God is good
149. Good dominates my every experience.
150. I am a strong being with many abilities and skills.
151. In every moment, I am inspired to take the right action, morally, ethically and spiritually.
152. I am focused on finding the best parts of nature and enjoying them.
153. God knows my needs and meets them.
154. Divinity dwells in me as the living, breathing spirit of me. Therefore, I am now whole, perfect and complete in every way.
155. I know the people around me are also magical forces of nature.
156. God lives inside my heart and in my subconscious
157. My life is part of an everlasting fabric that connects the world together.
158. I am part of a beautiful world that welcomes me.
159. God within me is mighty, powerful and unstoppable.
160. I believe in the creative power of nature to transform my life.
161. I am Divinely led, guided and inspired in all I think, do and say.
162. My life is enriched by the experiences of other people
163. Study, prayer, and meditation prepare me to live my faith.
164. I am a force of nature with the ability to control my circumstances.
165. My faith motivates me to take care of my well-being.

166. My faith defines my life and gives me purpose. I call upon my faith for routine chores and small gestures, as well as great demands.
167. My faith encourages me to give more. I share my time and resources with my family, friends, and community.
168. I am sheltered and enveloped by the perfect Peace of God.
169. I build a strong foundation that inspires and empowers me.
170. My faith fills me with gratitude. I give thanks for my blessings.
171. With you oh mighty and divine one, I feel at peace, ease and joyful
172. Nature gives me strength and energy, so I can enjoy the world around me.
173. My faith increases my patience. I accept delays and setbacks as a natural part of life. I remain calm and adapt to whatever circumstances come my way.
174. My faith plays a guiding role in my daily life. I put my beliefs into action.
175. My faith shapes the way I speak. I choose gracious words that convey my respect and affection for others. I promote peace and harmony through tolerance
176. I am sheltered by the mercy of Spirit
177. I develop the courage and wisdom to overcome challenges, and use my spiritual gifts to serve others and create a better life for myself.
178. Understanding and appreciating nature makes me happy.
179. I build a strong spiritual foundation that inspires and empowers me.
180. Today I am centered in my heart, and closer to Spirit.
181. I am perfectly blessed and I am a perfect blessing for the world.
182. Today, I recognize that I am a powerful force of nature. My life is filled with amazing opportunities made possible by nature.

183. I know that I am an everlasting force and part of a miraculous world.
184. Everywhere I go, everything I see, everything I experience provides visible proof that I am supported and sustained by the entirety of creation.
185. My heart and life are open to receive every divine blessing
186. The Spirit of God within knows the perfect way to answer and respond to my every need and desire. Therefore, all my needs are met.
187. Now is the time for my good
188. I patiently and respectfully ask for Divine guidance on anything and everything.
189. I am anchored in love. I am buoyed by love. The wings of love lift me into perfect communion with all life everywhere.
190. I live in the moment and am grateful for all my life experiences. All of them.
191. I see myself and the spark of divinity in others.
192. Today, I demonstrate my faith. My actions reflect my beliefs.

CHAPTER NINE

POSITIVE AFFIRMATIONS FOR THE CAREER MINDED

1. I further my career with every action I take.
2. I have my dream job.
3. I love every day that I work.
4. My career brings me closer to my family.
5. My job brings me financial abundance.
6. My coworkers love being around me.
7. My boss values the work I do.
8. I am a valued employee.
9. My clients appreciate and value my work.
10. I attract new clients every day.
11. My positive attitude, confidence and hard work naturally draws in new opportunities.
12. I am enthusiastic and excited about my work.
13. My enthusiasm about my job is contagious.
14. My workplace is peaceful and full of love.
15. I make decisions easily.
16. I speak positively about my coworkers and they respond by speaking positively about me
17. Work and Career Affirmations
18. My job adds satisfaction and fulfillment to my life.
19. I am exactly where I want to be. My career provides me the right opportunities to grow.
20. I am valued and appreciated at my workplace. My voice is always heard.
21. I ask for meaningful work and perform it with the greatest diligence and attention.
22. My work has a profound impact on this world.

23. Right now, the job I am looking for is looking for me.
24. I am a great employee. Any employer is lucky to have me.
25. I am an asset to any organization, and I prove it in every interview.
26. Every time I interview for a job, I exude confidence and energy.
27. Amazing opportunities are appearing in my life out of nowhere.
28. I am ready for my interviews. I am confident in my interviews. I am successful in my interviews.
29. I am creating the career of my dreams.
30. Career change is an opportunity to have the career I want. This time I choose a great career for me.
31. No more excuses! I deserve a job that fulfills me, and I am ready to find it.
32. I committed to my happiness in this job search, and my determination pays off.
33. Every time I say 'no' to the wrong job, I get closer to the perfect job.
34. I see myself in my ideal job.
35. I act with confidence and have a plan, and I accept that plans are open to change.
36. I love challenges because they bring out the best in me.
37. I easily and effortlessly learn new system and processes.
38. I am kind, loving, and compassionate. I truly care for other people.
39. It comes naturally to be confident in myself. I don't need to question my confidence.
40. I don't need to be perfect. I am already good enough and I am worthy of a great life already.
41. I do not have a need to compare myself to other people. I only judge myself by my own standards of success. I am enough just the way I am.

Positive Daily Affirmations

42. I channel love, positivity, and energy to all the people around me.
43. Positive Affirmations for Women While at Work
44. I practice self-care and recognize when I need to take a break. I feel good about taking care of myself.
45. I am successful and confident in my abilities to do my job.
46. I am a competent member of the team. I have the knowledge and skills that I need right now.
47. I move at the perfect pace. I do not need to speed up or slow down.
48. I embrace success. The words "I can't" are not something I say. I refuse to believe even my own excuses. I am unstoppable.
49. I take my goals seriously. I am aware that my time on earth is finite. I respect my life by doing the things I love.
50. I refuse to overcommit myself. I am able to say "no" when I need to. I protect my time because I deserve it and it is invaluable.
51. My work is a self-transformative process that brings me inner peace, proper health, and prosperity.
52. I'm almost at the finish line. I know I have what it takes to meet my goals.
53. My hard work, humility, and persistence will pay off. None of my work is going to waste.
54. The passion I have for my work allows me to create true value. I am lucky to have a job that provides me with the finances I need to live a good life.
55. I work extremely hard and always do my personal best. I believe in myself and I know I can do anything. I deserve all of the positive things that come my way in life.
56. The work that I do benefits the society in which I live, and I am a valuable part of my community.
57. I do not give up when things get difficult. I keep working until I finish what I started.

58. My work is fulfilling, inspiring, and enriching. I am not only helping myself, but I am also helping others.
59. I see myself reaching the pinnacle of success as I envision it and work hard every day until I am where I want to be in my career
60. I bring something unique to the table that no one else can and that makes me uniquely valuable to my company.
61. I am a capable leader. Others are attracted to my charisma at work and look up to me during times of crisis.
62. I stay true to my values and my authentic self. I do not compromise for anyone else. My success will come without compromise.
63. I do not need to prove my worth. My work is enough for people to see its value. People recognize my worth without having to be told.
64. Other people's successes empower me to keep growing. I am happy for anyone who accomplishes their goals and I will strive to continue to accomplish mine.
65. I cultivate a sense of gratitude and thank others for their kindness at work.
66. I appreciate my education, and the opportunity to do meaningful work.
67. No matter how busy I am, I am still actively involved in my community. I comfort a friend who is feeling blue and help an elderly neighbor with yard work.
68. My most important mission in life is to stay true to myself.
69. I embrace the energy I receive from work and my coworkers.
70. Even when unpopular, I choose to protect and uphold my beliefs because they keep me honest.
71. Sometimes my coworkers cause new employees to feel out of place. I avoid joining them by helping new persons to feel welcome.
72. Self-discipline is my forte. I conduct myself at work in a professional manner

73. I know how to strike a healthy balance in life. At the workplace, work is my priority and at home, family is my priority.
74. I am known for being industrious and seizing whatever opportunities that are available.
75. I am a master salesman for the company I work for
76. Career to me is a means to an end. That end is happiness and fulfillment of potential and my career is providing it to me in abundance.
77. I am always ready to learn and grow in my job!
78. Diligence in work, honesty in attitude and a positive frame of mind open up new horizons for me in my career.
79. The fruits of my labor are always so sweet and rewarding
80. My main aim is satisfaction of my customers and I strive my best to achieve that aim.
81. I accept constructive feedback and put it work for my benefit
82. Today I see the ways this job contributes to my growth.
83. I work hard at what I do. I work smart in wisdom and application of skills and I deserve the accolades I earn
84. I am passionate about my job. I recognize and seize opportunities as and when they appear.
85. The customers I cater to on behalf of the company love and trust me and as a result, my order book is overflowing with orders.
86. I am always enthusiastic and my enthusiasm rubs off on my co-workers and this results in a productive work day for all of us.
87. I always attract the best projects and the best people to execute them because of my positive mental attitude.
88. I am not frustrated as I have the freedom to either keep this job or find a better job whenever I want to.
89. My career is what I make of it and today, I have made the choice to make it a happy and successful experience.

90. Today I see the ways this job contributes to my financial well-being.
91. My career is mine alone and today, I am taking ownership of it
92. I know that I am blessed with the job that I have. I remind myself to be content with what I have.
93. Today, I choose to focus on positivity and enjoy the beauty that surrounds me. I take a walk around my neighborhood to marvel at nature and renew my energy.
94. I became a (insert current job role) to make a difference and today I am seizing every chance to do so
95. As I align my career with my true talents, passions and skills, the money I desire and the happiness from fulfillment flows to me
96. I am happy that the work I do benefits me as well as the society I live in.
97. I am a valued person at my workplace and my voice is always heard respectfully.
98. I climb the corporate ladder with integrity and confidence
99. I acknowledge my potential in this place and celebrate my accomplishments.
100. I am able to balance my career with my family life so that both are in harmony with each other.
101. I mold my current career to match my life goals
102. I am attracting into my life my dream job and most suitable work for me.
103. I am manifesting my dream job.
104. I always see possibilities, I refuse to see dead ends in my career.
105. I am enjoying working in my dream job.
106. Outside of work, I have a strong support system. I value my family and friends. I let them know that they are a vital part of my life.

Positive Daily Affirmations

107. I am aware that the Universe is making all the perfect arrangement for my dream job.
108. I am not overtly focused on just myself and my career growth. I share my riches, time and ideas with others.
109. A great company has offered me a dream job
110. I have a great relationship with the people I work with as well as my boss.
111. I have found a lucrative job and I love working there
112. Today, my affirmations are attracting to me the job I enjoy doing
113. Thinking about my recent victories builds my confidence and inspires me to aim higher.
114. Today, I declare that I am working in a successful company, at an excellent workplace with wonderful people
115. I am attracting the right job into my life
116. Today I choose to grow and get better through collaboration with my colleagues.
117. I am manifesting a great job, which I love and enjoy, and my job is bringing me a lot of money.
118. Doors of opportunities are open to me this day
119. I am the engine of my career success
120. I am making the right connections at work
121. I am a world-class (insert dream job position) and I am presented with the opportunity to prove it every day
122. I have found the dream work for me. I am at the right place, and I like the people that I work with.
123. Right now, I am working at my dream job.&
124. I manage work stress by listening to music that eases my tension and cheers me up.
125. Today and every day, I use my talents in productive ways
126. My work ethic ensures that I get regular promotions and monetary incentives.
127. I take full responsibility for my work.

128. I am excited to have this job and I work diligently to make the most of it.
129. There are no limits to the greatness I accomplish
130. My empathy for others is alive even at work. I pitch in when a coworker is swamped and take time to listen when a friend is going through a difficult time.
131. I always work for amazing bosses.
132. I take good care of my juniors and guide them appropriately. I am friendly with my colleagues and respectful to my seniors.
133. I am working at my dream job
134. I open myself to receive the offer to work in dream job
135. I put a lot of worth and value on committing to the things I believe in.
136. My job does not define me, but I have the power define my job
137. Today I see the ways this job contributes to my happiness.
138. My ideal employment is coming to me right now.
139. I love and enjoy my work because I find fulfilment in it
140. My knowledge, wisdom, and skills help me to make valuable contribution to my job, society and provide for my family.
141. I am the director of my career and I take the initiative to have the career I want
142. I am working in a job which I love and I am receiving very handsome salary
143. The ambience of my workplace is non-toxic and as a result, I grow in my career
144. I have unlimited potential and my dream job is looking for me
145. I am working at a job I love and enjoy, and which is very satisfying and fulfilling in every day
146. I love and enjoy my job. My job is is bringing me a lot of money and feeding my passion

147. When career challenges arise, I keep my attention focused on the good things going on in my workplace.
148. I am confident of my skills and abilities to attract my dream job
149. I am a great employee. Any employer is lucky to have me.
150. I am an asset to any organization, and I prove it in every interview.
151. I am appreciated and rewarded well wherever I work.
152. I am fully myself and completely authentic in my career.
153. It's not what I do, but how I do it… I treat every task as an opportunity to create more beauty, abundance and joy.
154. Today, I abandon my old work habits and take up new, more positive ones
155. I am doing my best in my career and giving my everything without reservation.
156. Amazing career opportunities are appearing in my life out of nowhere.
157. The Universe is making perfect arrangements to find right employment for me
158. I am attracting most suitable job opportunities
159. My career happiness is a choice I make everyday.
160. I am open to new opportunities that lead me to get my dream job.
161. I am confident radiating who I am in all situations at work
162. I love my career as it allows me to grow as well as makes me financially abundant.
163. My mistakes do not define me or dictate my future success.
164. I deserve to have an exciting, rewarding career. It is so much fulfilling
165. I am deeply fulfilled by all that I do.
166. What I do in my job makes a difference to at least one person in the world. I work in the knowledge of this truth
167. I unselfishly share my gifts with the world and give others permission to do the same.

168. I teach my peers to believe in me by believing in myself
169. The joy I find in my career is reflected in my overall happiness.
170. I am grateful for the discomfort of growing in my career, as I expand myself to create all that I've wished for
171. I am energetic and enthusiastic about my job. Confidence is my second nature
172. I have the courage to go after what I truly want
173. Right now, the job I am looking for is looking for me.
174. Everyday, I tap into more of my potential
175. I choose community over competition in my work and my life.
176. I serve others willingly, gladly and gratefully.
177. Harmony permeates my experience, and my work flows in productive and joyful ways.
178. I deserve to work in a dream job.
179. In my career and in my life, change is constant. I accept change and make the most of it.
180. I have everything I need to create my own opportunities at work
181. I manifest unexpected opportunities every day because I am aligned with my calling.
182. I am calm and comfortable speaking out in front of my colleagues. I have confidence in myself, thus, I relate easily with them.
183. I have found my ideal employment
184. I am opening my consciousness to a greater prosperity and part of that prosperity is an increased salary.
185. I am always open to opportunities to get me an ideal employment
186. Today, I am attracting into my life the best and most suitable job for me
187. I am creating and building the career of my dreams.

188. I am ready for my interviews. I am confident in my interviews. I am successful in my interviews.
189. I accept constructive criticism and welcome self-improvement
190. I am at a workplace that I love, and my job gives me satisfaction and good salary
191. I am now manifesting an opportunity for a wonderful and well-paying job
192. I offer constructive criticism to help others around me.

CHAPTER TEN

POSITIVE AFFIRMATIONS FOR CREATIVITY

1. I tap into the universal source of inspiration to boost my creativity .
2. I access and I use the vibrant energy that surrounds me on all levels.
3. I channel the positive life forces around me to increase my own creativity and become amore expressive individual.
4. I summon the creative energy of the stars and planets to surround and fill me.
5. Every being has creative energy from the universe and I have access to the source
6. I embrace new sources of energy as I grow and become stronger. The earth, water, and air are filled with powerful forces I can use.
7. Being positive improves my creativity.
8. I draw inspiration from the world around me It provides me with strength, so my abilities grow and change.
9. I am a powerful creator, and I create the life that I want starting today.
10. The artist is already present within me.
11. I am inspired, creative and productive.
12. I come up with new and innovative ideas easily.
13. I am a visionary.
14. Great ideas come to me easily.
15. I am part of an infinite universe with an endless supply of creativity.
16. Doing repetitive tasks frees my mind to consider creative solutions to problems.

Positive Daily Affirmations

17. I am a magnet for innovative ideas.
18. An endless reservoir of creativity lies within me.
19. The beautiful universe around me has abundant energy for me to use.
20. I find original solutions to problems.
21. I have an adventurous, imaginative mind.
22. I am grateful for the creative ideas that come to me.
23. I follow my creative inclinations.
24. I love inventing exciting new ways of doing things.
25. I am awake and see the world through fresh eyes.
26. I have infinite creative potential.
27. Today, I recognize the energy around me and appreciate the creative it provides me.
28. I will come up with amazing new ideas
29. Being creative makes me feel so alive.
30. Creative inspiration follows me wherever I go.
31. Ideas are starting to flow freely from my mind
32. I am creative and have the willpower to make use of my talents.
33. I always have lots of unique ideas for solving problems.
34. I am finding it easier and easier to come up with new ideas
35. I am surrounded by revitalizing forces that spread over me and reach every part of me.
36. I increase my inventiveness in all that I do.
37. My creativity is increasing
38. Today I am making time to create.
39. I am always tapped into my creative energy
40. My creative juices are a natural stimulant.
41. I am a brilliant and successful artist.
42. Today, I am happy that I have values to help me make wise decisions when innovating.
43. My imagination is becoming stronger and stronger
44. I am a creative thinker.

45. I know that being creatively true to myself always pays off in the end.
46. I am comfortable with alone thinking.
47. Divine inspiration surrounds me.
48. Creativity flows through every cell in my body.
49. I can feel new sources of creative energy enter my body and mind.
50. My creativity fills me with passion and purpose.
51. I have a fertile imagination.
52. Every creative thought I express provides me with great joy.
53. I am a fount of ingenuity.
54. I will tap into my creative energy
55. I attract brilliant ideas
56. I exercise my imagination at every opportunity.
57. Creative ideas come to me regularly.
58. I take inspired action to keep my creative spark alive.
59. Everything I create is inventive and unique.
60. I am clever and creative in all that I do.
61. Creativity makes it easy for me to step into my uncomfortable zone
62. I am easily able to come up with fresh, new ideas.
63. Creative energy flows through me at all times.
64. I choose to create.
65. My creative spirit has no boundaries
66. I easily tap into the Creative Force whenever I need to.
67. The abundant universe the resource to keep my creative spark alive.
68. I am an unlimited creative being.
69. My creative source never runs dry.
70. Brilliant ideas come to me all the time.
71. Creatively, I am spontaneous; I surprise even myself.
72. My creative energy radiates outwardly to myself and the people I meet.
73. I am creatively expressing my highest potential.

74. The art of mindfulness ignites my creative spark.
75. Every day I become more creative and inventive.
76. I am in love with my unique creative expression.
77. I am immensely grateful for my creative abilities.
78. I am inspired by the beauty in my life and all around me.
79. I am a creative problem solver.
80. My environment supports my creative thinking
81. I am grateful for the energy that feeds my imagination.
82. I am efficient and imaginative in my work.
83. I am open to new experiences
84. I give myself room for self- expression.
85. Being creative is one of the top priorities in my life, and I practice this feeling every day.
86. Every moment of every day I am becoming more and more inventive.
87. My creative thoughts boost my confidence and courage in my abilities
88. I am a creative problem solver.
89. I am endowed with great creativity and intelligence.
90. I easily connect with the infinite creativity of the universe.
91. Innovative thoughts keep me on my toes
92. Being creative is one of my great joys in life.
93. I give thanks for the creative inspiration I receive daily.
94. I am a naturally artistic individual
95. My creative energy is limitless.
96. I employ my power in inventive and helpful ways.
97. I am incredibly creative and inspired.
98. Divine inspiration blesses every day of my life.
99. I always follow where inspiration leads.
100. I exercise innovative thinking at all times.
101. Fresh ideas come quickly and easily to me.
102. Every day I let my imagination soar to new heights.
103. I am a powerful and resourceful creator.

104. I find inventive solutions for each problem I am present with.
105. I open myself to a life of creativity.
106. My mind is flexible
107. I am an innovative thinker.
108. My imagination and creativity are my dynamic duo
109. I create new masterpieces every day.
110. The wellspring of creativity runs deep in me
111. I express my creativity whenever possible.
112. I have abundant creative talent.
113. I am always developing great new ways of doing things.
114. I am a creator and an innovator
115. I easily tap the imaginative resources of my mind.
116. I love exercising my artistic side.
117. I expand my understanding of things and this feeds my imagination.
118. I'm ready to share my authentic expression.
119. My creativity is growing
120. I am imaginative and creative in all that I do.
121. I have a wealth of good ideas.
122. I easily find novel solutions to problems.
123. The natural beauty of life insures my creativity
124. I am ever receptive to the inspiration the universe sends me.
125. I am an innovator. My ideas are inspiring.
126. I am full of infinite, creative energy.
127. I wake up with good ideas every single day
128. I am continually developing new, innovative ideas.
129. I enjoy my natural creativity.
130. My creativity flows freely.
131. I allow my creative genius to shine.
132. Great new ideas come to me every day.
133. I love inventing things.
134. I will tap into my imagination

Positive Daily Affirmations

135. I approach all problems in an inspired and resourceful way.
136. I am becoming highly creative
137. I feel creative and inspired at work.
138. My creative self wants to come out and play.
139. Creative ideas just flow out of my mind naturally
140. I have a great imagination.
141. I have a powerful imagination
142. I employ lateral thinking in all that I do.
143. I will unleash my creativity today
144. I am confident and skilled in my creative work.
145. Creativity comes naturally to me
146. I allow my creative energy to flow freely at all times.
147. I have endless creativity
148. I am very resourceful and inventive.
149. I am effortlessly creative at all times
150. I can get into a creative state of mind whenever I want.
151. I love and embrace my inner creative child.
152. Today, I am filled with infinite, creative energy.
153. I play and create with the joyful exuberance of a child.
154. I am always thinking of new, original ways to do things.
155. My imagination runs wild
156. I find creative solutions to problems every day.
157. I am a wellspring of creativity.
158. My creative mind is my best resource for overcoming challenges
159. I exercise my creative genius every day.
160. I am infinitely creative.
161. I have a fantastic imagination
162. I love expressing myself creatively.
163. I am always developing as an artist.
164. I am open to perfecting my creativity potential
165. I have an endless supply of creativity.
166. I am one with the creative flow of life.
167. My creativity overpowers my fears.

168. I have instant access to unlimited ingenuity.
169. The universe is my creative playground
170. I am incredibly creative and imaginative.
171. I love losing myself in the zone of creative thought.
172. I find original solutions for all difficulties in my life.
173. Nurturing my creative mind is a priority.
174. I am a creative genius.
175. My creativity is for the betterment of mankind.
176. I honor my creative genius.
177. I am inventive and resourceful.
178. I love inventing original new products.
179. I love exercising original thinking.
180. I can always count on my imagination for inspiring ideas.
181. New ideas are always coming to me
182. I love having an outlet for my artistic abilities.
183. I am forever grateful for my imaginative mind.
184. My creative mind frees me from habitual thinking.
185. My mind is wired for creativity
186. I increase my creativity by being clearly focused in the present.
187. Living a creative life is important to me; it makes me a healthier, happier person.
188. I invent new things that are inspiring
189. I express my unique creativity in all that I do.
190. Fresh new ideas come to me daily.

CHAPTER ELEVEN

POSITIVE AFFIRMATIONS FOR WOMEN

1. I am happy, healthy, and centered.
2. Change provides me opportunity.
3. My life is an adventure.
4. Good enough is good enough.
5. Feelings are not facts.
6. I have abundant energy.
7. My child is happy and healthy.
8. Let go of "what if
9. I will not live in reaction to my child.
10. Balance in life is what I strive for.
11. I will take time to put myself first.
12. I will act after thought, not on instinct.
13. Calm is my primary state of being.
14. I am content.
15. Principles guide me. Not a moments fancy.
16. I give myself permission to take personal time.
17. Would I expect this of anyone else?
18. I am unique and a gift to the world.
19. I am at peace with my body and accept it as it is. It was created to do amazing things.
20. I love living in my unique female body. It has features that are distinctive and make me who I am.
21. I am attractive just as I am. I don't need to change anything. I'm not perfect, but I am still beautiful.
22. I love my body and I take care of it through healthy eating and exercise. I respect my body and am thankful for all it can do.

23. I am responsible for what happens to my body, so I treat it with love, respect, and care.
24. I exercise my body daily with ease and am amazed at the ways it can bend, move, stretch, and pose.
25. I am a strong, confident woman and will only continue to become stronger.
26. I am patient with my body when it needs rest, healing, and recovery.
27. I respect my body's needs and treat it with the kindness that it deserves.
28. I choose to release love, happiness and gratitude into the world today. Life is precious and beautiful, and I choose to focus on the positive.
29. I am grateful for this wonderful day and the endless possibilities it has to offer. I know something great is in store for me.
30. No matter what goes on today, I know the truth that I am a radiant, powerful, and free woman.
31. I embrace my best self today. I live in a way that brings tranquility, joy, and pleasure to myself and others.
32. I know I am alive for a reason. Today, I honor my purpose and inspire people around me to do the same.
33. I don't need anyone else or anything to complete me because I am already complete just as I am.
34. I am beautiful and I am worthy of every beautiful thing in this world.
35. I am overflowing with renewed confidence every day. I continue to grow and become a stronger woman for myself and for the people around me.
36. I accept that I cannot change the past. I focus on my future and move forward in my life. My past does not define who I am today.

37. I do one thing every day to make consistent progress toward my dreams. I surpass other people's expectations because I am exceptional.
38. I choose to learn from the positive and negative events of the past so that I continue to make progress towards my bright future.
39. I do not need to control everything around me. I focus on allowing the best things to happen. I know that whatever is supposed to be will be.
40. I am cultured and smart, yet able to stay humble.
41. Because of my high self-esteem, I easily accept compliments and give them in return.
42. I deserve everything that is good. I do not have any need for misery and suffering.
43. I accept my past mistakes and let them go. They don't define me. I move forward with confidence in my essential goodness and good judgment.
44. My mind is full of caring, healthy, positive, and loving thoughts which transform into my life experiences.
45. My voice matters and I am confident to speak up when I want to. People listen to me because my words are valuable.
46. Success is possible for me because I have the right opportunities, and I take advantage of them when I see them. I know the path I need to take in order to succeed.
47. I have more than enough value to offer in my job. I continue to flourish and gain experience and succeed to levels that I never expected.
48. My mind is focused, and I have clarity in all that I do at work. I do not succumb to distractions.
49. Others recognize my work for its excellence, and I am proud to call it my own.
50. I am on my way to greatness. I go the extra mile to meet people whom I admire and respect. I take one step farther than anyone else around me.

51. I avoid fretting about past disappointments or comparing myself to others.
52. I realize that I have all that I need to be happy in this present moment.
53. I wake up every day with a restored sense of well-being.
54. I am focused. I give my full attention to each task, whether I am setting the dinner table or writing a computer program.
55. I embrace the new day with love in my heart.
56. I take care of my body and mind so that I am strong enough to give to others..
57. I have new energy and a deeper understanding of my surroundings.
58. I am awakened with appreciation and stirred up in awe of the wonders of my body
59. I love the beautiful world and appreciate all my blessings as well as my place in it
60. I organize my schedule while remaining flexible enough to take advantage of promising opportunities that come my way
61. My sense of wonder at my strengths and discovery of my potentials are restored, so I can explore new experiences.
62. I am secure in my perception of my place in the world.
63. I volunteer in my community and extend my hospitality to newcomers and old friends.
64. My nurturing love grows with each moment I spend on this planet.
65. I set specific goals that guide my actions and add value to my life.
66. Today, I remember my love of the world is renewed every day.
67. I find new meaning and joy in daily tasks.
68. I value my family and friends. I let them know that they are a vital part of my life.
69. My love is daily extended to my family, friends, coworkers and others.

70. I appreciate the people, places, experiences and events that shape my life.
71. I appreciate each person and the lessons our interactions bring
72. I am grateful for the chance to change and find recovery every day.
73. I embrace the energy I receive from friends and family. Together, we form a strong and powerful group that has unique capabilities and talents.
74. I am stronger and better because I attract positive powers into my life.
75. I remind my family that it is my responsibility to be forthright even with my them.
76. I know how to value my present, accept my past, and plan for my future with love in my heart.
77. I avoid viewing the decisions of people I care about as acceptable when they are misaligned with my beliefs.
78. Each day I encounter family, friends, and acquaintances. I am conscious of differences in thoughts and actions and respect them. But I avoid adopting them just for validation.
79. When family members make questionable decisions, I hold them accountable
80. I am mature enough to know that genuine friendships are able to withstand tension that comes from differences in opinion.
81. My body and mind are connected to the deepest parts of the universe. They are renewed each night as I dream.
82. I have something special to offer my family and the world.
83. I let my friends know the lines I am unwilling to cross. I am happy that they respect my point of view.
84. I am a very brave, strong woman
85. I deserve to be happy and loved
86. I spread joy with every step I take on my journey
87. My true friends appreciate me even when our thoughts differ. Our diversity helps to keep our relationship interesting.
88. I am the better half. I am better in everything I do.

89. I take care of my body in healthy ways.
90. I embrace my wrinkles and lines of wisdom.
91. I recognize that opportunities exist to celebrate life anew each and every day.
92. I reconnect with my dreams and these dreams help me renew my love of the physical world.
93. The fountain of youth lies in my heart, mind and soul.
94. It's okay to live my dream today and to be a little selfish
95. I am thankful for every part of my body.
96. I am in a constant state of progress.
97. I love myself, respect myself and accept myself exactly as I am.
98. I am attractive as I am.
99. I adopt a healthy outlook on matters that relate to getting older.
100. I am doing my best every single day and it is enough.
101. I embrace the female cycles that my body experiences.
102. I get older gracefully.
103. I am wiser and wiser each day.
104. I am worthy of love and respect
105. I am the perfect age today.
106. I take full responsibility for my wellness.
107. I wear confidence in my smile and in the way I move my body.
108. I have a healthy relationship with time in terms of my age
109. My love for the world is nurtured by the universe. I am part of a magical collection of beings who are changing and growing each day.
110. I may be older but I feel young and alive
111. I give myself permission to be relaxed and happy
112. I am not afraid of getting older. Instead, I step into the next stage of my life with ease and confidence.
113. I choose today to begin to materialize my dream
114. My life becomes richer in meaning through the years.

115. I nourish my body with healthy thoughts each day.
116. I recognize the wisdom, strength, and compassion that within me.
117. I am thankful to be alive, to be well and to be breathing
118. I am honored to have so many friends in my life
119. I am well supported by the female tribe.
120. I let my love for myself increase each day
121. No success is too small to celebrate, and I revel in the tiny wins today.
122. I connect with my inner goddess who loves to shine.
123. I am always safe and protected
124. I benefit from the wisdom of the women who have come before me
125. It isn't selfish to be kind to myself.
126. I have a sisterhood of women who nurture and support me
127. I am at peace in my own body
128. I celebrate who I am and who I am becoming with each passing day.
129. I am a woman of substance. I take interest in everything. I take great care to develop my personality.
130. I deserve a loving, supportive partner
131. I am a sympathetic yet assertive and demanding boss and treat my employees equitably. I get the best out of each employee
132. I celebrate every aspect of my life with utmost joy.
133. I love myself and treat myself with kindness.
134. I allow my inner goddess to rock her magic.
135. Today I start loving myself more
136. I am amazed by the perfect creation of my physical being.
137. I am a loving and nurturing sister. I care for and dote on my brother.
138. I enjoy being a woman
139. I discover true joy with being a woman, even as I get older.
140. I align with the dreams of my inner goddess.

141. All my dreams are destined to come true
142. I am open to new adventures in life.
143. I commit to my success and I do not allow myself to be intimidated
144. I have been blessed with qualities that uplift others and even on my hardest days, I am the perfect mother for my children.
145. I am unique and complete by just being me
146. I am a productive employee. I take my job seriously and always give my best.
147. I am blessed to be a woman. I draw on my feminine qualities and gifts for success.
148. I can handle anything that comes into my life
149. As a woman, I deserve success as much as any man who works hard out there.
150. My body shape is perfect in the way that it's intended to be
151. I am so in love right now with my true self
152. I listen to my body's needs attentively.
153. I embrace every imperfection that I perceive in my appearance
154. I am confident in my sexuality.
155. I am blessed with the gift of living and I appreciate this
156. I find deep inner peace within myself as I am
157. I embrace my curves. I love being me.
158. I am driven and motivated for success and in shows in my work ethics
159. I enjoy expressing myself as a woman totally.
160. I am a strong, confident and capable woman.
161. I am gentle with myself
162. I wear my confidence as a woman with pride.
163. Every cell in my body is perfect, complete and whole
164. I love myself fully, including the way I look
165. I embrace my life each and every day, even as I get older.

Positive Daily Affirmations

166. I am committed to my success and will not back down. I enjoy taking action when I have a goal so I can acquire the lifestyle that I dream of.
167. I am well supported by my loved ones and the people in my community.
168. My breast size is perfect in the way that it's intended to be.
169. My self-esteem is high because I honor who I am
170. I embrace my grey hair with grace
171. I am enough as I am
172. I strive to improve myself
173. My inner goddess is magic, crystals and sunshine
174. I am the best friend that anyone can have. For me, friendship is the ultimate relationship.
175. I discover everlasting beauty from the inside-out.
176. I choose to understand and forgive myself
177. I enjoy being in this female body.
178. I am a being of unconditional love and compassion
179. I am a loving and caring wife. My partner is my soul mate. We complement each other.
180. I have persistence in what I believe
181. I can do anything that I put my mind to
182. I am a model daughter. I love and respect my parents and discharge faithfully my duties toward them.
183. I appreciate every moment of my life
184. I am perfect as I am.
185. I love and enjoy being the best of myself
186. I am a woman of love. My touch heals all wounds.
187. I combine feminity and intelligence beautifully
188. I adore motherhood. I am an ideal mother and my children love me.
189. It's okay to be a powerful woman
190. With every breath I become more peaceful

191. I am calm when I am faced with conflict. I can brush off negativity easily, and I can agree to disagree. I enjoy being the bigger person and taking the high road.

CHAPTER TWELVE

POSITIVE AFFIRMATIONS FOR MEN

1. I am respected and appreciated and deservedly so.
2. I am moving closer to my dreams.
3. I surrender my ego and pride to the universe. I embrace humility
4. I am outgoing and charismatic.
5. I have a positive body image.
6. Today, I deserve to have a great job success.
7. I know that I am worthy of financial stability.
8. I am grateful for the abundance I have.
9. I am connected to my inner emotions and I am not ashamed of this
10. My confidence grows stronger each day.
11. I love myself and I accept myself as I am.
12. I love being a father. I am an ideal father and my children love me.
13. I am brave and I courageously take on my responsibilities
14. I can change any negative perceptions I have about myself
15. I am a good person.
16. I am a great provider for my family.
17. I am the creator of my life. I refuse to be stereotyped into a role
18. I am worthy of happiness, wealth and peace.
    I can't control others.
19. I am successful, prosperous, healthy, and happy.
20. I am a man of substance. I am interested in everything.
21. I feel sexy, charming and attractive.
22. I am assertive and at the same time, considerate about others.

Positive Daily Affirmations

23. I am a strong advocate for myself. I strongly believe in my abilities.
24. I am not a failure. I learn from any challenges I encounter.
25. In my field of work, I am a productive employee. I take my job seriously and always give my best.
26. I bravely strive to better myself in every way
27. I am proud and happy to be the man that I am
28. I am strong, courageous and independent. I live my truth
29. I am in control of my life.
30. I attract new business opportunities easily.
31. As a child, I love and respect my parents and faithfully discharge my duties toward them.
32. I treat myself right because I love myself.
33. I am confident in my looks. I am a sexy and attractive man.
34. People genuinely enjoy being around me because of my positive energy
35. Every day I am getting more confident I myself. I take on new adventures
36. I am looking healthier and stronger every day because ai am making the right eating choices
37. I balance my masculine and feminine energies.
38. I will continue to grow and learn.
39. I am everything a son can be. I make my parents proud in everything I do.
40. Whatever I am called to do, leadership comes to me instinctively
41. I am bold and confident. I refuse to be pressured into making poor choices
42. Today, I am grateful for the man I am becoming.
43. I am living the life I always wanted.
44. I am a successful and thriving family man. I am a loving husband and a doting father.
45. In my relationship, I am the other half. I am best in everything I do.

Positive Daily Affirmations

46. I am manly in my appearance, caring in my attitude and loving in my personality.
47. I am in touch with my emotions and I am not ashamed to be vulnerable
48. I am connected to my inner motivation. I wake up each morning with intention and purpose.
49. Today is meaningful, important, and special. I live it with purpose
50. I radiate love with smiles and I feel it reflected back to me
51. I love myself in a healthy and wholesome way
52. Health is a priority for me. I take good care of my body.
53. Today, I base my happiness on my own accomplishments and the blessings I've been given.
54. I am a loving person. I give out love and I receive love unconditionally.
55. My emotions and feelings are worthy of attention
56. I am excited for what is to come. Because the gest days are ahead
57. I love, appreciate and value the person I am becoming
58. I am smart, generous and good at my job.
59. Creative energy surges through me and leads me to new and brilliant ideas.
60. I am worthy of love and deserve the good kind of love
61. I love the way I look and I put in the work to look good
62. Success and wealth come effortlessly to me.
63. I have great ideas that are transformative
64. I am not aggressive. I am assertive and strong.
65. I listen to my needs and prioritize self-care because I deserve it
66. Happiness is a choice. I am choosing to be happy today.
67. Today, I am closer to making my dreams come true than I was yesterday.
68. I am a man who creates responses to circumstances not just reactions.

69. Everything that is happening now is happening for my ultimate good.
70. I am a man who receives wisdom from my subconscious 24/7.
71. I am blessed with an incredible family and wonderful friends.
72. I actively listen to what other men say without interrupting them.
73. I have all the qualities of a strong man.
74. I am guided in my every step by the spirit who leads me towards what I must know and do.
75. Today, I abandon my old habits and take up new, more positive ones.
76. I have been given endless talents which I begin to utilize today.
77. As a leader, I am a sympathetic yet assertive and demanding boss and treat my employees equitably.
78. I am a man of substance.
79. I am a glorious creature. I radiate beauty, charm, and grace.
80. My efforts are being supported by the universe; my dreams manifest into reality before my eyes.
81. I am the ideal male figure.
82. I am actively involved in building my community
83. I can do anything I put my mind to.
84. I love and nurture the people in my life with strength and empathy.
85. Today and every day going forward, I acknowledge my own self-worth; my confidence is soaring.
86. My thoughts are filled with positivity and my life is plentiful with prosperity.
87. I radiate with self-confidence and a charming energy.
88. I am a man of my word.
89. As a provider, I seek to provide for my loved ones.
90. My fears of tomorrow are simply melting away.
91. I am resilient, nothing really breaks me

Positive Daily Affirmations

92. I am the creator of my entire life and experiences
93. Successful people are attracted to me.
94. I forgive those who have harmed me in my past and peacefully detach from them.
95. My marriage/relationship is becoming stronger, deeper, and more stable each day.
96. I believe in myself.
97. I am open to abundance, joy, pleasure and positive experiences in life.
98. I am ready to create amazing memories that will be worth remembering
99. My future is an ideal projection of what I envision now.
100. I am the best male friend that anyone can have. For me, friendship is the ultimate relationship.
101. I am naturally masculine, graceful and handsome.
102. I am a giving man who knows how to make others feel happy about life.
103. I am highly resilient. I can withstand tough times
104. I am the architect of my life; I build its foundation and choose its contents.
105. I define my own happiness and success; not the world or society dictates to me
106. I am a confident man with a hunger and desire to achieve my goals every day.
107. All the things that are happening in my life are to benefit me.
108. I am superior to negative thoughts and low actions.
109. I take much pride in being a man.
110. I am a loving and caring husband.
111. I am In awe of the person that I am and I am proud of the person I am becoming
112. My partner is my soul mate. We complement each other.
113. My body is healthy; my mind is brilliant; my soul is tranquil.

114. The world needs my uniqueness because everything about me is special
115. I am a loving and nurturing brother. I care for and dote on my sister.
116. I am a man who is confident and strong yet caring and corroborative.
117. I deserve to be employed and paid well for my time, efforts, and ideas.
118. I believe I can do anything in this life.
119. My obstacles are moving out of my way; my path is carved towards greatness.
120. I am a man who knows how to relax and have a good time.
121. I am a great protector of the people in my life and of my family.
122. I am great at my job and I am acknowledged for this
123. I am a man who laughs at himself with childish joy.
124. Many people look up to me and recognize my worth; I am admired.
125. I am a man who finds opportunities and advantages behind every door I open.
126. A river of compassion washes away my anger and replaces it with love.
127. My ability to conquer my challenges is limitless; my potential to succeed is infinite.
128. I am a prepared man who has a results-oriented daily plan.
129. I am a man with passions and I pursue them with intensity and fervor.
130. I am not consumed by work. I create time for my hobbies and activities I enjoy.
131. My mental and physical strength are incredibly strong.
132. I am a peaceful man who creates synergistic and positive relationships.
133. I am manly and perfectly enough.

134. Today, I am brimming with energy and overflowing with joy.
135. I have complete faith that everything is going to turn out perfectly I my favor
136. My subconscious properly prepares the subconscious of every other man I meet for positive interaction
137. I am powerful in so many ways and I celebrate this power daily
138. I am a man who is youthful and adventurous and spontaneous.
139. I am a vibrant powerhouse; I am indestructible.
140. No one negative is allowed to be in my life.
141. My life is just beginning.
142. When I speak to other men I focus on their interests not mine.
143. I am a man who takes direct action towards goals to build massive momentum.
144. Each day, I am closer to finding the perfect job for me.
145. I am grateful for everything in my life.
146. I follow my dreams as if my life depends on it, because it does.
147. I create harmony with other men through cooperative effort not competition.
148. My business is growing, expanding, and thriving.
149. I have made up me mind and decided that I'm going to relax and have fun with this day, no matter what the outcome may be
150. I am a responsible and trusting man who sees the good in others.
151. I encourage other men to talk about themselves and I listen intently when they do
152. Everywhere I go people are drawn to my dynamic masculine personality.
153. I possess the qualities needed to be extremely successful.

154. I am a strong man who is an outstanding and confident leader.
155. My nature is Divine; I am a spiritual being.
156. I am a great leader who can see the point of view of other men.
157. I accept, love, and appreciate myself, exactly as I am with no conditions.
158. I am worthy. I love and respect myself and always make life supporting loving choices in all areas
159. The perfect partner for me is coming into my life sooner than I expect.
160. I treat myself with kindness
161. Prosperity and masculinity are my birthrights and it shows through my actions.
162. I am sure of myself.
163. The tone of my masculine voice communicates strength and confidence.
164. I am supported, safe, and free to be myself
165. I make the choice to love and accept myself exactly as I am
166. I am at peace with all that has happened, is happening, and will happen.
167. I have a magnetic, warm, and masculine presence and handshake.
168. I am a man with enough time, energy, and wisdom to accomplish my desires.
169. My magnetism and masculine charm are noticed as soon as I walk into a room.
170. Today, I am ready for a healthy, loving relationship
171. I take great care to develop my personality.
172. When I speak with other men they notice how confident and fun I am.
173. I am a leader and influential man who gains respect through my actions.

174. I am a tower of strength, vitality, and masculinity and women notice it.
175. I wake up today with strength in my heart and clarity in my mind.
176. I express my honest and sincere appreciation for other men easily and often.
177. When I am around other men I feel content and strong.
178. I am conquering my illness; I am defeating it steadily each day.
179. I am a leader and I sincerely recognize the value in every other man I meet.
180. Every day, I learn and continue to grow into the best version of myself.
181. My personal experiences have made me the strong man I am today.
182. I am courageous and I stand up for myself.
183. I am a man who follows his gut instinct and I always find a reward.
184. I am a man who releases the need to be right all the time and to judge others.
185. I am a serious career person and I work hard to further my career.
186. I am confident about the way I look.
187. I am smart and witty and I am okay with myself
188. In my workplace where I lead, I get the best out of each employee.
189. My skills are unique and have enormous worth.
190. I love myself and the people around me.
191. I am a natural leader.

CHAPTER THIRTEEN

POSITIVE AFFIRMATIONS FOR TEENAGERS

1. I know it is okay not to have all the answers for my life right now, I take one day at a time.
2. All my school goals are being accomplished with ease.
3. I find it easy to be myself around new and old friends.
4. I am responsible teen. I own up to my actions
5. Spending time with my peers feels fun and invigorating.
6. I feel so great in my own skin.
7. I have the ability to choose any feeling I am feeling, therefore I always choose confidence.
8. I grow more confident from the challenges that life brings me.
9. I know that mom and dad want the best for me so I listen to what they have to say and respect them.
10. I tune out the voices of peer pressure and I listen to my parents because I know they want the best for me.
11. I have learned to stay calm in stressful situations.
12. I am so thankful for the ability to learn and grow from my teachers.
13. I sleep very soundly helping me have more energy in the day.
14. I am a genius and smarter than anyone I know.
15. Every new thing I try, I do really good at it.
16. I am not a social outcast
17. I feel great in who I am becoming.
18. I accomplish great things when I put my mind to it
19. I am blessed and God keeps me safe and secure.
20. I am super proud of myself.
21. I embrace my imperfections and grow from them.
22. I am really compassionate and passionate about the world

Positive Daily Affirmations

23. I am fearless
24. I easily let go of negative people in my life, they have no place in my life.
25. I am incredibly gifted, unique and special.
26. I am very determined.
27. I use my powerful ability to love for myself and give it to others as well.
28. I naturally find and embrace my talents and passions.
29. I have a really good attitude.
30. In school, I am a quick learner.
31. I am so creative and I get better every day
32. I have an awesome sense of humor and love to make my friends laugh.
33. I play so well with new and old friends.
34. I feel total relaxed when I go to parties.
35. I am a great friend. I have healthy that lasts a long time
36. I love eating health and exercising.
37. I love trying and learning new things in and out of school.
38. I create good habits in my life that will help propel me nicely into adulthood.
39. I love my family and love helping them with things.
40. I am learning a lot about myself right now and I keep doing so because it is so important to know thyself.
41. I am confident about myself and my abilities.
42. I choose how I feel and choose to feel loved and great all the time.
43. I have a retentive memory. I retain everything I study with ease.
44. I discover new talents that I have all the time.
45. There is nothing that I can't set my mind to and not achieve.
46. My dreams are possible to achieve.
47. I feel great and at ease eating in front of others.
48. I always do my best in everything I do

Positive Daily Affirmations

49. I feed my mind with positive content which transforms my mind and life for the better.
50. I am worthy of living my best life.
51. I am powerful kid
52. I naturally let go of relationships that are not supportive of me creating and keep high levels of self confidence.
53. I never try to act or be like anyone else because I love myself just the way I am.
54. I am appreciative to be at this young stage of life where there are so many possibilities.
55. I am very helpful around the house.
56. I am enough.
57. I am a great and valuable person with a lot to offer.
58. I am becoming a better me every single day.
59. I do my homework super fast right when I get home.
60. I choose my emotional state and therefore I always choose a state that makes me feel great about myself.
61. I am a great listener.
62. I can trust mom and dad with anything on my heart.
63. I feel like I am in a judge free zone when I am in social situations.
64. I am a fast learner, failing is a part of that process
65. I know that the more I like and accept myself, the more others will too.
66. I am so smart and intelligent.
67. I have all that it takes.
68. I love my life so much.
69. I feel so at ease in social situations.
70. I love being in social situations.
71. I can let go of worries I have anytime I want to. I have that power.
72. I attract other confident people into my life who I model and learn from which grows my level of confidence .

Positive Daily Affirmations

73. My courage overpowers any feeling of lack of self confidence.
74. I care about others and love to show my kindness.
75. I don't resist people trying to help me, I trust that they want what is best for me.
76. I am a very hard worker and always do my homework on time
77. I bless confident people because what I bless comes back to me.
78. I get better I school because I am a quick learner.
79. I am a natural at all the subjects and classes I take.
80. I love being myself and being around people who value the real me
81. My best self always comes out in social situations.
82. I am highly intelligent and bring a lot of value to my interactions.
83. I love being a kid
84. I make new friends so easily
85. People believe in me and think I am great.
86. I know I am loved by God.
87. I may not know what is best for me at all times, and I accept that and seek help when I need to do so.
88. I respect all my friends, teachers and family.
89. I am never a victim of my circumstances.
90. I am not afraid to try new things and challenge myself.
91. I am so thankful for my friends and family.
92. I let go of any anxiety and fear I have right now.
93. I know that honesty is always the best policy.
94. I am gifted and blessed and share it with the world.
95. All my problems have perfect solutions. I do not let worry consume me
96. I use my body to create a feel of confidence by standing tall and proud and opening myself up.
97. I have the right people to counsel me when I need it
98. I am contented with what I have and I am happier for it

99. I allow myself to learn great life lessons at this time of my life.
100. I wake up each day with energy and happiness.
101. I am a highly competent student.
102. I believe in myself.
103. I am always honest. Honest is the best policy.
104. I am safe in the here and now.
105. I am enough and I will not be made to feel less
106. I can share the truth with my parents and teachers about my life.
107. I naturally hang out with people who want the best for me and inspire me to grow and become more.
108. I can do anything I set my mind to.
109. I see all of the good things I have done in this life and it makes me feel great about myself.
110. I love myself.
111. I am so naturally gifted.
112. It feels great to be at ease whenever I am at a social gathering.
113. I believe in my capabilities.
114. My mind is strong and powerful.
115. I believe and trust myself.
116. I respect my teacher and love learning from him/her.
117. I allow myself to engage in my passions each day because it helps me live in the moment.
118. I love my friends and family and love to show them that I do.
119. I know mistakes only help me get better.
120. I am completely consumed and dedicated to my studies.
121. I always use my words to communicate during arguments.
122. I have no fear of speaking in public.
123. I do not hold grudges. I forgive people who are mean to me.
124. I accept myself completely.

Positive Daily Affirmations

125. I am confident enough to speak up for myself
126. I accept my body as it is changing and growing.
127. My teachers see the greatness in my that I may not even yet see.
128. Whether my parents at present or not, I try to adhere to the values they teach me
129. I have so much worth.
130. At home or at school, I feel safe and secure.
131. Confidence oozes out of me in social situations.
132. I am a knowledge seeker. I love learning new things in and out of school.
133. I trust my intuition to guide me in making good decisions.
134. I trust that I will do good in school and in life.
135. I am unique, truly one of a kind.
136. I have the best and most positive friends.
137. I already see myself graduating with honors and walking across the stage victorious.
138. I am always so happy.
139. I pay attention to the things I feed my mind with
140. I feel good about who I am and who I am becoming.
141. I allow myself to feel lost at times for I know I will find myself.
142. I feel so loved and protected by my family.
143. People always tend to really like me.
144. I am making deliberate choices about my future
145. I find it easy to sink into very good study sessions.
146. I am a wise teen
147. I always find myself not even thinking about my social anxiety.
148. In am divinely protected from any form of abuse
149. I love meeting new people.
150. I am a happy and generous person and people do not take advantage of that
151. I strive for purpose and progress, not perfection.

Positive Daily Affirmations

152. I am a child of excellence
153. I give myself permission to only study things that bring me happiness and fulfillment
154. Even though I am young, I still am grateful for each day for I know life is short.
155. I choose good and healthy foods because I love my body.
156. My mind always chooses positive and uplifting thoughts that help me feel great about myself.
157. I love hanging out with my family and sharing my love with them.
158. My breath is perfectly controlled when I am social situations.
159. Everything will be okay
160. I am enough.
161. Failure is not the end of the road. I know I can always do better next time.
162. I don't judge myself, I love myself.
163. I feel very beautiful/handsome at all times.
164. I love exercising my body and love the way I feel because of it.
165. I naturally see myself doing things in life with grace and perfection, hence I go into these situations feeling very confident.
166. When people say negative things to me, I don't care because I love and respect myself.
167. I feel like a natural talking to people in social situations.
168. I can make really good choices, and if I make a poor choice, I have the right support system to help me through it.
169. I am thankful that I have such a great teacher.
170. It is safe for me to open up in front of people.
171. I am whole, perfect and complete.
172. The universe supports and wants to help me feel the most confident.

Positive Daily Affirmations

173. I am not confined by fear as I always break through my fears.
174. I am proud of myself and the accomplishments I have made so far
175. I come to class with a wide open growth mindset.
176. I am not easily distracted as I have really good focusing skills.
177. Everything I do makes me feel even more proud of myself.
178. Life is an adventure do me because I am brave and confident.
179. I am very responsible. I carry out my chores diligently
180. I ace my tests with ease.
181. The mistakes I make do not define me. I learn from all of my mistakes.
182. I let go of all my feelings of low self-esteem, right now.
183. I am in charge of my emotions, no one else.
184. I am in my element in social situations.
185. I enjoy learning because I grow when I do
186. There are so many opportunities for me in life and I embrace them all
187. It feels great to be a child of God.
188. I choose to let my life overflow with joy and self confidence.
189. I see life as a classroom which helps me crush my school goals.
190. I make easy connections with the subjects I am studying help me memorize and learn better.
191. I am making a positive impact in this generation

CHAPTER FOURTEEN

POSITIVE AFFIRMATIONS FOR PREGNANCY

1. My birth is going to be perfect and quick.
2. I am committed to consciously raising this child. All the unconscious generational negativity stops with me
3. Birth is safe for me and my baby.
4. I choose to enjoy every second in this journey of pregnancy, even in difficult days.
5. My baby loves me.
6. I welcome the challenge of motherhood with grace, gratitude, and a warm heart filled with love.
7. I have the right support system to help me through this pregnancy and beyond
8. I accept my labor and birth.
9. I am a strong woman.
10. My husband/boyfriend and I will become deeply connected during and after the birthing process.
11. I assertively use my voice to express what I want and need and to say no when I'm uncomfortable.
12. My baby feels my love.
13. I educate myself to make the best possible decisions for my pregnancy and my baby's birth.
14. I am the best parent for my baby.
15. The world welcomes my baby into this world with love and open arms.
16. I have no fear about the birthing process, I let go of it now.
17. I feel blessed, privileged, and favored to carry my baby inside of me.

Positive Daily Affirmations

18. I am bringing a perfectly healthy, whole, and strong child into this world.
19. I love my baby even though we are yet to meet
20. I believe in myself and my natural ability to give birth easily, peacefully, and in comfort.
21. I know how to take care of myself in pregnancy.
22. My baby loves me fully and completely.
23. My body knows exactly how to care for my growing baby.
24. My baby is in the perfect position to come to the world efficiently and smoothly.
25. I love and approve of myself and I welcome, honor, and embrace the changes in my beautiful pregnant body as it shifts to accommodate my baby.
26. I am surrounded by those who love and respect me.
27. I was divinely chosen and called to be the mother of this child and I am good enough to care for her/him
28. I will be ready and prepared for a safe, beautiful, and effortless birthing experience.
29. My love and connection with this child within me humbles me every day. I am blessed and I know it.
30. My baby cannot wait to get to this world!
31. My body is accepting my baby and my pregnancy will end with the safe birth of a healthy baby.
32. As the motherhood chapter of my life begins, I am ready to make it a beautiful chapter in my life.
33. My pregnant body is beautiful.
34. I am in perfect health. My baby is in perfect health. This pregnancy comes to a perfect end.
35. I rely on millennia of maternal instincts embedded in me. I know how to take care of my baby.
36. Breathing in, I know I am a great mother. Breathing out, I am a great mother
37. My body knows how to give birth.

Positive Daily Affirmations

38. I cherish and celebrate the gift of pregnancy, life, and motherhood.
39. The concept of labor doesn't scare me as I know that contractions help to bring my baby.
40. I deeply trust my instincts and my body, and I trust I am capable of safely delivering my baby.
41. I have an amazing support system! When I ask for help, I receive help.
42. My baby will be born at the perfect time.
43. I allow myself to see the beauty and joy in this process, to enjoy this precious time with my baby, and to be empowered by all it brings.
44. I visualize myself after a perfect delivery. I am at home loving and playing with my beautiful baby.
45. I have a close bond with my baby. My relationships with my baby is so strong.
46. My doctor and I are on the same page. We are partners in delivering a healthy, happy baby.
47. My baby knows the true birthday.
48. I trust my body to make the labor process as easy and effective as possible.
49. I am remaining alert, in tune, and aware of my needs and I intuitively know the needs of my baby.
50. I protect myself and my baby by allowing only positive thoughts and words about pregnancy and childbirth.
51. How my child is born is solely my choice and I choose natural birth!
52. I will make plenty of breast milk for my baby.
53. This pregnancy is not a complicated one
54. My body knows when to give birth.
55. My baby is loved and she senses my love as our bond and connection grows stronger every day.
56. I am proud myself for the contribution of carrying, nurturing, and sustaining a life within me.

Positive Daily Affirmations

57. I feel powerful and healthy during the birthing process.
58. My body was made to nurture a baby.
59. I am happy and excited about my pregnancy and I'm looking forward to a calm, quiet, and beautiful birth.
60. My neuro-muscular system is working in perfect harmony during my delivery.
61. I choose the see the beauty in this whole process of bringing a new life into the world.
62. My midwife is a beautiful friend and wise counsel throughout my pregnancy. I am lucky to have her
63. I am deserving of an easy and uncomplicated pregnancy.
64. My pregnancy is a gift.
65. I am calm, cool, and confident throughout my pregnancy. This is the most beautiful nine months of my life
66. My baby is developing normally and will be born healthy, whole, safe, and at the perfect time.
67. My growing body is beautiful because of its power.
68. I know this is the right time for my baby to come to the world and bless our family.
69. My baby is growing just as she/he should.
70. My most important job in pregnancy and childbirth is to simply relax, stay centered, serene, and balanced, and to allow my baby's birth to happen.
71. I have built a harmonious union with my doctor/midwife/doula.
72. Despite difficulties, I remain energized, strong and healthy.
73. I am an amazing mother about to have an amazing baby
74. I am well cared for by myself and my loved ones.
75. My pregnancy is perfect. I am delivering a happy, healthy baby
76. My body accepts and protects this baby.
77. I am a strong women perfectly capable of a healthy and perfect birth.
78. Without any doubt, I believe that I am a great mother

Positive Daily Affirmations

79. My body was designed to nourish, protect, and grow my baby in my belly.
80. I am excited about my journey
81. I make the best decisions for myself and my baby.
82. I am strong and healthy and sailing right through this pregnancy.
83. I feel confident that every change my body goes through is for my baby's good.
84. I conceived a beautiful baby and I am delivering a beautiful child.
85. Today, I declare that my womb is functioning optimally.
86. My baby is receiving all the nourishment and nurturance that it needs.
87. My baby and I are working together to prepare for her birth and we are both grateful for this powerful experience.
88. I declare that I am healthy; my body is healthy.
89. My baby is so special to me and so is my body.
90. With each contraction I feel stronger and more powerful.
91. I am having fun with my pregnancy. I enjoy each week. I savor each milestone.
92. I am a great mother. My new baby is lucky to have me
93. My body is a relaxed and a warm home for my growing baby.
94. I will listen to my intuition and what it is telling me to make the process more natural and easy.
95. Today, I am feeling energized.
96. My body is a loving, safe home for my growing bundle of joy.
97. As my healthy baby grows within me, I am more attuned than ever to the perfect rhythms of nature and my body.
98. I trust that my body knows exactly what it is doing.
99. My baby knows how and when to be born and I patiently await for her arrival.
100. I will be a great mother.
101. My body was made for this experience

Positive Daily Affirmations

102. My life will soon be better because my baby will be in it.
103. I choose to be happy for me and my baby.
104. I crave healthy nutrition throughout this pregnancy
105. I am going to be perfectly relaxed during the birthing process.
106. I crave nutritious foods and I enjoy every meal that I share with my baby
107. I transcend all pain during the birthing process.
108. My womb is full of love.
109. I trust my body knows how to safely guide my baby out of the womb and into my arms.
110. My body is strong and capable.
111. My partner is uniquely equipped to care for me and the baby
112. There may be difficult days during this pregnancy, but I am strong, I am determined, and I am resilient.
113. I take deep breaths and feel the presence of my baby inside my body.
114. I am forming plenty of milk for my baby and I appreciate all the work from my breasts.
115. From conception to birth, I am having a wonderful experience
116. I release the discomfort of pregnancy, I let go of the worry, tension and the fear of birth and I am focused on the joy of meeting my child.
117. I release all my fears and trust that I am ready for this
118. Giving birth is normal and natural and my baby and I will be healthy and happy when it is over.
119. I am mentally, financially, emotionally and spiritually equipped for this pregnancy
120. I envelope myself in a warm and positive blanket that comforts and nurtures the life growing inside of me
121. An amazing mother lives within me. That mother is born along with my baby.

122. No Matter the sex of the baby, my baby is perfect.
123. I am absolutely committed to providing my child with a safe and happy home environment.
124. I am a perfectly functional engine for the creation of life
125. I will be patient and courage throughout the entire birthing process.
126. My uterus is full of life-giving energy.
127. I am attentive to this experience. I am committed to optimal nutrition, exercise and rest.
128. My body is powerful and full of light
129. I was made to be a mother. I trust my body.
130. It's so exciting to know that a new life is growing inside me.
131. I love my pregnant body- it is radiant, beautiful, and blissful because it is equipped everything I need to take care of my baby.
132. My pregnancy scars tell a story of my journey to creating life
133. I see myself right in the here and now, holding my beautiful baby in my arms. We are both happy, healthy and better yet intimately connected.
134. I welcome every experience on this journey to motherhood
135. I will be active to ensure a great delivery and a healthy baby.
136. Each pregnancy is a unique and beautiful experience. I am consciously enjoying this unique journey
137. Every kick is a reminder of a developing blessing inside of me.
138. A warm feeling fills me as I think of the amazing miracle forming inside my body.
139. I choose to experience the beauty of a natural birth and so that IS what I will experience
140. Just breathe and know that everything will be okay.

Positive Daily Affirmations

141. I take a deep breath and I smile every time I think of my pregnancy
142. The bond between me and my baby is inseparable.
143. There's life inside of me that I will care for the rest of my life.
144. I am not afraid of labor. I feel closer and closer to my baby with each contraction.
145. I will think positively, for everything will be fine and my baby is going to be fine.
146. My baby knows the love I have and is feeling this inside its entire body.
147. All the parts of my body are working together in harmony for a healthy, smooth and happy pregnancy.
148. There's beauty in the growth of my belly and the rest of my body.
149. My whole family is going to be deeply and intimately connected after our birth.
150. I caress my tummy and sense my baby enjoying this time inside my womb.
151. My choices throughout this pregnancy are based on facts not fear
152. My body is accepting this baby and will protect it.
153. On this journey to birthing, I accept the help of others.
154. Any day now, my life will change for the better with you in it.
155. My body is beautifully nourishing the child I carry. My child is perfectly healthy.
156. My body is perfectly qualified for this journey
157. I consult with my doctor, but I listen to my body and my heart when deciding how I will give birth.
158. I am enjoying my pregnancy one butterfly flutter at a time.
159. I am blessed and favored to be able to have this baby inside of me.
160. I am envisioning a healthy delivery of a healthy baby.

Positive Daily Affirmations

161. I let go of all worries, pre-birth, during birth and post-birth.
162. I am capable of delivering this baby.
163. I share affirming, warm and loving words with my baby.
164. My baby is safe and forming perfectly.
165. I will make the right decisions for my baby.
166. An amazing mother lives within me and will be born along with my amazing baby.
167. This is a great time. This is a miraculous experience. I'm excited to become a mom.
168. My love for you will grow every day just like you will.
169. My baby's head fits snugly into my pelvis.
170. I trust my body to help guide my baby into this world, into my arms.
171. I feel connected to my baby and my baby feels connected to me.
172. I am strong and ready to give birth to a beautiful healthy baby.
173. My baby is developing into a strong, happy and secure person.
174. My happiness is within my womb and will be here in 9 months.
175. I can endure all and will endure all that comes my way.
176. I look forward to developing a loving relationship with my baby and watching him/her grow to be a successful and happy adult.
177. I will cherish every little toe, finger, bone, face expression, and more.
178. As I care for myself well, I care for my baby well.
179. My soul loves you baby.
180. My baby senses the peace I feel.
181. I maintain peace go myself and my baby. I am the peacekeeper of my life.
182. My baby will find the perfect position for birth.
183. Every week is a step closer to meeting my bundle of joy.

184. I speak loving words to my child and I speak loving words to myself.
185. I am a highly-capable mother-to-be! If there are hard decisions to make, I can and I will make them
186. Everything I need to take care of this baby is already within me.
187. My morning sickness is the overwhelming emotions of happiness my baby has because I am their mother.
188. I am good enough to be the mother this child needs and care for this child within me.
189. The foods I eat are nourishing my child's body.
190. I am a good mother.
191. I conceived this baby in love. I am delivering this baby in love. I will raise this baby with love.
192. I cannot wait to bond with my little one.
193. My body is perfectly capable of nourishing the life within

CHAPTER FIFTEEN

POSITIVE AFFIRMATIONS FOR TOUGH TIMES

1. Regardless of the challenge, I'm creating value in the world through my business.
2. Challenges are opportunities to learn and grow.
3. My bills are paid and I will live freely. I refuse to worry
4. I can get through anything in my life.
5. I will learn what I need to from today which will make me a stronger person.
6. When I have done all I know how to do, I choose to let my mind rest.
7. I know when to persevere along a path and when to let go and change course.
8. Whatever I am going through is guiding me to where I want to go.
9. I create a joyful, peaceful world to live in regardless of the challenges
10. The challenges I face give me energy and purpose.
11. Though these times are difficult, they are only a short phase of life.
12. This business is growing at the right speed for it to become successful.
13. I easily flow with the changes I experience
14. I am safe and secure no matter what.
15. Hard times do not get the best of me.
16. I have the strength and courage to get through any situation.
17. I welcome fear as a sign to be careful, but choose to let go of it when it no longer serves me.

Positive Daily Affirmations

18. My commitment to showing up tomorrow overshadows the mistakes I have made.
19. There are no problems, only challenges.
20. When I have a crisis at work, I remind myself that I earn plenty of money and love what I do.
21. Today, money comes to me effortlessly.
22. I let go of any stress and anxiety from today.
23. I welcome challenges into my life.
24. I can get through anything.
25. I have the ability to overcome any obstacle
26. I know that life is not meant to be easy so I brace myself for the seasons
27. Today may be tough, but tomorrow is a brand new day.
28. I can and will survive anything life throws at me.
29. I am doing what I can with the knowledge and skills I have to survive this.
30. Nothing lasts forever. This experience too will pass
31. I am worthy of love and my life is meaningful despite my losses.
32. I can get through anything.
33. My income is constantly growing. I am not worried
34. I am ready to become the best version of myself.
35. I am getting stronger everyday.
36. I don't have to go this road alone. I have, or can find, people in my life and examples to support and inspire me.
37. I welcome challenges into my life.
38. When circumstances change, I will feel all the more grateful for what I have.
39. I am holding on in the dark to what I know to be true in the light, in better times.
40. I boldly face my fears as courage does not mean having no fear of danger, but facing the danger despite that fear
41. I can solve any problem.

42. Life's problems are not solved by perfect people, but by those who show up. I am someone who shows up.
43. I will not let fear take control of me.
44. I don't have to have this all solved today.
45. I attract financial abundance into my life.
46. I am flexible and can adapt when life doesn't go according to plan.
47. I am doing the best I can, and thus choose to release myself from guilt and shame.
48. Life is full of constant change. My pain, though very real, will not be as acute forever.
49. I am slowly becoming the kind of person who can survive this storm.
50. This is just one chapter in my life's story.
51. I am protected; I am safe
52. The freedom that I gain from running my own business is my biggest reward.
53. There is a huge demand for my particular skills and abilities. I will not be frustrated
54. I am not a burden on anyone as I earn good money and enjoy what I do
55. I know that I deserve love and I accept it even now
56. I am a strong and capable person.
57. I laugh at life and choose not to be offended by anyone or anything
58. My ability to achieve greatness within this challenge is limitless.
59. I am not alone. I make friends easily wherever I go
60. I am not carrying emotional baggage. I release old hurt, resentment and anger easily
61. I forgive myself for past failures.
62. No matter what happens, I am gentle kind and patient with myself
63. I go with the flow, my life is easy and filled with joy

64. The present challenges cannot define me. The past has no power of me
65. Breathing in I am calm. Breathing out I smile. I remain calm
66. Helping others get what they want is the first step in getting what I want.
67. I release all negative emotions from the day.
68. My family's needs are met and more through the work that I'm doing.
69. I am not deterred by the troubles confronting me. My dreams for my business align with my core values in life.
70. On this journey, I trust myself and I trust life
71. No matter what I see in the news, I am safe wherever I turn
72. My success is inevitable if I keep working hard to reach my goals.
73. I am thankful to others who have helped me. I am thankful to myself.
74. The universe sends positive vibes my way
75. My passions sustain me as I'm doing what I love and my income is growing every day.
76. I am a strong person.
77. Today I'm creating opportunities to grow myself and my business. Nothing can hold me down
78. Despite the negative voices, what I'm doing is making a difference in the world.
79. Challenges in business cannot stop me. I am a natural entrepreneur. This is my calling in life.
80. I am filled with joy and ease right now.
81. I am not exhausting myself. The value-generating aspects of my business are where I put my effort.
82. Where others see a challenge, I see new opportunities.
83. I will be proactive in discovering obstacles to my accomplishments.
84. I couple courage and action with high hopes to enjoy the best life possible.

Positive Daily Affirmations

85. I know everything works out for me in the end.
86. I know that my situation right now is temporary and it is only getting better every day.
87. I release all negativity from my life.
88. I am not a failure, but a survivor. I am daily in the process of surviving.
89. I am surrounded by hopeful and positive people.
90. I completely surrender and let go of any illusion about control
91. I desire to learn new things.
92. There is a a plan for my life and this is just something I need to overcome.
93. I can, I will, I must overcome this.
94. I laugh at my feelings of depression which makes them dissipate.
95. I am constantly improving.
96. I know that I will become a stronger version of myself for what I am going through.
97. Time is my friend. I finish all the tasks I need to finish.
98. I choose to completely transcend these feelings of depression.
99. Answers about how to feel better come to me with ease.
100. I am not the only one to have faced this sort of trauma, and I will not be the last.
101. I believe in myself and love myself.
102. This is not the life that is designed for me.
103. I am standing up inside myself for myself
104. I feel heavy feelings lifting.
105. My mind and body feel clear and positive.
106. I choose to be easy on myself.
107. The outer world cannot shake my inner peace. I trust that all is well and everything is working out for my highest and greatest good.
108. I am constantly finding new activities that help me feel positive and motivated.
109. I know that all my wishes are being fulfilled.

Positive Daily Affirmations

110. People support me on my journey and lift up my spirits because they love me.
111. My life gets better everyday
112. I have no fear of asking loved ones to support and help me along my journey.
113. My challenges are real, but I can stay positive through them.
114. God is lifting my depression.
115. Mindfulness will help me get the most from my time.
116. I decide that I can heal myself completely.
117. I take responsibility for my successes and my failures.
118. Everything is temporary. Success is temporary. Failure is temporary.
119. Everything that happens to me is another opportunity to choose love.
120. This too shall pass.
121. No fear can scare me: I am bold!
122. I naturally use my body to counteract feelings of depression. I maintain strong stances that help me feel happy and confident.
123. I will not be discouraged. This is my calling in life.
124. No matter what, I love working. It energizes me and brings me focus.
125. No matter the challenges I face, I remain strong, calm and at peace!
126. I always remain strong
127. I always remain bold
128. andI always remain determined and with faith in my heart!
129. I am a strong person and I go on. I always go on!
130. My life is a bold life!
131. I naturally seek growth and personal development for it makes me feel better and more positive.
132. The success that I want is the natural end of the work that I'm doing.

133. I am the most powerful person I know and nothing slows me down
134. Each minute of my life, I am bold
135. All my wants and needs are being fulfilled by the universe.
136. My passion and my purpose drive me through challenges and towards success.
137. I naturally let go of people aren't contributing to the creation of positive mental health for me.
138. My experiences are bold experiences
139. I feel more and more positive each day.
140. I am a brave person
141. I naturally let go of all negative thoughts that are contributing to my depression.
142. In this economy, my business makes me stronger and happier.
143. There is nothing that I can conceive that I cannot achieve.
144. I have great powers within me
145. I naturally think positive, empowering and uplifting thoughts.
146. I am stronger. I can move mountains.
147. I have the ability to manifest my goals and dreams whenever I choose.
148. I know how to remain bold and unshakable!
149. I am thankful for the lessons life has taught me for they have made me stronger.
150. What I speak comes into fruition into my life, therefore I only speak positively.
151. No situation can come on my way
152. I am transforming my life for the better in every area of my life.
153. My life is made for joy. I will live with exuberance.
154. I completely forgive and love myself in the here and now.
155. I overcome all obstacles

Positive Daily Affirmations

156. I know that I am guided in this life and have faith my life will turn out perfectly.
157. There is nothing I cannot overcome.
158. I easily let go of people who are negative and not supportive.
159. I am not forgotten. My energy attracts the customers and clients that I need to be successful.
160. I have so much value to add and give to the world.
161. I naturally attract more success and happiness every day.
162. I am not dependent on anyone else. But I accept help when it is offered
163. I have hope for a better future.
164. I have what it takes to make my dreams come true.
165. I am likeable and positive.
166. The comeback is always greater than the set back.
167. I am aware that I am the creator of my existence.
168. I know that no challenges is too big for me to take on and triumph over.
169. I always have so much hope.
170. I don't listen or pay attention to negative people and what they say.
171. I feel so positive about the direction my life is going.
172. I follow through and persevere towards my dreams no matter what.
173. I am thankful for the ability to have hope.
174. I let go of all the worries I have for it drains me of vital energy.
175. I have the courage to keep moving forward.
176. I love how my passions give me hope for a better future.
177. I am decisive and always make excellent decisions in these times
178. I have more strength that I know.
179. I attract people into my life that are positive and uplifting.
180. I seek happiness from within.

181. I do not define myself by my diagnosis, it is just an opinion.
182. I feel completely at ease with the world.
183. I feel great in my own skin.
184. I create positive changes in my life with ease.
185. I choose to replace negative thoughts with positive thoughts with ease.
186. I love who I am, completely.
187. Hope is always a solution to all my problems.
188. I have a growth mindset.
189. I am completely renewed with high levels of hope each day.
190. I admit my true feelings. This is not a weakness, it is a strength that simply hasn't been revealed to me yet.
191. I will not be crushed by my circumstances

CHAPTER SIXTEEN

POSITIVE AFFIRMATIONS FOR WEIGHT LOSS

1. I believe I can lose weight
2. My health is the most important thing to me
3. I am avoiding excessive carbs
4. I am happy and grateful to have lost ____ pounds
5. There is no need for rich or sugary foods
6. I have the power to control my weight through healthy eating and exercise
7. My body is a temple. I will keep my temple clean
8. I can go with the flow.
9. My body is my best friend.
10. When I eat well, exercise and get enough sleep, I am investing in myself.
11. I am proud of all my body does for me, every single day.
12. I listen to what my body needs.
13. I do not compare my body to other peoples' bodies.
14. I love what my body is capable of doing now and in the future.
15. I am thankful that my body is both beautiful and strong.
16. I use my body with love, pride and care.
17. I am allowed to have bad days.
18. I am brave to endure days like today.
19. I am patient with and kind to myself.
20. Tomorrow is more than another day; it's another chance to shine.
21. I look forward to feeling better about things again.
22. Life is tough sometimes, but so am I.
23. I am a survivor and that makes me proud of myself.

Positive Daily Affirmations

24. On hard days like this, I love myself more than ever.
25. My bad days and unhappy moments will always pass.
26. I can see the end of this hard time, and I move towards it with every breath I take.
27. I deserve to feel good about myself right now.
28. This positive energy is of my own creating.
29. I am excited by and for life.
30. I savor feeling good about myself.
31. It is important that I take a moment to cherish feeling at peace with myself.
32. These good days feed my soul and help me prepare for harder times.
33. I celebrate myself and what I have achieved today, and every day.
34. The future is bright, and so is the light shining inside me.
35. I aim to share with others the positivity and love I feel for life.
36. I smile with confidence in myself and in the future.
37. I do not have to change for anybody.
38. There is nobody else in the world like me. That is my magic.
39. I am not afraid to be different.
40. I go to bed early so I can wake up rested and strong.
41. I attract nature's limitless abilities to help me alter my current body weight
42. My body can heal and reach new goals, thanks to nature.
43. My body and mind are being restored as excessive and a toxic mindset exits it.
44. I acknowledge that nature has a nutritious healing strength that fills my body and soul.
45. The foods nature provides are transforming my body and making me whole.
46. I recognize that each day in nature is a gift from the universe and try to spend time outdoors.
47. I eat a balanced diet, and exercise daily.
48. I embrace the energy food provides me each day.

Positive Daily Affirmations

49. I completely understand that unhealthy foods do not help me lose weight, so I eat only healthy, nutritious foods.
50. The sounds, smells, and visual aspects of nature have powers that revitalize and promotes health and I am drawn to them.
51. Healing is happening in both my body and mind.
52. I no longer feel the urge to stuff my body with unhealthy foods, and I can easily resist temptations.
53. I am the best version of myself, and I am working hard to become even better. I will lose weight because I want to, and I have the power to do this.
54. I manage stress by doing things that are healthy but effective like taking a warm bath or watching a funny movie.
55. I feel excitement when life brings challenges to me, and I gladly accept them without any guilt or anxiety.
56. I enjoy life by staying fit and maintaining my ideal weight.
57. Being myself is good and rewarding, and I always perceive challenges as opportunities to prove my abilities.
58. I have an appreciation for the great outdoors. This helps my body connect with nature so it can transform.
59. I understand my goals and let go of any negative thought patterns that discourage me from attaining them.
60. Every time I inhale, confidence fills my entire being and every time I exhale, all guilt and shyness get washed away.
61. I always chew my food properly so that my body can digest it and take out the nutrients
62. I am letting go of any guilt I hold around food.
63. I treasure my health and well-being. With a strong body and sound mind, I can take on challenges and fulfill my goals.
64. I have the right mindset. I am a focused person, and I will not quit doing anything when I feel challenged or wronged.
65. I know that I need to lose weight.
66. I acknowledge both my qualities and defects, and I always strive to improve.

67. I set myself free from all the guilt I carry around the food I chose in the past.
68. I choose to accept myself exactly the way I am, and be happy with my life.
69. I am closer and closer to my ideal weight with each and every day.
70. I have a strong urge to eat only healthy foods, and let go of any processed foods.
71. Every day is a new day to begin on a positive and stable foot.
72. I am intensely driven toward achieving my weight loss goal.
73. I believe in my ability to love and accept myself for who I am.
74. I believe in my ability to change my habits and create new, positive ones.
75. I love and embrace the weight loss journey, enjoying every single step of the way.
76. It is perfectly clear to me how all the positives about weight loss outweigh the negative.
77. I dwell on all the long term positive effects that my weight loss will bring me, and it inspires me
78. Every cell in my body is healthy and fit, and so am I.
79. I burn fat with ease.
80. I pay no attention to people telling me my goals aren't possible.
81. My weight goals are achievable because I invoke the power of nature.
82. I always envision myself at my ideal weight.
83. I love the idea of me being at maintaining my perfect body weight with ease.
84. My health is improving more and more every day, and so is my body.
85. I am arriving closer and closer each day to my perfect weight.

Positive Daily Affirmations

86. I feel stronger knowing nature's nutrients are working on my system and mind. I trust in their power to make a difference in my physical condition.
87. All the weight I lose, I lose permanently.
88. I am naturally raising the standard on myself and my health.
89. I can do this, I am doing this, my body is losing weight right now.
90. I give thanks for having a body that is capable of exercising and effectively losing weight.
91. I naturally eat in perfect and proper proportions.
92. Today, I recognize the healing power of nature in my life and feel grateful for this wonderful gift.
93. I easily work my workouts and exercise around my work and life schedule.
94. Every day I am exercising and taking care of my body.
95. I listen to my body when it tells me I need to eat, I do not eat out of boredom.
96. I am so happy and grateful now that I weigh _____ kilograms/pounds.
97. I am fully committed to getting down to my ideal body weight.
98. Nature is activating my body's self-repair mechanisms, so my weight loss goals are easier to achieve.
99. Not only is my health improving, but so is my entire life. And it feels great!
100. I am in complete control of my weight.
101. I am mastering my weight loss and health more and more each day.
102. Weight loss is as easy and natural for me as breathing in and out.
103. I love setting new goals for myself that keep me inspired and motivated to keep going with my weight loss.
104. My body is repairing and rebuilding itself because I embrace the naturally healthy things and this is helping.

105. I am being cleansed and unburdened by nature.
106. I am grateful for this new lifestyle change and love losing weight.
107. My focus and drive never wavers on my weight loss journey.
108. I accept my body exactly the way it is and I constantly work on improving it.
109. I belief in my abilities and know I have what it takes to transform my body and mind.
110. I see food as fuel, not as something to suppress emotions with.
111. I love the journey of health and commit to a lifestyle change, not just a diet plan. It is who I am now and forever.
112. I am closer and closer to my ideal weight with each and every day.
113. I easily let go of relationships that don't benefit my weight loss and health.
114. My metabolism is high and effective at burning fat and helping with weight loss.
115. I feel my desire for unhealthy fat-rich foods dissolving.
116. I enjoy eating healthy foods.
117. I have all the mental and physical power needed for effective and long lasting weight loss.
118. My fat loss is progressing each day, and progress feels so great
119. I feel my body losing weight in every single moment of the day till I hit my goals.
120. I am so thankful that there are so many tools and tips that I can use to get me fit for life.
121. I am becoming more physically active each day.
122. It is safe for me to change my body.
123. I inspire people with my dedication and commitment to fitness and weight loss.

124. Eating healthy foods helps my body get all of the nutrients it needs to be in best shape.
125. Everyone is different and I don't hold any expectations to my weight loss, only that it is and will keep happening.
126. I make choices with ease that support my weight loss journey.
127. I appreciate every single thing I have in my life, and I live in absolute joy.
128. My cardiovascular system is running perfectly, helping me reach my weight loss goals with ease.
129. I commit to loving myself throughout this entire journey.
130. I am capable of achieving my weight loss goals, and I will not let anything stay in my way until then.
131. I am literally watching fat melt of my body, more and more by the day.
132. I am craving healthy and whole foods more and more each day.
133. The whole universe conspires to help me with my weight loss and fat loss.
134. All my feelings and emotions are predicated around my weight loss.
135. I am attaining and maintaining my desired weight.
136. I sink into deep states of sleep and relaxation, helping my body recover perfectly each day.
137. Everything I eat heals and nourishes my body, which helps me reach the ideal weight.
138. My heart and soul is so passionate and driven toward achieving my weight loss goals.
139. I love going to the gym and eating healthy.
140. My body is my temple, and I attentively take care of it every day by eating only healthy foods that heal and nourish me.
141. Each and every cell in me feels healthy and vibrant.

142. I accept myself the way I am, and I am getting better and better in everything I do.
143. Being alive makes me a happy person.
144. I replace "I must," "I have to" and "I should" with "I choose."
145. I am true to my wonderful self.
146. I am loved for who I am right now.
147. In the future, all will be well with my beautiful soul.
148. I trust that I am strong enough to face whatever the future brings.
149. I commit to a new lifestyle that is beneficial not only for weight loss but for higher self confidence and self esteem.
150. I inhale self-confidence and exhale fear and anxiety.
151. I am perfectly full and satisfied with the perfect amount of food I need for fat loss
152. I am grateful to my body for all the things it does for me.
153. I listen to what my body tells me it needs.
154. All the people around me are in complete support of my weight loss.
155. I am aware that my metabolism is working in my advantage by helping me in gaining my optimal weight.
156. I love my body completely right, which helps me in my journey of losing weight.
157. I am fit and confident in my own body. tell my body and mind what to do. Not the other way around.
158. Meeting new people is easy. I can creative supportive relationships and make new friends without feeling anxious.
159. I prioritize working for progress and not perfection.
160. I can trust myself to go through with my weight loss plans
161. My mind is filled with positive thoughts
162. I set realistic but challenging goals for myself that inspire me to lose weight and feel great.
163. I naturally read and watching content that helps me gain knowledge and ideas for effective weight loss.

164. I have the power to easily control my weight through a combination of healthy eating and exercising.
165. Working out comes natural to me.
166. I trust myself, and I have the confidence that I am a worthy person everyone respects.
167. I trust myself fully and completely to make the right choices that create great weight loss.
168. My thoughts are constantly positive and revolve around positive images of me being fit and healthy.
169. I share with people my insights and tips for weight loss as I know they reinforce my new beliefs.
170. It matters little what other people say. What really matters to me is how I react and what I believe in.
171. I am kind, loving, compassionate, and I truly care for the people around.
172. I breathe in relaxation and breathe out stress.
173. I have all that it takes to lose weight and achieve my ideal body weight.
174. I am a confident person who is respected by everyone around.
175. I am a unique and worthy person, and I deserve everyone's respect.
176. I am enthusiastic and energetic, and confidence is an important part of my nature.
177. I respect myself, and so do others around me.
178. I accept myself, and I love myself for who I am.
179. I trust and believe in myself, and I let go of the negative.
180. I thrive on my absolute self-confidence. My body is beautiful, and I enjoy every single thing about it.
181. I deserve all that is good in this world. I release any need for suffering, and I can feel happiness, confidence and love getting into my body, mind, and soul.
182. I never compare myself to others, as I understand my uniqueness.

183. I have integrity, as I am a reliable person and I always do exactly what I say.
184. I am healthy, well-groomed, and good-looking, and I acknowledge both my inner and outer beauty.
185. Every time I inhale, fresh energy fills my entire being and every time I exhale, all toxins and body fat leave my body.
186. Change is inevitable and I accept it wholeheartedly.
187. I am a person who easily accepts new challenges.
188. I deserve good things in my future.
189. I look forward to living tomorrow, and tomorrow's tomorrow.
190. My metabolism rate is at its optimum level, and this helps me reach my ideal body weight.
191. Even in my dreams, ideas and inspiration come to me about weight loss.
192. Sometimes I don't know where I'm going, but I will find my way. And it will be fabulous.

CHAPTER SEVENTEEN

POSITIVE AFFIRMATIONS FOR MANIFESTING DESIRES

1. The Universe always has my back.
2. Opportunities arrive at the right time in the right place
3. Whatever I can conceive, I believe
4. Everything works out perfectly for me. I am creating my dream life.
5. I have a powerful and natural ability to visualize things that I desire
6. Something wonderful is about to happen to me
7. I listen deeply to the goals and dreams that are whispering to me now
8. Miracles manifest everyday in wondrous ways
9. It is ok for me to have everything I want. Every day I move towards having everything I want.
10. I live in the house of my dreams; in tranquil surroundings filled with love, a blessed family and happy kids
11. I am a master of converting the energy of my dreams into fuel for powerful action
12. Whenever I breathe, I inhale health and exhale misery. I attract a wonderful life.
13. I am worthy of receiving my yes. I now release everything that is not serving my highest purpose.
14. I am worthy enough to follow my greatest dreams and manifest my deepest desires
15. I always think about the other person first. Hence, my relationships are safe and secure.
16. If I see it in my mind, I am going to hold it in my hand.

Positive Daily Affirmations

17. I am worthy of love, abundance, success, happiness and fulfillment.
18. I now release any fears or limiting beliefs I may have about achieving my yes.
19. There is no place for negative self-talk in my life. I am completely and utterly in love with myself.
20. Always possibility, never lack
21. My higher self rules over my ego.
22. I am creating my dream life, and everything works out perfectly for me
23. My inner home is a peaceful retreat, a storehouse of practical wisdom.
24. I am worthy enough to follow my dreams and manifest my desires.
25. I effortlessly and frequently visualize living my life exactly as I desire
26. I use visualization to reprogram my subconscious
27. Increasingly confident in my ability to create the life I desire.
28. I am acting on inspiration and insights and I trust my inner guidance.
29. I don't play small, I refuse to.
30. I open myself to receiving abundance of the Universe.
31. I have the Midas touch, everything I touch turns to gold.
32. I work where I want, when I want and with people I want to work with.
33. I attract people into my life that help me do big things
34. I set big goals and make a plan for how I am going to accomplish them.
35. When my "why" is strong and clear enough, my "how" appears easily and instantly
36. I always radiate thoughts about my dreams and that helps me attract people and events necessary to achieve them.
37. I celebrate life

Positive Daily Affirmations

38. I have the traits, qualities and mindset to achieve great things in this life.
39. The universe is conspiring on how to bring massive wealth and abundance into my life.
40. I have all that I need right now and keep getting more.
41. Today, inspiration flows easily to me
42. I feel abundant in the here and now.
43. There is nothing in this life I cannot have.
44. I am generous. I help those in need
45. I am attracting prosperity now in expected and unexpected ways.
46. I have unlimited potential.
47. The Universe provides me with all that I will ever need.
48. I understand that giving is as important as receiving and I constantly strive to contribute as much as I can.
49. I am abundant in my finances, in happiness, and in love.
50. I believe in myself fully
51. I find myself in situations and with people who are going to add more to my net worth.
52. My body will feel strong, capable and competent all day.
53. I will set new and inspiring goals today.
54. I am richly blessed.
55. I will find laughter and humor today.
56. I will accept every single person and situation today as is.
57. I surround myself with positive and genuine people who help me and encourage me to reach my goals.
58. I enjoy absolute freedom
59. My confidence is growing more and more each day.
60. The universe has my back
61. I trust the Universe. It gives me exactly what I need at exactly the right time.
62. I am creating a life of passion and purpose.
63. I am love.
64. My attitude will be positive and empowering all day.

Positive Daily Affirmations

65. I have the power to choose my emotional state and I choose a beautiful, happy and successful state ...always
66. Every day I am moving towards my best life.
67. I will attract success and love wherever I go today.
68. I inhale trust and exhale fear
69. My business gets better and better every day.
70. I welcome this day with open arms and thankfulness.
71. I follow bliss. I experience bliss. I am bliss.
72. What I desire and what I ask for is fueled by an unlimited and unwavering belief in myself
73. I step out of my comfort zone to achieve my goals. I find comfort in change and new
74. I will see old relationships get strengthened today and new relationships come into existence today.
75. Everyday I am moving toward my best life
76. New and deeper love will come into my life today.
77. I am One with Spirit
78. My body and mind will overflow with positive energy all day today.
79. I do not believe in rejections, only divine redirections
80. I love myself. I support myself. I believe in myself.
81. Each of my body is awake and charged for a great day.
82. I love myself. I support myself. I believe in myself.
83. I know exactly what I want and constantly remind myself about my goals.
84. My spirit dances in step with joy in my heart.
85. I am divinely guided in all that I do.
86. My intentions are clear, powerful and in complete alignment with my life purpose
87. I use the power of visualization to manifest the life I want
88. I am receiving infinite, inexhaustible and immediate abundance.
89. What I seek is seeking me

Positive Daily Affirmations

90. I think power thoughts! I take power action! I achieve power results
91. I am smart, creative, and motivated. I only take yes for an answer.
92. I have share in the vision of my community and I serve the community with love
93. I am willing to believe that by focusing on feeling good, I make better choices that lead to desired results.
94. I am whole and in perfect health
95. Everything feels so right, and I trust I am on the right path
96. I am wealthy and prosperous in every aspect of my life.
97. I experience the world in all its glory.
98. I am willing to believe that by raising my vibration, I will attract more of what I desire.
99. I constantly think about the thing that I want to attract and this constant thinking attracts the desired thing into my life.
100. I am receiving abundance now in expected and unexpected ways.
101. I am giving and receiving all that is good and all that I desire.
102. Every cell in my body vibrates with health and positive energy.
103. I am attracting more and more wealth and success into my life each day.
104. Whatever I can unify in my mind and my heart I can manifest in my world
105. I am confident of my ability to create the life of my desire and am constantly at it.
106. My life unfolds beautifully before me as I navigate my path with grace and ease
107. My teachers and mentors inspire me to live in the now
108. Each one of my pores radiates with abundance.
109. I transform my mind with the power of visualization
110. I see beauty everywhere I go.

111. I am completely worth of all the good things that life has to offer.
112. I attract an abundance of love and happiness in my current and new relationships.
113. Money and success come into my life so easily and naturally.
114. I am constantly striving to raise my vibration through good thoughts, words and actions.
115. My soul is ready to live the life of my dreams.
116. I attract the life of my desires. I take whatever action necessary for the same.
117. I have deep courage to walk my own path and follow my dreams
118. I am completely ready for my life to overflow with abundance.
119. Each and every day provides me with the perfect mix of sun and rain to grow my dreams into realities
120. In my mind's eye, I see a new and vibrant life for me and attract that life for me.
121. Faith in my future lifts me higher than fear
122. All the pieces of my life are falling perfectly into place now
123. I am constantly and unwaveringly thinking about my goals and thereby attracting them.
124. My life has massive meaning and I am working on leaving a huge legacy.
125. Today is a great day it is to be alive
126. Beauty is the breath of my soul.
127. My dreams correspond to my beliefs and my life corresponds to my dreams.
128. I am creating my life according to my dominant beliefs; and I AM improving the quality of those beliefs.
129. My intentions for my life are clear. What I am seeking is seeking me.

130. I am making a meaningful contribution to the world and I AM wonderfully compensated for my contribution.
131. I am financially wealthy
132. I am attracting all the abundance I desire, fulfilling all my wishes
133. I understand that I and only I am responsible for the quality of my life.
134. I am willing to believe that I am the creator of my life's experiences.
135. I am powerful.
136. My constant thoughts and subsequent actions create my life experiences.
137. My positive attitude always attracts success in whatever endeavour I undertake.
138. I will find adventure in the day today.
139. I will make the best choices today
140. I am a magnet to happiness. I only attract cheerful and happy people in my life.
141. Checks arrive in my inbox every single day.
142. I open myself up to all the wealth and happiness life has to offer.
143. My wisdom will grow today.
144. My gut feeling and the inner guidance that I receive help me inch towards my goal.
145. I am grateful for all that is and all that will be.
146. My wealth grows in ever increasing amounts.
147. I am going to get so much done today.
148. My food and physical activity is such that I attract the best of health.
149. I will manage my time perfectly today.
150. I have developed the habit of feeling good under any circumstances as this helps me in seeing life in a different perspective.
151. I love my blessings

152. I am grateful for_____
153. I greet today with gratitude.
154. I am limitless in my ability to have the things I want in this life.
155. I deserve success, prosperity and happiness and I attract them all.
156. I greet today with excitement and confidence.
157. I attract love everywhere
158. My dreams are much bigger and greater than my fears.
159. I weigh _____ pounds/kgs. And I am happy with it
160. I am always climbing higher and higher in every area of my life.
161. I feel healthy and strong.
162. My life is one big adventure
163. I am surrounded by people who want the best for me and are going to push me to reach my goals and dreams.
164. I am the creator of my own existence and today I choose to create miracles in my life.
165. My mind is completely clear of self doubt, I have unshakable belief in myself.
166. My soul is ready to manifest and live the life of my dreams
167. I am at peace with the world and the world is at peace with me.
168. I will find success and meaning today.
169. My relationships are harmonious
170. I attract positive circumstances and positive people into my life.
171. I trust my journey.
172. My business is a resounding success
173. I am the greatest.
174. I work as and when I want to, anywhere I want to
175. My dreams are coming alive today
176. I am a skilled communicator and I convey my ideas easily. That helps me attract the desired people in my life.

Positive Daily Affirmations

177. My life plays put the way I have envisioned it
178. Today will be a peaceful day.
179. I am exceptionally good at pursuing my dreams
180. I choose to dwell in the realm of possibilities
181. My life is rich and colorful
182. My dreams are manifesting in many ways
183. My success is known in many lands
184. I have witnessed so many personal miracles and I am in a constant state of awe
185. I am doing more than thriving
186. Today, I step into a protective bubble of positivity
187. My life is good
188. I have a wealth of fond memories
189. I can. I will. End of story.
190. My prayers are always answered, in support of my dreams
191. I have the visual insight to see the future that I desire

CHAPTER EIGHTEEN

POSITIVE AFFIRMATIONS FOR MEDITATIONS

1. My mind is clear and focused
2. I can let go of my thoughts at will
3. I value the art of listening.
4. In silent meditation, I can hear the voice of the divine, the beauty of nature, and my own subconscious.
5. A quiet mind brings me peace and happiness.
6. Meditation helps me to see my world and my choices more realistically.
7. My mind is calm even in chaotic times.
8. I monitor my self talk.
9. Kind and loving thoughts guide my speech and actions.
10. Loving others reduces stress in my life
11. I am free from stress and worry
12. If I become tense or irritated, I use my breath to restore my loving thoughts.
13. I look at the world around me and can't help but smile and feel joy.
14. I cherish myself as I breathe in. I cherish others as I breathe out.
15. I admire the good qualities of others.
16. I see that the happiness of others is just as important as my own.
17. By allowing myself to be happy, I inspire others to be happy as well.
18. I refuse to listen to the inner voice that tells me to be afraid.
19. I have the power to stop fear before it takes over.
20. I can tap into a wellspring of inner happiness anytime I wish.

Positive Daily Affirmations

21. My body is relaxed and calm
22. I have a peaceful mind
23. By listening carefully, I learn about myself and the world around me.
24. I feel joy and contentment at this moment right now.
25. I recognize how much I have in common with others.
26. I am happy to accommodate others.
27. Fear is an illusion in the mind, and I know I can overcome it.
28. I listen more than I talk.
29. Loving others strengthens my relationships.
30. I put together a list of all of my fears so I can be on the lookout for them and stop them in their tracks.
31. I am at peace within myself
32. My mind is naturally calm and tranquil
33. Through meditation, I gain insights into my thoughts and behavior.
34. I feel at peace even if things turn out differently than I had planned.
35. If people are discussing something sensitive and I am there, I choose a quiet place and time.
36. I can let go of my fears.
37. I am grateful for my education and health care.
38. My mind is strong and able to see beyond a moment of fear.
39. I may disagree with some of what I hear, but I know that someone may need a chance to express themselves without being judged.
40. If I am unclear about a message, I paraphrase the words of others and ask clarifying questions.
41. I am detached from everything
42. I can detach from all concerns and worries
43. Listening is one way of expressing my concern and respect for others.
44. I appreciate people in the service industry

45. I appreciate the workers who build roads and supply electricity.
46. I clear my mind with meditation and prayer.
47. I recognize my talents and pursue my dreams regardless of any fears that may arise.
48. To generate loving thoughts, I focus on my family and friends.
49. Today, I am free. Free to go after my dreams.
50. Today, I gather information to make sounder decisions.
51. I am committed to my meditation practice
52. My meditation practice is an important part of my life
53. Regardless of my expertise on any topic, I can give someone my attention.
54. My mind is open to the truth about self-imposed limits.
55. I accept that I may sometimes feel uneasy or irritable, but I choose constructive actions that enable me to regain my composure quickly.
56. I avoid creating boundaries for my spirit.
57. Instead of allowing my fears to be in charge, I control my body and mind.
58. I have fun with all of my endeavors, even the most mundane.
59. Fear is an illusion.
60. I leave fears behind and let my creativity blossom.
61. I meditate deeply
62. Meditation comes naturally to me
63. Lending my ear helps me to connect with friends, family, and coworkers on a deeper level.
64. I choose to reduce stress
65. I can avoid panic because I know I am strong and powerful.
66. My mind is a unique vessel that functions without fear.
67. Fear is one of these limits, but I am stronger than the illusion.
68. I am thankful for the kindness of people
69. I am free from the illusion that tries to make me afraid.

Positive Daily Affirmations

70. During difficult times, I listen to my intuition and follow its advice.
71. My mind is at ease
72. Releasing mental tension feels nice
73. I use my ears more than my mouth.
74. I discover more opportunities for building relationships.
75. Remaining calm builds up my strength and confidence.
76. I have the freedom to create the life I desire.
77. I reveal my vulnerabilities.
78. Loving thoughts fill my mind.
79. My intuition guides me to the answers to my issues.
80. I view others with compassion and affection.
81. My thoughts are quiet
82. Meditation improves my health and well-being
83. My ability to listen attentively grows stronger with practice
84. To still my mind, I slow down.
85. My faith in my abilities stabilizes me.
86. Meditation provides calm and clear instructions for action.
87. I stay calm.
88. I choose words that are encouraging and cheerful.
89. I manage my emotions.
90. I find joy and pleasure in the most simple things in life.
91. I am focused on the present moment
92. Mental serenity is mine
93. I hear others out instead of rehearsing what I want to say next.
94. Meditation is a powerful assistant on my journey to happiness.
95. Daily meditations enhances my physical and mental health.
96. I accept feedback graciously.
97. I have a relaxing routine. I take a long walk or a warm bath. I turn off my phone and savor the silence.
98. I remember the good things that people contribute to my life.
99. Downtime makes me more effective.

100. I know the difference between my intuition's voice and my mind's general voice.
101. I will let go of all worries
102. I am naturally gifted at meditation
103. I note two sides of an issue and meditate it over before making decisions
104. I focus on my intuition for guidance.
105. I teach myself to be brave by proving that I can cope with whatever comes my way.
106. I take a step back from the daily rush and collect my thoughts.
107. I step away briefly from a difficult situation to evaluate it.
108. I am able to hear my intuition speak during difficult times.
109. Today, I rejoice in feeling at peace.
110. During meditation, my intuition is given the chance to find answers.
111. My mind is becoming quiet and relaxed
112. During conversations, I avoid interrupting.
113. I reconnect with nature and my friends to help me examine tough situations.
114. I pay attention to my gut feelings and listen to my intuition talk.
115. I face challenges head on and seek solutions calmly
116. Today, I intend to focus on the power of my intuition in a challenging situation.
117. My victories and setbacks become more meaningful because I go through them with family and friends.
118. I am sensitive to the needs of others.
119. I avoid allowing fear to paralyze my intuition or be in charge because I maintain control of challenging situations.
120. I acknowledge all of my feelings, and then focus on the wise whisperings of my inner guide.
121. I am releasing the tension from my body
122. Today, I listen deeply and effectively.

123. My intuition provides valuable lessons about the past, present, and future.
124. Today, I offer my good wishes and practical assistance to those around me.
125. I know the steps I need to take to find success and happiness.
126. My intuition supports me on this journey.
127. If my performance is criticized, I use their feedback to excel the next time.
128. I notice the needs of others and empathize with them in their struggles.
129. I make people feel comfortable as they share their challenges.
130. I surround myself with positive energy.
131. I will focus my mind on the present moment
132. I show my respect and appreciation for others, and gain greater knowledge and wisdom for myself.
133. I love when the energy around me is positive.
134. Meditation makes me feel able to accomplish all I set out to do.
135. I am an observant listener. I pay attention to the tone and voice of the participants during the conversation.
136. Discussions with my friends cover thoughts and plans for a fulfilling future.
137. I make it a point to understand the needs of my family, coworkers, friends, and strangers.
138. I focus on my breath and allow deep breathing to soothe me.
139. I expand my own support group as I support others.
140. Today, I focus on the needs of others. In return, they do the same for me.
141. My meditation practice is improving
142. Today, I also work at listening even when I am alone.

143. I listen to my friends' stories and communicate my concern.
144. Joyfully, my network of friends becomes a circle of love.
145. I help people. I lend a listening ear, offer a shoulder to cry on, and do whatever I can to uplift them.
146. I relax my body and tune out distractions.
147. I notice the minor details while friends talk. This helps me provide wise advice for their situations.
148. I am generous. I share my time and resources freely when they need help.
149. I treat people with kindness and help them work on solutions for a brighter future.
150. I go in search of people, things, and places that exude that positivity and encouragement.
151. I will meditate every day
152. My loved ones know that they can always count on me.
153. Today, I pledge to play my part in bringing positive energy to all situations.
154. I am sensitive to my loved ones' emotional states.
155. When I focus on others, I feel at peace.
156. I understand how to comfort and support people.
157. Positive energy motivates me to achieve important personal objectives.
158. I am full of love and compassion, so my friends know they can turn to me.
159. My commitment to bright and cheery living comes across in all my interactions. I am a positive being.
160. Meditation builds my confidence and willingness to embrace other people's viewpoint.
161. My mind is becoming highly focused and perfectly calm
162. I know I am unable to completely eliminate negativity, but I avoid encouraging it.
163. Whenever I am able to pacify a situation, I take action to calm things down.

Positive Daily Affirmations

164. At times my workplace can be contentious. I remind myself to stay away from conflict.
165. My friendships are based on healthy and supportive communication.
166. It is much easier to focus on my responsibilities when I avoid negative energy.
167. I refrain from judging or criticizing and listen to people with an open heart.
168. The bond I share with my friends helps me to think optimistically.
169. I know that team work produces better results when everyone is on the same page so I encourage it.
170. The positive influence of people sparks ideas.
171. I am finding it easier to detach from my thoughts
172. Meditation helps me to make the most of my opportunities
173. I open my heart before I open my mouth.
174. My sincerity shines in my words
175. I express my true feelings.
176. Today, I practice sincerity. I speak my mind with love
177. I recognize the positive actions and personality traits of others
178. I follow through on what I promise.
179. My words and actions show my friends and family that I am there for them. I listen patiently and validate their experiences
180. I balance criticism with compliments and ask coworkers for their suggestions.
181. I will release all stress and tension when I meditate
182. I live up to my commitments.
183. I earn the trust of others.
184. I provide comfort.
185. I create a calm environment before I deliver criticism that could be difficult to hear.
186. I share constructive feedback.

187. I let my family and friends know how much they mean to me.
188. I focus on collaboration and helping others to enhance their performance.
189. I awaken in the morning feeling happy and enthusiastic about life.
190. I align my mind and thoughts with the intentions of my deepest being
191. Meditation is becoming easier every time I practice

CHAPTER NINETEEN

POSITIVE AFFIRMATIONS FOR BIRTHDAYS

1. Today is the first day of the rest of my life
2. Today, I am worthy and deserving of good things
3. Love is everywhere, and I am loving and lovable.
4. I am a radiant being of love.
5. Today and every day, I do at least one thing that stretches me
6. Struggle is my boot camp preparing for bigger and better things
7. Today I am attracting the people, places, and things that are perfect for my growth
8. Each and every day I reach deeper levels of self-realization.
9. Today what serves me stays and what fails me goes
10. I now see that roadblocks are simply shortcuts to something better than I had planned
11. I am joyous and happy and free.
12. Today I live with a purpose and my purpose lights my path
13. I enter into this new life with ease
14. I trust the process of life to bring me my highest good
15. The obstacles on my path are there to build my strength and understanding.
16. I am a work in progress, but what a work I am!
17. I refuse settle for where I am, when I know I have better within me
18. Today I am taking one step beyond where I have gone before! In no time at all, I'll be far down the road
19. My purpose is to learn to love unconditionally.
20. Today, I love and accept myself exactly as I am.
21. Today, what matters is who I am not who I've been

Positive Daily Affirmations

22. My way forward is paved with the strength of an open heart and the power of an open mind.
23. I experience love wherever I go in this new year
24. Today I am the acorn courageously engaged in the process of becoming the oak
25. I am stronger, wiser and more confident with each new day.
26. I am the captain of my ship. I choose how my days and life unfold.
27. I am now very well organized.
28. I bring my best game to all I do.
29. I now create a wonderful new life
30. I allow myself to receive.
31. My limits yesterday are my starting point today
32. I believe in my talents and skills to make things better wherever I go.
33. Today old paradigms are falling as I find new and better ways to live
34. I am filled with love and affection.
35. My consciousness always expands to embrace the opportunities and challenges in my life
36. Every challenge has called on me to be a better, stronger person and today I am
37. Today I release older lesser versions of myself and grow into my greatness
38. I am in the process of positive changes.
39. I am the best I have ever been
40. I give myself completely to my purpose and my purpose gives me completely to success and happiness.
41. Today I am building bridges from the world that is to the world I choose
42. . I face this challenge with strength and know that I will get through this.
43. In this new life, I flow with life easily and effortlessly.
44. I am following my bliss to inspire others.

Positive Daily Affirmations

45. This season, I pursue my goals with diligence and determination.
46. I have decided that I will enjoy every moment of my life.
47. I intend to live this day to the fullest and practice gratitude.
48. I have a wonderful new relationship with myself
49. I thrive on every opportunity to become more than I have ever been before
50. I now begin a project that will change my life forever – I am unstoppable
51. I pursue peace in all of my relationships.
52. I now move to a better place.
53. I am looking forward to the bright future God has planned for me.
54. I am totally healthy and I am grateful
55. I have the perfect living space.
56. Today I am aware of my desires and intend to pursue them.
57. I declare that I am courageous and brave.
58. Today I exchange my need to always be right for my need to always be growing.
59. I am in a joyous relationship with a partner who deeply loves me.
60. Playing it safe keeps me safe from every dream I have. Today I take risks for my reward
61. I am at peace with others and myself.
62. I go to God first and He directs my steps.
63. I release myself of anger, hate and bitterness – I am free
64. I appreciate all that I do.
65. I have a happy body that pleases me.
66. I choose peace in this situation – I am responsible for my emotions.
67. I embrace fear and self-doubt, not letting anything stop me from what I want.
68. Today I am planting the seeds of growth in my life. I am absolutely committed to watering them every day.

69. Today, I pay attention to my inner longings and act on them.
70. My life is filled with one positive experience after another. I make use of every experience in my growth.
71. I forgive myself from past errors
72. With each breath I take, I feel deeply at peace.
73. Bring the rain. I'm eager to grow! Bring the sunshine. I'm ready to bloom
74. I am co-creating my destiny with my inner wisdom and the universe.
75. Even as I stretch and strive to be who I can be, I am happy with who I am now!
76. I am in love with myself. I love my hair/ nose/ body.
77. This change comes right on time and is exactly what I needed.
78. I use my talents and skills to fulfill my purpose in life.
79. Each and ever day I learn new lessons, expand my awareness, and develop my abilities.
80. I love and accept myself.
81. Today, my thanksgiving extends far beyond my thoughts; I bring a grateful spirit to each step and action I take.
82. I trust myself to be better
83. I may not live forever, but today I strive for better
84. I am eternally young. In mind and body
85. I am grateful now, and that is keeping the door open for more blessings.
86. The universe supports my success
87. Wealth is now my portion. I am prosperous.
88. Today I am the person I came to the planet to be
89. I am on the path to achieving my goals.
90. There is the life that I live and the life that I want. Today I am taking action to bring them into alignment
91. I radiate acceptance.
92. I stand up for myself by saying how I truly feel with kindness.
93. I am my own person.

Positive Daily Affirmations

94. The summit of every success is the foot stool for my next success
95. I thrive on every opportunity to become more than I have ever been before
96. My body is beautiful
97. I now step out of my comfort zone to become the person I believe I can be.
98. Today I'm strong and I understand
99. I feel secure in myself. I am safe.
100. Today I make the most of who I am and what I have to become who I can be
101. Today I am working consciously toward a greater opening of my heart and my mind.
102. Today I am entering new and exciting realms in my life
103. I am strong, courageous and worthy of all good things.
104. I am grateful for my life, the people in it and all that is possible for me.
105. I am full of peace, love and happiness.
106. Every weakness I think I have is an angel whispering, "grow, grow.
107. Everything that happens in my life perfectly prepares me to fulfill my purpose
108. I am ready to make positive change.
109. Today I open my heart to others by seeing the good in them.
110. This week I am breaking new ground in my life and it feels great
111. The past is a blessing because it is my teacher. The future is a blessing because it is my opportunity.
112. I take daily action on things that matter to me.
113. Day by day and thought by thought, I am creating my ideal life
114. Today, I am overflowing with joy, love and gratitude.
115. I celebrate all that is right in the world

116. Today I am liberating myself from the shadows of my past. A bright new day dawns for me
117. New and exciting opportunities are ahead of me – I am creating my destiny.
118. I breathe good thoughts in and breathe bad thoughts out.
119. I release old habits that are limiting my potential.
120. I am grateful for all the good that surrounds me – I attract goodness
121. I am letting go of what I cannot change.
122. Today, I am thankful.
123. I am grateful for the helpful guides that sometimes appear in disguise to usher me back to love.
124. I let go of fear of the past and embrace love and joy the present
125. I forgive myself and release my past.
126. Today I release old habits and blaze new trails
127. In my life, I'm willing to see beauty where others see nothing; I can look beyond a rock and uncover the diamond.
128. I am ready for a healthy, loving and lasting relationship.
129. Today I am aligned with energies that heal my past and grow my future.
130. I am starting fresh by forgiving this person.
131. I deserve love, trust and peace in my life.
132. I forgive for a better life.
133. I struggle, but I grow. I fall, but I get up. Even amid adversity, I succeed and I prosper
134. I give and receive love openly and freely.
135. I welcome all of the ways the universe wants to bless me.
136. On this day, I shine the light of appreciation on an otherwise dark situation; there is no darkness that can escape that light for long.
137. I am brave enough to ask the universe for the life I desire
138. I radiate confidence in all I do

Positive Daily Affirmations

139. Henceforth, I choose to be kind to everyone I encounter – I am kind.
140. I am creating the best possible life for myself and those I love.
141. Today, I can be anything I wish to be.
142. I inspire people with my kind words and actions.
143. I am the master of my destiny
144. I exude kindness and love in my heart.
145. By releasing what is, I open the door for something better
146. Today and every day, I am on a heroic journey from where I am to where I am destined to be
147. I create my own life everyday and I work hard to create a life full of growth and expansion.
148. Abundance comes to me because I am grateful.
149. Today is a new chapter and a fresh start.
150. Each day is a new opportunity to be amazing.
151. I am a magnet for good and for that good... I am grateful.
152. I will create the life that I desire.
153. I am eternally grateful for the love I am capable of giving, and for the love I have yet to receive.
154. I choose to be thankful for the light of this new morning, and for renewed energy and strength to be who I know I can be.
155. This new year, I accept my burdens an I accept my blessings, and so I transform my burdens into my blessings.
156. I partner with peace today, and I do this through the power of keeping a grateful heart.
157. I am willing to trust that my life is exactly as it's meant to be.
158. I choose to see this season of my life, then, through the eyes of appreciation, as best as I can.
159. Whatever has happened, and whatever does happen, I'm certain that I can be grateful again.

Positive Daily Affirmations

160. This year, my thanksgiving is going to be perpetual; it survives every obstacle because I am willing to keep it alive.
161. I am learning to be grateful for what I have while being excited for what has yet to come.
162. I let go of negative confrontations. I choose to see peace instead.
163. I feel profound gratitude for all I am and all I have.
164. Today, my gratitude is an absolute magnet for the manifestation of all that I want
165. I am willing to trust that my life is exactly as it's meant to be.
166. Regardless of whatever I see, I trust that the universe is supporting my highest good.
167. I know gratitude is a daily choice and today, I choose to be grateful.
168. I can relax a little and be thankful for what I have now.
169. Gratitude opens the door for my essence to flow through my life, and spirit blessings to
170. Today marks the beginning of a new dispensation in my life
171. I fully accept the joy that wants to surface in my life, and I accept it now in gratitude.
172. I just feel grateful this morning.
173. I am attracting good into my life.
174. I am grateful and thankful for all goodness God has given me.
175. Starting today, my daily attitude is one of gratitude.
176. I give thanks daily for blessings that flow into my life.
177. For the rocks and the diamonds, I am thankful, because life is a rich experience that includes everything.
178. I am grateful for my life and growing consciousness within it
179. I realize that I am blessed in so many ways and am deeply grateful

180. I am feeling that I have a grateful heart.
181. The feeling of gratefulness expands my perspective and opens me up to new ways of living happily in this world; it's as if the whole universe is in my heart.
182. I am grateful.
183. The more grateful I am, the more blessed I am.
184. My soul continuously rejoices and unites with my experience as I engage in gratitude.
pour into all that I choose to create.
185. I see abundance all around me. I am grateful.
186. I see the benefits of gratitude. I now immerse in gratitude and cultivate it as a habit.
187. I am grateful for my health.
188. I am shining brighter and brighter unto perfection
189. This year, I am doing great exploits
190. I rise triumphantly with grace
191. By my gratitude, I am close to the source of abundance.

CHAPTER TWENTY

POSITIVE AFFIRMATIONS FOR THE TRAVELLER

1. I enjoy peace and tranquility on my dream holiday.
2. I am taking a trip to the most amazing holiday destination in the world.
3. I am constantly marveling at the worlds many wonders.
4. Incredible things are headed my way.
5. I deserve the happiness that this new start offers to me.
6. I am grateful for the opportunity to travel the world.
7. I will create sunshine for the joy of others.
8. I always spread joy and love wherever I go.
9. I am lucky for the opportunity of a fresh start, full of love and laughter.
10. The best is yet to come.
11. I attract the vacation of my dreams.
12. There is no limit to what I can do or to the love I can receive.
13. My bags are packed and I am ready to go.
14. I live and breathe excitement and seek out new experiences.
15. I release harmful thoughts of my past and look to the future with excitement.
16. I am in charge of the trajectory of my adventurous spirit.
17. I visit lands far and wide while discovering the world.
18. Through travel, I learn to embrace happiness in the largest and smallest of places.
19. I am happy with the me I am right now in this moment.
20. I face the challenges of today with a positive and cheerful spirit.
21. The perfect trip away is within my grasp.
22. Money for travel flows into my life effortlessly.

Positive Daily Affirmations

23. I walk into this situation expecting love and openness.
24. I am the happiest I have ever been.
25. I am open to receiving an abundance of love and wild adventure.
26. Taking time out for rest and relaxation at a beautiful resort is where I am meant to be.
27. The more love I give to my endeavors, the more I receive.
28. I sail the deepest oceans and fly over the highest mountains to reach my dream destination.
29. I am so grateful for the opportunity of knowing a new home.
30. I invite new opportunities into my life.
31. I visualize my dream holiday every day.
32. I am prepared to prosper beyond my wildest dreams.
33. I enjoy the company of my loved ones while enjoying my dream vacation.
34. I appreciate my abundant life.
35. I am a magnet for new journeys and adventures.
36. My desire for new experiences inspires others to break free.
37. My getaway is calling me closer each and every day.
38. I am open and willing for new adventures.
39. I give back to the world as love flows into me.
40. Every day holds new opportunities for great things to happen.
41. A fabulous vacation is being drawn toward me.
42. I feel grateful to be able to manifest my dream vacation.
43. Travel teaches me to look on the bright side.
44. Today, I am grateful for all the good things in my life and for those yet to come.
45. Travel makes everything seem
46. Today I choose to let go of all past negative influences.
47. I have unlimited choices.
48. I am the energy that I wish to attract.
49. Travel fills my days with laughter.
50. I find pleasure in the hidden and most secret of places.
51. My dream vacation is on its way.

52. I am grateful for this journey. I am enough, and I have enough.
53. I wake up in a new place joyful and inspired to make this day great.
54. The universe provides me with unlimited resources to be able to travel where I want and when I want on my dream vacation.
55. I am grateful for every single one of my adventures and opportunities to grow.
56. I am free to design the life of my dreams, and my imagination knows no limits.
57. I live life to the fullest.
58. The past holds no power over me.
59. I welcome adventure into my life.
60. I greet all life with love in my heart.
61. I indulge in luxury relaxation packages while on my dream vacation.
62. Travel cultivates cheer in me every day.
63. I have all that I need and more.
64. I am open to new and exciting adventures.
65. Travel makes me an optimist.
66. I create the life I deserve.
67. I ask, I believe, I receive.
68. I am surrounded by beauty.
69. Every day in every way, travel is making me happier and happier.
70. Travel makes me radiate positive energy.
71. I am waking up to another relaxing day in paradise.
72. I am worthy of everything good that comes my way and I will accept it with gratitude.
73. I am grateful and open to the abundances of the universe.
74. I attract success and wild adventure.
75. My dream holiday destination draws closer to me each and every day.

76. My heart seeks a journey.
77. Travel helps me to inhale with positivity and peace and exhale negative thoughts.
78. The universe will provide me with adventure and love.
79. Others are attracted to my adventurous spirit.
80. My world is brimming over with joy and love.
81. My energetic signature is an exact match with a wonderful holiday.
82. I allow the abundance of the universe to flow through me.
83. I am worthy of adventure and love in all its forms.
84. I visualize unpacking my bags in the most beautiful location in the world.
85. I simply decide to be excited for the day.
86. I celebrate this life
87. I commit myself to take well deserved holidays often.
88. I always have what I need when I need it in my adventurous heart.
89. All of my dreams are coming true.
90. I am expanding on my cultural awareness while discovering the world.
91. I invest in myself wholeheartedly.
92. The stresses of life all melt away when I vacay in paradise.
93. I graciously accept gifts of the universe with gratitude.
94. I am flying to faraway lands full of excitement.
95. My gratitude knows no limit.
96. I was born to fulfill my travel dreams.
97. A well-deserved break leaves me feeling rested and renewed.
98. The universe loves to show me it's beautiful landscape as I travel around the globe.
99. I am allowed to prosper and accept abundance into my world.
100. As I allow more abundance and love into my life, more doors will open for me.
101. I am jet-setting around the globe.
102. Wealth of the world flows freely into my life.

103. I am creating a life of adventure and happiness.
104. I will not be limited.
105. My happiness grounds me and I allow my fears to drift away.
106. Something incredible is going to happen to me on this trip
107. I visualize eating at the finest restaurants while on my dream holiday.
108. I attract positive events and opportunity into my life.
109. I am carving out the wild and true lifestyle I desire.
110. A river of perfect wealth always runs toward me, washing over me.
111. I am grateful for this journey and the exquisite beauty it brings to my life.
112. I know everything will work out how it should.
113. The downtime I deserve is granted to me in the form of a beautiful getaway
114. Adventure makes me strong and peaceful.
115. I am the architect of my travel fortune.
116. Travel teaches me courage and to embrace my vulnerability.
117. I enjoy sightseeing while taking amazing trips to exotic land.
118. My journeys are always safe, relaxing and enjoyable experiences.
119. I am so very full of peace and gratitude for this journey.
120. I am an adventurous spirit who experiences the Earth's wonders daily.
121. I enjoy plenty of spending money while on holiday in my dream destination.
122. I am so very full of peace and gratitude for this journey.
123. I feel fulfilled for I am certain that all my travel desires are being met.
124. I am deeply fortunate to be in the position to travel.
125. I deserve a long break away from work.

Positive Daily Affirmations

126. I am a traveler.
127. My spirit is pure adventure.
128. The path that I take today leads me to a place of fulfillment and greatness

CHAPTER TWENTY-ONE

POSITIVE AFFIRMATIONS ABOUT EMOTIONS

1. Today, I dig deep into my soul to discover the source of any resentment that accumulates in my heart.
2. I am able to block resentment from feeding on my thoughts and feelings. I release it back into the universe and replace it with positive thoughts.
3. I understand how to discuss my feelings.
4. I can express my emotions with confidence.
5. Meditation shows me how to be content and relaxed.
6. I tune out emotional distractions and focus on creating balance.
7. My concentration on my real feelings grow stronger. I pay attention to how my mind works. I listen to my inner voice.
8. I choose to be in control of my actions instead of operating emotionally on autopilot.
9. I remember that I am in control and I have a choice.
10. I focus on my core values and spiritual purpose to keep me grounded
11. I connect with my true emotions.
12. I put aside any form of judgments and regard myself with compassion.
13. Every single day, I make the decision to love and accept myself just the way I am.
14. I recognize the power I have over my life and I decide how to respond to whatever circumstances come my way.
15. I devote my time and emotions to activities that are meaningful to me.

Positive Daily Affirmations

16. I am fully aware of myself and my worth. I know that I am worthy of love and success.
17. I realize that observing my thoughts and feelings about certain things, prepares me to live the life I really want.
18. I cultivate a sense of inner calm and serenity that I can carry with me through traffic jams or tense business meetings without breaking down emotionally
19. I give myself the gift of freedom from resentment. I let go of anger, forgive others, and make room for love.
20. I embrace my feelings and begin the process of healing.
21. I live my life mindfully and deliberately.
22. I define myself in a way that goes beyond my age, gender, profession or even past experiences
23. When things start to get frantic, I slow down and breathe deeply.
24. I am ready to put in the work to overcome obstacles.
25. I understand the power of resentment and its ability to harm my mind and body. Therefore, I work actively on letting go
26. I set aside time for meditation and prayer to nourish me emotionally
27. Today, I tackle challenges without overwhelming myself with too many responsibilities.
28. I take a walk outdoors to enjoy nature to relax myself and connect with my center.
29. My relationships remain secure while I express my thoughts and feelings
30. My center is a source of strength that gives me the determination to persevere.
31. To let go of past hurt, I focus my awareness on the present moment.
32. In chaos, I reach for my center. To connect with my center, I still my mind.
33. I find the source of my resentment so I can let it go.
34. By staying centered, I can accept the natural changes in life.

Positive Daily Affirmations

35. I am living in the present
36. My center is strong and this is the place where I feel in balance emotionally.
37. I attract calming situations and people into my life
38. I am confident when I'm around others
39. I clarify my thoughts as I sieve through my emotions. My mind slows down.
40. I trust in my inner wisdom
41. I control my emotional outbursts and at the same time, I experience the stability that comes with being in touch with my authentic self.
42. I release anxiety because I know it is just passing through
43. Today, I gladly let go of any resentment in my heart and move forward toward a happy life without this negative emotion.
44. I replace feelings of worry with hope
45. I identify with my feelings of anxiety as much as I do peace
46. I look deeper than the surface. I see beyond superficial labels and roles.
47. I am capable of adjusting to new situations
48. I am confident in my future
49. My confidence, inner wisdom and self esteem increase daily
50. I refuse to allow the pain of resentment to fester inside me.
51. I am more than my genetics
52. I react to my anxiety calmly and effectively
53. I inhale confidence and exhale self doubt
54. I learn from my anxiety
55. I learn strategies that I can use to release negative emotions in a healthy way and I practice them daily.
56. I know my intuition is my best guide
57. I know that being direct is the most effective approach so, imbibe it.
58. I vibrate at a higher emotion than anxiety
59. I interpret my emotions and have the final say in how I react

60. I release habits of worry
61. I reduce the risk of misunderstandings and delays by keeping communication clear
62. I embrace stress, it steers me away from what drains me
63. My beliefs and values create a strong foundation for my life. I am centered and grounded.
64. I am courageous and confront my fears
65. To maintain balanced communications, I ask myself what would serve the common good rather than just my own interests.
66. I ask for what I want.
67. I face difficult situations with courage
68. I am more than my family history of mental illness
69. I am proactive. To help me let go of resentment, I study positive communication methods.
70. Meditation gives me an opportunity to discover my true self.
71. To put myself in a sincere frame of mind, I examine my motives.
72. I allow myself to be vulnerable and this deepens my relationships.
73. I check that my thoughts are free from resentments and anxiety.
74. Meditation helps me to unleash my true emotions as well as my true potential.
75. My toxic self-doubts fad away.
76. I have the ability to create change in my life.
77. I let go of the past for it no longer serves me.
78. Where I am mentally and emotionally is OKAY
79. As I release stress and anxiety, my mind grows still and peaceful.
80. I speak only positive things.
81. I choose to respond to emotions that build me.
82. I stop comparing myself to others, and work on leveraging my own unique strengths.

83. I do not indulge in self pity.
84. I can also let go of bitterness because I understand that my past can only affect my present or future if I let it.
85. I enjoy the emotional journey I am on. I love who I am becoming.
86. I approve of myself.
87. I am my own rock emotionally
88. I am a warrior and a soldier when it comes to protecting my mental health
89. I have no fear of my future.
90. I am in love with this life so much
91. I am completely fearless as I discover the real me
92. I am a gift to the world.
93. Today, I cultivate a strong center that guides my decisions, my actions and my reactions.
94. I am not oppressed. There is no mountain I can't climb.
95. I like how far I have come emotionally. I am an inspiration to others.
96. I make the choice is to learn what I can from unfortunate situations, leave them in the past, and move forward without them.
97. I love myself fully and completely.
98. I love and approve of myself.
99. I am brave and grateful to have learned it.
100. I surround myself with positive vibes and allow travel to lift my spirits.
101. I choose to be relaxed and happy.
102. Today, I sit down to meditate. I explore my feelings and learn to appreciate myself.
103. I will not stress over things I can't control.
104. I pause and reflect before reacting.
105. I am superior to negative thoughts.
106. I let go of all the worries that drain my energy and feel as light as a feather.

Positive Daily Affirmations

107. I accept and embrace all experiences.
108. I am becoming more calm, positive and loving everyday
109. My happiness is contagious.
110. I prove to myself that daily that happiness comes from within rather than depending on material possessions or approval from others.
111. I am centered, peaceful, and grounded.
112. I am surrounded by supportive loved ones always.
113. Today is a good day.
114. I am content and at peace.
115. Negative thoughts are not me.
116. I invite peace into all my interactions with others.
117. I am peacefully allowing this moment to pass.
118. I am happy right here, right now.
119. I am grateful for this moment.
120. I am complete, with nothing to prove.
121. I am not alone.
122. I am gentle with my words and my thoughts.
123. I observe my emotions with calm detachment.
124. I do not judge my own thoughts.
125. I forgive myself for past mistakes.
126. I am alive in this moment.
127. My heart is bursting with joy.
128. My mind is at ease.
129. I choose to be calm.
130. I am here, now.
131. I allow my soul to shine.
132. I discard all expectations.
133. I am peaceful in my place.
134. I find joy in stillness.
135. I am calm and content.
136. Today is fresh and new.
137. I am in charge of how I feel.
138. I am in control of my emotions and feelings today

Positive Daily Affirmations

139. I exude warmth and kindness.
140. I am pure sunshine.
141. I focus on what I can control and I let go of what I can't.
142. I love my beautiful mind.
143. I am allowed to have bad days.
144. I am a survivor and that makes me proud of myself.
145. I have a beautiful laugh.
146. I stay calm in frustrating situations
147. I invest in myself through big and small acts of self-care and self-love.
148. I am brave to endure emotional days like today.
149. Life is tough sometimes, but so am I.
150. My smile makes others smile.
151. I am choosing love over other emotions
152. My inner strength knows no bounds
153. I am patient with and kind to myself.
154. I look forward to feeling better about things again.
155. I am proud of the person I am today, and the person I will be tomorrow.
156. I am in control of my emotions
157. I breathe in energy and love, I exhale negativity and doubt.
158. Life is tough sometimes, but so am I.
159. Tomorrow is more than another day; it's another chance to shine.
160. I rock at being me!
161. I am attracting the love my heart desires
162. I look after my mental health because it deserves my love
163. My bad days and unhappy moments will always pass.
164. I am trusting in my ability to set myself free
165. I bring joy to the world.
166. I choose my peace of mind
167. I'm not ashamed or alone in having mental health struggles.

Positive Daily Affirmations

168. I can see the end of this emotional time, and I move towards it with every breath I take.
169. I am attracting kindness from others
170. My hugs are full of love and warmth.
171. When chaos surrounds me, I remain calm
172. My mental health is just as important as my physical health.
173. I take time to know my needs, limits and boundaries better.
174. I am attracting people who treat me well
175. Love is what I believe in most of all.
176. I am manifesting love and happiness from within
177. Good mental health is a journey, not a destination.
178. On hard days like this, I love myself more than ever.
179. I am making responsible decisions
180. I sow seeds of peace wherever I go
181. I inspire others to be happy when I allow myself to be happy
182. I open my heart to healing
183. I breathe in peace and breathe out dysfunction
184. I grow more at peace each day
185. My good days prepare me for my harder days
186. I stay calm in frustrating situations
187. I am processing my hurt and anger in healthy ways
188. I surround myself with people who care about my wellbeing
189. Life is tough sometimes, but I am tougher
190. I am considerate of how my decisions affect others
191. My heart is full of love for who I am.

www.ingramcontent.com/pod-product-compliance
Lightning Source LLC
Chambersburg PA
CBHW031056080526
44587CB00011B/706